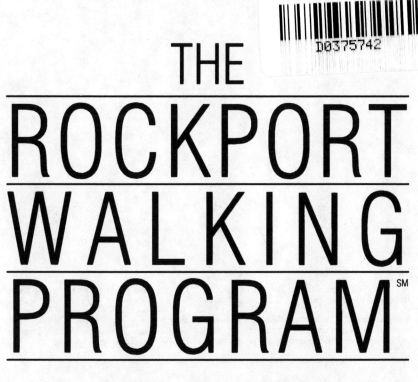

THE ROCKPORT WALKING PROGRAM

James M. Rippe, M.D.,
and Ann Ward, Ph.D.,
with
Karla Dougherty

Recipes developed by Judy Fredal Pang, M.P.H., R.D.

Prentice Hall Press
New York • London • Toronto • Sydney • Tokyo

The charts and graphs on pages 30–40, 219, 226, and 227 are reprinted courtesy The Rockport Walking Institute, copyright © 1986.

Rockport and the Rockport ProWalker are registered trademarks of The Rockport Company. The Rockport Fitness Walking Test is a trademark of The Rockport Company. The Rockport Walking Program and The Rockport Walking Institute are service marks of The Rockport Company.

Prentice Hall Press
Gulf + Western Building
One Gulf + Western Plaza
New York, New York 10023

Library of Congress Cataloging-in-Publication Data

Rippe, James M.
    The Rockport walking program^{SM} / James M. Rippe and Ann Ward with Karla Dougherty.
      p.   cm.
    Bibliography: p.
    Includes index.
    ISBN 0-13-782301-0 : $9.95
    1. Health. 2. Physical fitness. 3. Walking—Health aspects.
4. Reducing diets. I. Ward, Ann, 1950–   . II. Dougherty, Karla.
III. Title.
RA776.R57   1989
613.7'176—dc20   89-32149
                                                     CIP

Designed by Barbara Cohen Aronica

Manufactured in the United States of America

10 9 8 7 6 5 4 3 2 1

First Edition

The Rockport Walking Program^{SM} is designed to help you lose weight and maintain better health regardless of your age. But before starting this or any weight-loss and exercise program, we do suggest you consult your physician— especially if you have a medical problem.

ACKNOWLEDGMENTS

Without the invaluable contributions of the entire team at the Exercise Physiology and Nutrition Laboratory, the University of Massachusetts Medical Center, The Rockport Company, and all the people close to us who have kept our focus clear and our spirits up, this book—and the study on which it is based—would never have existed.

First and foremost is Diane Morris, Ph.D., R.D. An extremely important part of making the study and the book a reality, Dr. Morris provided information for the book as well as editing expertise. She had the overall responsibility for the study's nutritional aspects, including the nutrition data base and the design of the nutritional counseling and materials given out to our 80 subjects. She also was responsible for hiring and supervising registered dietitians Paula Cuneo and Merry Yamartino.

Merry Yamartino, R.D., and Paula Cuneo, R.D., in turn, developed objectives and goals for each subject, counseled subjects, and provided both group and individual instruction. They developed nutritional education materials, analyzed food diaries, maintained the nutrient data bank, and provided moral support for the study subjects—and all of us at the Exercise Physiology and Nutrition Laboratory. They also developed materials for the book and read drafts of the manuscript for accuracy.

Judy Fredal Pang, M.P.H., R.D., developed all the recipes and supervised the testing of each one. She developed the meal plans and was a joy to work with—even long-distance in California.

John Porcari, Ph.D., our postdoctoral fellow in exercise physiology, had the formidable responsibility of the day-to-day management of the study, including the recruiting and screening of subjects, scheduling, testing, training, data reduction, and statistical analysis.

The rest of the exercise team also deserve our thanks:

Maureen Maher, B.S., was responsible for drawing and handling blood for cholesterol analysis. She also helped with scheduling, testing, training subjects, and data reduction.

Carol Shustak, R.N., our staff cardiovascular research nurse, helped with drawing and handling blood.

Cara Ebbeling, M.S., Stephanie O'Hanley, M.S., Martha Lozeau, B.S., and Kathy Bell, M.S., helped with recruiting, screening, scheduling, testing, and training. They also took care of data reduction and data analysis.

Also helping us with exercise training was Don Sussman, Ph.D., our postdoctoral fellow in biomechanics. Further training and testing was conducted by Carmen Cononie, M.S., Christine Ebbeling, B.A. (a graduate student at the University of Massachusetts at Amherst) and by the medical students from the University of Massachusetts Medical School who were on summer fellowships with us: Chris Curdo, Michael Zackin, Susan Hastings, and Emmett Clemente.

We owe a great deal to our friends at The Rockport Company, especially Alex Hofstetter, director of marketing, Reina O'Connor, field marketing manager, Debbi Kravetz, marketing supervisor, Robert Infantino, vice-president of product development and Bob Slattern, president. Thanks to their unflagging support, this study—and all the research leading up to it—became an exciting reality.

A special thanks to Elizabeth Porcaro, editorial assistant extraordinaire. Because of her organizational and editorial abilities, she literally made everything happen.

Jane Hodgkinson, administrative assistant, and Mary Sosvielle, laboratory coordinator, made all of our professional lives run smoothly and made our hectic schedules easier to juggle.

Without Carol Cone, the president of Cone Communications, Inc., the vision for this book would have been lost.

Last, but never least, we give thanks to our exceptional 80 subjects. Because of their cooperation, enthusiasm, courage, and conviction, this study—and this book—is an inspiring reality.

CONTENTS

INTRODUCTION:
HOW IT ALL BEGAN

On February 24, 1988, we witnessed an extraordinary phenomenon at the University of Massachusetts Medical Center in Worcester.

It started out as a typical day. We had met with the staff in our Exercise Physiology and Nutrition Laboratory and had gone over some test results. We were discussing some new ideas for research projects as we returned to our sixth-floor offices. We entered the elevator from the exercise physiology lab, located in the basement of the hospital. When the elevator opened on the first floor, a well-dressed man in his late forties entered, nodded politely, and also pressed the sixth-floor button. We assumed he was visiting a patient and wouldn't have given him any more notice except for the fact that he was holding a newspaper article almost reverently in his hand. Not only was it odd that he carried an article ripped out of the paper, but it was crumpled as if he had read it several times. As the elevator continued up at its usual slow place, he kept glancing at the article and at the lit-up floor numbers with impatience. We got off at six. He got off at six. We entered our offices. He entered my office. To our amazement, he stopped at the assistant's desk and showed her the crumpled article. It was a story that had appeared only that morning in the local Worcester paper. It described a major study our Exercise Physiology and Nutrition Laboratory was about to conduct on weight loss and cardiovascular fitness. He had come to the hospital to volunteer.

We wanted to hear more, but it was difficult. The phone was ringing off the hook—with virtually no hiatus between calls. The place was in pandemonium—and that was only the beginning.

Within the first few days after the article was printed in the local paper, we received more than 400 phone calls from people asking to be put into the program—even though the article had not listed a phone number or a staff member to contact if the reader was interested. Others, like the mystery man in the elevator, became frustrated at the busy phone lines and actually drove to the hospital to find someone who could help them—anyone who could enroll them into our study. And still others wrote impassioned letters requesting a spot. It seemed as if everyone in Worcester had read the story that morning—and wanted to volunteer.

It soon became apparent that what had begun as a small article that we hoped would interest the 80 adults necessary for our study had become a major event. Clearly, we had struck a chord in hundreds of people. We were on to something that had a major importance in all of our lives.

The Rockport Walking Program^{SM} is the result of that study, which was announced so inauspiciously that wintery February day.

A Pure and Simple Message

The basic principles that we have proven in our laboratory are:

1. Walking is a form of exercise that will provide cardiovascular and mental benefits.
2. When a walking program is combined with a moderate low-fat diet, people will lose weight, keep it off, feel better, and gain control of their lives—some for the very first time.

It isn't magic and it isn't complicated. But it is powerful.
And it works.

Who We Are

DR. RIPPE: My interest in walking began when I was director of the University of Massachusetts Cardiovascular Rehabilitation Program. It was there, when I saw the tremendous benefits walking had on recovering heart-attack patients, that I began to wonder if it would provide these same benefits for stronger, healthier individuals.

DR. WARD: I joined Dr. Rippe in 1985 as director of research in exercise physiology. During my Ph.D. program, I founded the University of Wisconsin Health and Fitness Program in Madison. I had been involved in several exercise training studies related to cardiovascular training and had been especially interested in the role of exercise and diet for weight loss.

THE LAB: The largest walking experimentation laboratory in the world, the Exercise Physiology Laboratory has made a name for itself not simply by generating a body of facts about health and fitness, but by showing how these facts can be put into practice by the American public. In our five years of existence we have researched everything from measuring aerobic capacity with a one-mile walk test to getting fit through walking, from walking with weights to the biomechanics of a good walking shoe. We have tested more than 700 individuals ranging in age from 20 to 79 in our studies and, in only three years, we have published and presented more than 30 scientific papers in the areas of walking and fitness to the American College of Sports Medicine, the American Heart Association, the American Association of Cardiovascular and Pulmonary Rehabilitation, and countless others.

Dr. Diane Morris, the study's research nutritionist, was hired in 1986. As a research associate at the Harvard School of Public Health's Department of Nutrition and a faculty member at the medical school, she was extremely well qualified to set up the nutrition design of our study. By 1988 the rest of our nutrition and exercise physiology team was in place, including exercise physiologists, a postdoctoral fellow, a meal planner and recipe writer, a nurse, and registered dietitians—10 staff members in all.

The Rockport Walking Program study was about to begin.

Who The Rockport Walking Program
Subjects Are

We started out with 80 unknowns, 8 men and 12 women in each of four groups: diet alone, walking alone, a diet-and-walking combination, and a control group who wouldn't change their habits during the course of the study. They ranged in age from 30 to 59 years old. All 80 subjects were at least 20 percent overweight, and most had tried many diets and/or exercise plans in the past. They were housewives and executives, salespeople and computer programmers, single and married men and women, all with busy lives, all coping with the vicissitudes of modern life, all trying to juggle their time, and all of them sincerely wanting to do something right for themselves—with no idea how to go about it.

By the end of four months of extensive diet counseling and exercise supervision, members of all three experimental groups—the diet only, the walking only, and the diet-and-walking group—lost weight. But the combination diet-and-walking group had the best results, proving in a laboratory setting what we have always believed to be true: that what people do on a day-to-day basis in their daily lives will have a profound impact on their long-term health.

Based on the results of the combination diet-and-walking group, The Rockport Walking Program is as much a product of our subjects' determination and desire as our knowledge and expertise. Here's definitive proof:

• The diet-and-walking group showed an average weight loss of 17 pounds—with 90 percent of that loss in body fat, as opposed to lean muscle tissue.
• Those with high blood pressure dropped within a normal range of less than 140/90.
• Their level of fitness improved. Measured by the amount of oxygen consumed, the combination diet-and-walking group showed an average increase of 4.9 milliliters of oxygen per kilogram of body weight per minute in all.
• Their cholesterol readings dropped on the average from 208 mg/dl to 191 mg/dl.

After two months of unsupervised study where all our subjects were on their own, all three groups continued to keep their weight off—and the combination diet-and-walking group lost even more weight—an average of another 2½ pounds.

In addition, the success they found in their healthy eating and daily exercise would translate into control over every aspect of their lives. As Rockport Walking Program subject Phil Burgess says, "Alcohol is down to a minimum. I had a couple of sips of a margarita and it put me right on my ear." Another subject, Nick Rioux, has changed his old "couch potato" habits for good. As he says, "I'd be crazy to devote this much time only to give it up. I've learned something here."

Our subjects now feel younger than they have in years. They've made improvements in their cardiovascular systems. They've improved their mood and sense of well-being. In short, all 80 subjects—even the control group who received the diet-and-walking plan at the conclusion of the six-month study—got something out of the program. By the study's end, all of these 80 strangers had become inspiring individuals, each one of them a success story of how habits can be changed, how lives can become balanced, and how wishful thinking can become exhilarating reality. What worked so powerfully for them can work for you. Without crash diets. Without radical changes in your daily life. And without exhausting exercise regimes.

How to Use This Book

Motivation, maintenance, and measurement of success are the three keys to success on The Rockport Walking Program—and all are specifically built into and spelled out in our program. They are the reasons why The Rockport Walking Program works so well, even among people who have tried countless diets and on-again, off-again exercise regimes.

The Rockport Walking Program is designed to be used—easily and effectively—with the 3 Ms in mind. To reinforce your own individual "3 Ms" (motivation, maintenance, and measurement of success), it is divided into three separate sections—"Part I: Starting a Better Life"; "Part II: 30 Days to Change Your Life"; and "Part III: For the Rest of Your Life."

The first section details the latest information on diet and health and explains why we structured The Rockport Walking Program the way we did. In the same way that a person who has an understanding of the elements of grammar will have more success in learning a new language than someone who only memorizes a few key phrases, this section will provide you with the "whys" for better understanding—and staying power. And, just as the people in our study went through a series of tests before they started their program, you'll also find a chapter with simple tests that you can do at home to evaluate your body fat, the "hidden" fat you might be eating, and your cholesterol and blood-pressure readings. You'll also find our landmark Rockport Fitness Walking Test, an exciting step-by-step way to determine your level of fitness and specific exercise program, based on your individual age, sex, level of fitness, and weight. There's also a simple test to determine which of our three separate diet plans will bring you maximum results.

The second section of the book is designed to get you going. To make sure your first 30 days on The Rockport Walking Program are successful, we've designed an easy-to-follow day-by-day calendar containing one full month of your specific daily walking goals, daily meal plans, and, to keep your "3 Ms" on track, a daily inspirational quote. You'll also find hints and tips for dining out, company dinners, and much more. Like our 80 subjects, you can start to change your life in only one month!

The third section of the book takes you beyond your first month. Here you'll find sixteen more weeks of walking goals plus a complete list of the wide variety of foods you can include in your diet plan. You'll also discover important motivation tips for sticking with your Rockport Walking Program and maintenance programs that will keep you healthy and slim after you've reached your weight-loss goal. And you'll find answers to the questions commonly asked about The Rockport Walking Program, along with 109 mouth-watering gourmet recipes.

The Rockport Walking Program is a program for adults, for all of you who, like the people in our study, have reached a point in life where you want to do what's right for yourself, who want to change the way things are—but who feel too overwhelmed to do anything about it. Whether you are an aging "baby boomer" or a recent retiree, a person with more than 20 pounds to lose or someone who can't get rid of those same 10 pounds, an executive "juggler" or a beer-and-football devotee, a person who considers exercise a walk to the kitchen during commercials or a person who likes the idea of exercise but never seems to find the time . . . The Rockport Walking Program will work for you!

I
STARTING
A
BETTER LIFE

1

THE ROCKPORT
WALKING PROGRAM
PHILOSOPHY

- Ceile Burgess was 30 pounds overweight when she was accepted into the program. A nurse in her late forties, she had recently quit smoking and had gained quite a bit of weight. Her husband, Phil, is an electrical contractor in his late fifties who had found the weight creeping up over the years. Both Ceile and Phil enjoy life and enjoy eating. Because they travel extensively and dine out in restaurants more than they eat at home, they couldn't imagine a diet that would be anything but deprivation. But within four months of beginning The Rockport Walking Program, Ceile lost 18 pounds and Phil lost 23.

- Katie Allen is approaching 40—and wondering exactly when that heavy image started staring back at her in the mirror. When she was 18, Katie had no weight problem, and, throughout her twenties, she managed to attend a local health club at least five times a week. But when she got into her late thirties, something happened. Her life was busier than ever, and her responsibilities both at home and at work continued to grow. Suddenly she had no more time to exercise—but she continued to eat the same amount she did when she was in her teens. Her weight started to go up—and up. Before Katie knew it, she was 40 pounds overweight. She'd start diets only to get discouraged and gain even more weight. She'd begin exercise classes only to quit, exhausted and sore, after one or two sessions. But two months into The Rockport Walking Program, she was walking 2½ miles every day effortlessly. And her weight had dropped by 10 pounds.

2

- Roger Messier is a 45-year-old vice-president of a manufacturing company. Over the last five or six years, he noticed that he was putting on 10 pounds each year. He'd tried other diets when he saw the scale first start to creep up, but he never lost much weight—and always gained back more than he had lost. By the time we saw him, he was discouraged and worried about his health. Despite the fact that he ate out in restaurants all the time, he went from 244 pounds to 220 in four months on The Rockport Walking Program.

Contrary to what we see on our television screens, most Americans are not those lithe, smiling characters doing what's right for themselves with little or no effort. They are people like Roger Messier, Katie Allen, and Mr. and Mrs. Burgess—people concerned with creeping weight gain, dragging their feet, and growing old before their time.

In our extensive travels across America as involved spokesmen for the walking movement, we have seen this concerned public firsthand. We've listened to what motivates them, what they care about, and what they need to hear. And this "heartbeat of America," more than anything else, beats with the desire to do what's right. Almost all the people we have spoken to want to eat better and more healthfully. They want to integrate exercise into their daily lives for fitness and health—and they are more knowledgeable about health, nutrition, and exercise than people at any other time in our history.

But some of this knowledge is misguided, mired in what was once believed true and in "old wives' tales" that have stayed with us over the years—despite the latest scientific findings.

Fat Fable 1:

If you are giving up red meat, cheese is a good high-protein substitute.
Believe it or not, if you're on a diet, you're better off with a lean roast-beef sandwich—which has, ounce for ounce, more protein than fat. Most people don't realize it, but cheese is not a diet food, and it can sabotage the most motivated diet plan. Many popular cheeses are made from whole milk, which contains the equivalent of 2 pats of butter in every cup. And since it takes a whole gallon of milk to make 1 pound of cheese, that "low-calorie" cheese will have 32 pats of butter in it in all! Of course, we don't eat a whole pound of cheese at one time, but even eating a 1-ounce serving means eating 2 pats of butter!

This doesn't mean you have to turn your back on cheese forever. It is a good source of calcium and protein and, with the low-fat cheeses lining the supermarket shelves, you can buy your cheese and eat it too! The Rockport Walking Program shows you how to choose the right types of cheese to give you the maximum health benefits—and the maximum weight loss.

Fat Fable 2:

If I really want to lose weight, I'm better off running than walking to burn off the most calories.
I remember one of the women in our study who said that she always thought walking was for "old people." She felt it was great for the over-70 crowd, but not for her. Unfortunately, she is not alone. People don't realize what a potent form of exercise walking really is. Here's proof: If you walked briskly for only 45 minutes four times a week and didn't increase what you ate, you'd lose 10 to 15 pounds in a year without even trying!

There are three elements to a good workout: how hard you are working, how long, and how many times a week you do it. Since you can walk further than you can run without pushing yourself, you can stay with it longer—and you won't quit in exhaustion after day one. And, as an added plus, you will be burning more calories as you walk because you can exercise longer without getting tired.

Walking is a particularly good exercise if you are overweight because anyone, at any fitness level, can put one foot in front of the other and, as famous walking enthusiast Harry Truman once said, "walk as if you have somewhere to go." In the next chapter you'll learn exactly what your fitness level is and which walking program will give you the best results. Combined with our low-fat diet, a steady—and healthy—weight loss is guaranteed.

Fat Fable 3:

If you are overweight, the plain fact is that you just eat too much!
As anyone who has ever been overweight knows, this isn't always true. Studies have shown that obese people eat about the same amount as their leaner counterparts—and sometimes even less.

Yes, if you consume more calories than you burn up, you'll gain weight—but there are other factors that come into play. One is heredity. Children have an 80 percent risk of becoming obese if their parents are. A study of identical twins reared in different environments found that the heavier children had heavier natural parents— even if their adopted parents were thin. But environment can enter into the equation. A sedentary life-style doesn't give those calories you're eating a chance to burn up. And research shows that children with inactive parents have a tendency to become "couch potatoes" themselves when they grow up.

Whether genetic or inherited, environmental or biochemical, the good news is that obesity can be controlled. Fat cells can shrink and ingrained habits can be reversed. The key is diet and exercise. Because The Rockport Walking Program combines a nondeprivation diet with low-impact activity, it's easy to start—and it feels too good to stop.

Fat Fable 4:

The best diet to lose weight fast is an extremely low-calorie one. Look how well these diets work for celebrities!
Here's the real truth: More than 95 percent of the people who have successfully lost weight with these diets will be back to prediet weights within two years. And worse, they will come back fatter— with a higher percentage of body fat and a lower percentage of lean muscle tissue.

A certain number of calories are needed for metabolic function. The brain alone needs 400 calories of blood sugar (glucose) every day to function—which comes from the foods we eat. When you go on a restricted diet that is below 1,200 calories a day, your body can't supply these crucial calories of blood sugar from stored fat tissue alone—and it turns to your lean muscle tissue to pick up the slack.

There is a psychological component as well. People who have lost weight with these fast-weight-loss diets are, in effect, "fat people living in temporarily thin bodies." They haven't made a fundamental change in the way they approach food and physical activity. A University of Pennsylvania study of 50 women and 9 men who went on "crash" diets found that without this change in thinking, the weight always came back on. To make matters worse, most people gain back even more weight than they lose!

And, because of metabolic changes in their bodies, it becomes easier to gain and harder to lose. This will prompt them to "crash" diet again, which starts the deadly yo-yo syndrome of dieting and eating we all know so well.

Unfortunately, the more times a person goes on a "crash" diet, the harder it is each subsequent time to lose weight. Why? One reason is because each time you diet, your metabolism slows down, and your body burns calories at a much slower rate.

Long ago, there was a good reason for this slowing of the metabolism. Low-calorie diets and scales were nonexistent and, when warriors ate less food, it meant starvation. To conserve a depleting energy reserve, their bodies slowed down the rate at which they burned the calories in whatever meager foods were consumed. Unfortunately, our modern bodies can't differentiate between starvation states and dieting. The brain only knows that less food is being eaten, and our metabolism will go into its "survival mode" and slow down. In fact, various studies have shown that when people are put on a severe diet, they show actual signs of starvation—from eating too fast to feeling constant hunger pangs, from depression and irritability to lethargy and physical inactivity—until they have gained all their weight back.

The *setpoint theory* that has recently received so much attention is directly related to this slower metabolism. A setpoint is a kind of internal thermostat within the brain that determines how much fat a person should carry. The controls of this internal thermostat are as individual as the thermostats you set in your house. Different people have different setpoints. When you try to lose those extra pounds, your body will fight you every step of the way to keep you at your current setpoint weight.

According to the setpoint theory, people who lose weight successfully will gradually regain their weight because of internal signals to eat until all the weight is gained back—and the internal setpoint is met. The only way to keep weight off is to reset the setpoint control at a lower body-fat content.

But there is hope. And it's called exercise. Some research suggests that one's setpoint can actually be lowered by exercise. With a healthy exercise regime like walking, you don't have to cut as many calories from your diet to lose weight. And, because you're not drastically restricting your calories, your metabolism won't severely drop, and your setpoint thermostat will be more content. Further, exercise helps increase and/or sustain muscle mass, which is more active metabolically than fat tissue.

When it comes to weight loss, it's the slow and steady tortoise who wins the race—and stays on top. A healthy combination of diet and exercise is the only way to lose weight safely and keep it off.

Fat Fable 5:

Starch means fattening!
If asked to name two "fattening foods" to avoid when trying to lose weight, most people will respond: bread and potatoes. Somehow starchy foods have gotten a bad reputation. Many consumers believe that bread, potatoes, and pasta are high in calories and should be used sparingly, if at all, in a weight-loss meal plan. We'd like to lay this issue to rest. Starchy foods aren't themselves high in calories and by themselves aren't high in fat. The problem for most weight-conscious consumers is the company these starchy foods keep, namely butter, margarine, sour cream, mayonnaise, or cream sauce. Many people have a hard time enjoying a *plain* baked potato; their tendency is to add a little something to jazz it up. Consider the caloric cost of this choice: plain baked potato (medium size)—95 calories; baked potato (medium size) with 3 tablespoons of sour cream—185 calories. The sour cream adds nearly as many calories as the potato alone. Thus, starchy foods such as bread and potatoes aren't necessarily fattening; it's the butter and sour cream we add to them that add fat. In the recipe section of the appendix, you'll find delicious ways to enjoy starches and breads—without fattening fats.

Fat Fable 6:

You can't undo a lifetime of bad habits—especially in middle age.
A woman in our study wanted to go on The Rockport Walking Program because she had "reached the age of 50 and felt and looked older than [she] wanted to." By the time she completed four months on the plan, she felt years younger. It wasn't magic or some kind of hocus-pocus, it was simply because she had started to walk. Being active can make all the difference between weakness and

strength, lethargy and energy, brittle bones and suppleness. A few years ago, a study was done of active and inactive women between the ages of 70 and 79 and a group of average 19- to 20-year-olds. In terms of strength, reaction time, and balance, the active older women more closely resembled the young 19- to 20-year-olds than they did their inactive counterparts! Feeling old is more a function of inactivity than it is of the aging process. And, no matter what your age, beginning an exercise program such as walking right now can improve your general fitness, elevate your mood, and, like the woman in our Rockport Walking Program, make you feel years younger.

These, then, are some of the beliefs that have shaped our diet and exercise habits. We hope that The Rockport Walking Program will help dispel these myths, sweeping them back into the past where they belong.

But now it's time for the future—your future of good nutrition and good health.

The Fats of Life

There is a quiet revolution going on in smart American kitchens today. It is the fight against fat. And, if any phrase sums up The Rockport Walking Program, it is "cut out the fat!"

Why is fat on the "most unwanted" list? Because:

1. A diet high in fat, especially saturated fat, has been linked to high blood-cholesterol levels—a known risk factor for the nation's number-one killer, heart disease. According to the latest Surgeon General's Nutrition and Health report, saturated fat is the major health hazard in the modern American diet.
2. Fat has more than twice the calories, gram for gram, of protein and carbohydrates. Excessive fat consumption can therefore lead to obesity. A high fat intake can also lead to a greater risk of certain forms of cancer.

Fried foods, fast foods, and rich foods are all taking their toll on our health. The average American consumes 38 to 40 percent of his or her daily calories as fat. At least 40 million of us weigh 20 pounds more than we should and *an adult who reaches the age of 50 with 40 extra pounds cuts an average of 10 years from his or her life.*

Sobering statistics, but not hopeless. Reducing the amount of fat in your diet directly translates into weight loss and better health.

But *reducing* does not mean *eliminating*. Like almost everything else in life, fat isn't all bad. It is, in fact, essential to life:

- Fat is nature's most concentrated source of energy.
- Fat is necessary for proper growth and development.
- Fat aids in the absorption and digestion of vitamins A, D, E, and K.
- Fat is an important component of our cell tissue.
- Fat works as a shock absorber, cushioning our bones and vital organs.
- Fat insulates the body against cold.

The Cholesterol Connection

Cholesterol is news. Good news and bad news. First the good: Cholesterol is a waxy substance manufactured by the body and is a vital component of many body functions. It is found naturally in all animal products. And now the bad news: By consuming foods of animal origin, an excess of cholesterol may build up and then the good turns ugly.

Cholesterol is carried throughout our bloodstream by lipoproteins, substances made of protein and fat, which are formed in the liver. The major lipoprotein that carts cholesterol from the liver to other parts of our bodies is called LDL—low-density lipoprotein cholesterol. Unfortunately, if these LDLs are not removed from the blood or processed by our body cells, the cholesterol and fat in them "float" through the bloodstream, eventually coming to rest in artery walls and clogging them—leading to atherosclerosis and heart disease. That is why LDL cholesterol is called "bad cholesterol."

But there is another lipoprotein that does a hero's job. It's called HDL—high-density lipoprotein cholesterol—and its job is to carry cholesterol back to the liver for further processing or removal. HDL cholesterol acts like a vacuum cleaner, picking up the cholesterol left by the LDLs and keeping our arteries open and smooth.

A buildup of LDL cholesterol and the resulting high blood cholesterol can come from a genetically induced faulty disposal system; from eating too much cholesterol-laden foods, such as liver or eggs; or from loading up your diet with too many saturated fats.

Public Food Enemy Number One

Saturated fats tend to raise your LDL cholesterol levels and, hence, your total blood-cholesterol levels.

Most saturated fats are found in animal products and are solid at room temperature. But there are exceptions to every rule: Palm oil and coconut oil are both plant sources of saturated fat. Further, a chemical process called *hydrogenation* can turn unsaturated liquid oils into more solid or saturated fats.

The best way to avoid saturated fats is to replace them whenever possible with . . .

The Unsung Heroes: Unsaturated Fats

There are two types of unsaturated fat—polyunsaturated and monounsaturated—both of which can help lower cholesterol levels in your blood. Studies done in metabolic wards have confirmed that polyunsaturated fats tend to lower *total* cholesterol levels, while monounsaturated fats tend to lower only the "bad" LDL cholesterol, and leave HDL levels unchanged.

ALL FATS ARE NOT CREATED EQUAL

SATURATED	MONOUNSATURATED	POLYUNSATURATED
Butter	Olive oil	Safflower oil
Dairy fat	Peanut oil	Sunflower oil
Beef fat	Canola oil	Corn oil
Lard		Soybean oil
Chicken fat		Cottonseed oil
Vegetable shortening		Margarine (made
Hydrogenated		with liquid oil)
vegetable oil		
Palm oil		
Palm kernel oil		
Coconut oil		
Cocoa butter (found		
in chocolate)		

The Hidden Fat on Your Grocery-Store Shelf

But wait. . . . Let's check the labels. Things are not always what they seem. Your cart is filled with luncheon meats, margarines, salad dressings—foods all proudly proclaiming themselves *lite* and *low-calorie*. For maximum results, you must be a "supermarket detective" and learn to read the fine print.

(a)   (b)

It all comes down to fat. The two labels pictured here are for two different types of luncheon meat. Label *a* is for a package of smoked cooked ham—which you'd normally think of as a high-fat item. Wrong. Look at the calories per serving: There are only 25 calories per slice. Look at the fat content: There's only 1 gram. Label *b* is for turkey bologna which, at first sight, seems a better deli meat to choose—especially because the label proclaims *33 percent* less fat! But glance at the label again. There are 70 calories per slice—and the fat content is 6 grams.

A good way to judge the "hidden" fat content of food is by following these three simple steps:

1. Multiply the number of grams of fat by 9.
2. Divide the result by the number of calories per serving.
3. Multiply that result by 100.

You now know the percentage of calories that come from fat.
    Let's use the smoked cooked ham as an example:

1. 1 gram of fat × 9 = 9
2. 9 ÷ 25 calories = .36
3. .36 × 100 = 36 percent

Thirty-six percent of the 25 calories come from fat—less than half the total calories.

Not a bad choice. But now let's try the turkey bologna:

1. 6 grams of fat $\times$ 9 = 54
2. 54 $\div$ 70 calories = .77
3. .77 $\times$ 100 = 77 percent

More than three-quarters of the total calories come from fat! Not a good choice at all.

You can go through your supermarket and, using this simple equation, determine which foods are best to purchase. You might be surprised. You'll see that slices of ham and chicken have similar fat contents—about 25 percent of the total calories. You'll also find that cream cheese is loaded with fat—and that a lean roast-beef sandwich makes a great low-calorie lunch. Remember that while a food might be relatively low in calories, those calories can be packed with fat. A better choice is always the food item with less fat—even if it has a few more calories!

Here are some rules to guide you through the grocery-store maze:

1. Choose luncheon meats with no more than 3 grams of fat per ounce.
2. Margarine should have at least twice the amount of polyunsaturated fat as saturated fat and a liquid oil should be listed as the first ingredient.
3. Choose cheese products with no more than 6 grams of fat per ounce. Some very low-fat cheeses contain as little as 2 to 3 grams of fat per ounce. Check your labels!
4. Choose products that list fat way down on their ingredient lists. Check to see that the oils or fats are polyunsaturated and/or monounsaturated rather than saturated. And beware the word *hydrogenated*—which turns "good" vegetable oils into saturated fats.
5. Don't be fooled by the words *no cholesterol* on food labels. Remember, cholesterol is found only in animal products! Foods with no cholesterol may still be high in fat, saturated fat, and calories.

The American Heart Association recommends that you take no more than 30 percent of your daily total calories in as fat and, whenever possible, that you substitute polyunsaturated and monounsaturated fats for saturated fats. The Rockport Walking Program combines these guidelines with an easy-to-follow exchange program based on the American Diabetes Association and The American Dietetic Association's suggestions for healthy dieting.

Tips for Healthy and Safe Weight Loss

By this time, you're well aware of the dangers of fat—and how it can sabotage a diet. Here are a few more suggestions to keep in mind for better health and safer weight loss.

Limit Sugar

Sugar by itself is not fattening. Believe it or not, it has only 16 calories per teaspoon. The difference between regular sodas and diet sodas is about 100 calories per 12-ounce serving. The same holds true for presweetened fruit drinks versus low-calorie fruit drinks. To decrease calories, substitute artificially sweetened foods for regular products. But beware: Some people feel they're saving so many calories with their diet colas that they'll "con" themselves into eating an extra slice of pizza.

Increase Fiber

One of the benefits of increasing the carbohydrate content of your diet is an increased intake of fiber. Many people don't realize that low-fiber diets have been linked to problems with constipation and diverticulitis. Substituting fiber-rich foods for high-fat foods translates into fewer calories, larger portions, and better health. Studies have suggested that insoluble fiber, such as that found in wheat bran and whole-grain cereals, reduces the risk of colon cancer. Water-soluble fiber, found in oat bran, oatmeal, dried beans and peas, fruits, and vegetables, has been shown to help lower blood cholesterol. By following The Rockport Walking Program, you'll be assured of getting more than enough fiber in your diet.

Limit Salt

Unless you are sensitive to salt, there's no direct correlation between salt consumption and high blood pressure. But on the whole, we Americans consume far too much salt. The American Heart Association suggests that people consume no more than 3,000 milligrams of sodium a day. The Rockport Walking Program does not have a strict rule regarding salt intake, but a prudent approach to any healthy diet is to cut down on sodium. It's a good rule of thumb to taste your food before you salt it, use very little salt in cooking, substitute more natural foods for sodium-laden processed foods, and take the salt shaker off the table.

The Exercise Connection

Nutrition is only half of The Rockport Walking Program story. Let's turn now to exercise and see exactly what walking can do for you. Our Exercise Physiology and Nutrition Laboratory has by far the largest experience measuring walking of any facility in the United States. Walking will help you lose weight, improve cardiovascular health, slow down the process of osteoporosis, reduce stress, and improve your outlook and mental functioning.

Help You Lose Weight

Walking is an aerobic exercise—the type of exercise that most effectively promotes weight loss because it burns calories. *Aerobic* literally means "in the presence of air." During aerobic exercise, oxygen is utilized to keep our large muscle groups moving in a continuous, rhythmic fashion at an intensity that can be maintained for at least 20 minutes. This is in contrast to *anaerobic* activities, such as sprinting, throwing, and weight lifting, which burn very few calories. These types of activities are maintained for only a few seconds at two- or three-minute intervals. Another aerobic plus: A brisk walk will not only burn calories, but because it is a low-impact exercise, there's minimal chance of injury.

Like other aerobic exercises, walking also tends to curb your appetite. In a study of laboring mill workers, it was discovered that the least active of them ate around 500 calories *more* per day than their active counterparts.

Walking has also been shown to raise metabolic rates for one to four hours after an exercise session is over—translating into an expenditure of more energy and more burned calories. In fact, some studies have found that the energy our bodies use to digest food—a physiological process called *thermogenesis*—is kept at higher levels if one takes a brisk walk right after a meal.

Further, The Rockport Walking Program proved that walking will maintain more lean muscle mass and reduce more body fat than diet alone.

RISKY BUSINESS

A ground-breaking study done in Framingham, Massachusetts, followed more than 5,000 of its townspeople for more than 25 years to see whether any risk factors for developing Coronary Heart Disease (CHD) could be assessed—and possibly circumvented. The results pinpointed three major and five minor risk factors. The major risk factors double your chances of getting CHD and multiply each other if you have more than one. Two factors and you have four times the risk. All three major factors and you have nine times the chances of CHD. But almost all these factors are based on *habits that you can change.*

The Three Major Risk Factors

1. High blood pressure
2. Elevated cholesterol
3. Cigarette smoking

The Five Minor Risk Factors

4. Sedentary life-style
5. Stress
6. Obesity
7. Diabetes
8. Family history of coronary artery disease

Improve Cardiovascular Health

It's a simple truth: Exercise is connected to weight reduction. And weight reduction is connected to lower blood cholesterol.

What is more, we are beginning to find that exercise by itself may reap lower-cholesterol-level rewards.

Aerobic exercise raises the "good cholesterol"—HDL—which, as we have seen, helps retrieve cholesterol deposits from arteries and helps lower total cholesterol levels in the blood.

Walking also lowers blood pressure directly—and indirectly—as an important component of weight loss. With every two pounds you lose, you'll also take one millimeter of mercury off your blood pressure.

And walking improves our aerobic capacity—or VO_2max. No, this is not a new *Star Wars* robot. VO_2max stands for *maximum oxygen consumption* and, simply put, means the maximum amount of oxygen you can consume per minute. Exercise physiologists use VO_2max to measure a person's fitness level. The better shape you're in, the higher your VO_2max. An average 20-year-old woman will have a VO_2max of 35 to 40 milliliters of oxygen for every kilogram of body weight per minute when she's at her maximum capacity. An average 20-year-old man will have a VO_2max of 40 to 45 milliliters. But a marathon runner will have a VO_2max of approximately 70 milliliters per kilogram per minute. Here's how it works:

When you exercise, your brain complies with your muscles' request for energy by stimulating the heart to deliver oxygen to them via the red blood cells. This oxygen then combines with glucose, glycogen, or free fatty acids (from fat), which are broken down by enzymes to produce more energy.

Exercising at 60 to 70 percent of your VO_2max "overloads" or stresses your oxygen delivery system, which—though it sounds bad—is highly desirable. If you do this regularly, wonderful adaptations occur:

1. Your heart's ability to pump oxygenated blood throughout your system improves.
2. Your exercising muscles are better able to extract oxygen from this oxygen-rich blood.
3. These two factors translate into a higher aerobic capacity and more energy to do your daily chores!

Seventy to 80 percent of your potential VO_2max is inherited, but you can improve what you've got—with walking. We have proven that walking will increase VO_2max in individuals of all ages. And, in The Rockport Fitness Walking Test™ (which you'll be taking in the next chapter), we have devised a way to estimate your initial VO_2max so that you'll be able to start a walking program at the appropriate level—not too low for you to get all the important benefits and not so high that you'll get discouraged or hurt.

Slow Down the Process of Osteoporosis

Osteoporosis literally means "porous bone." It is a loss of bone mass—the amount of bone tissue—as well as a loss in bone strength. The weakened bones become prone to fractures. But its progression can be prevented or slowed by a weight-bearing-exercise regime like walking combined with appropriate calcium intake and estrogen levels. Why? Because walking will increase the amount of minerals in your bones and slow the rate of bone loss.

Reduce Stress

We don't know the actual links between mind and body, but we do know that when you're under stress, substances called *catecholamines* are released—with nowhere to go. Unlike our ancestors, who used these surges of energy to fight or flee ferocious foes, we're left with irritability and stress. But an aerobic exercise like walking can help release the catecholamines built up from a bad day at the office or at home.

Improve Outlook and Mental Functioning

Exercise has been proven to be a powerful way of releasing tension and anxiety and improving your mood. In fact, a survey of 1,751 primary-care doctors done by *The Physician and SportsMedicine* found that more than 80 percent of these doctors prescribed exercise for depression and more than 60 percent for anxiety—and more than 90 percent of them prescribed walking as the exercise of choice!

In one of our studies, we asked various individuals to walk for a total of 40 minutes at a slow speed, a medium speed, a fast speed, and a self-paced speed. Regardless of the speed, each person significantly reduced his or her anxiety and tension and elevated his or her overall mood—and the benefits lasted for at least two hours after they finished walking!

From mental benefits to cardiovascular health, from feeling good to looking good, we have proven that walking can't be beat! It is a low-impact, low-injury sport. It is sociable. It can be easily fit into your daily routine. And people of all different ages and all different levels of fitness can do it together—making walking ideal for a lifelong program of good health.

Walking and a Low-Fat Diet: A Winning Combination

There is only one way to lose weight: by burning more calories than you take in. But there are three basic ways to achieve this: diet alone, exercise alone, or a combination of the two.

We've already seen the disadvantages of an extremely low-calorie diet. But even a less-restrictive diet will result in the loss of more muscle tissue than is desirable. And, without exercise to help maintain metabolic levels and readjust your internal setpoint, your body will fight your good intentions with every pound you lose.

Exercise alone also has its drawbacks. Since it takes 3,500 calories to burn one pound of fat, you'd have to do a lot of pumping every day to lose a significant amount of weight. However, research does show that beginning an exercise regime is a great place to start for making overall changes in your life.

But a combination of diet and exercise will give you the best results. With exercise burning up some of those 3,500 calories, you can afford to be on a more manageable diet—without feeling hungry and without compromising your nutritional needs. And because you're eating more than someone who is only dieting, your metabolism won't drop drastically. Further, an exercise regime will assure you of losing more unwanted body fat and less lean muscle tissue than if you were only dieting.

Diet and exercise work together, reinforcing and complementing the positive mental and physical results you get from each. And studies have shown that people who combine exercise with diet maintain weight loss better.

2
TESTING, TESTING

Testing is a prerequisite for success on The Rockport Walking Program. It is also a powerful tool. Not only will tests show you where you are before you start your Rockport Walking Program, but testing yourself after only one month on the program will show you the vast improvements you have made.

To this end, we have developed a battery of self-tests to help you evaluate your body composition, diet, and aerobic capacity. The following six self-tests are highly accurate and simple to perform. All you need is a little time and a nearby pad and pencil.

Let's begin.

Self-Test 1: How Much Body Fat Do You Have?

Obesity is really a condition of excess body fat. Although height-weight tables are typically used to determine if you're overweight, these numbers alone cannot show how much of your weight is body fat. A physically fit and muscular person can weigh a lot more than the figures given in standard tables of "average" weight. For example, an athletic man who is six feet tall might weigh in at 180 pounds. His desirable weight for his frame is 166, but he isn't overweight because his extra pounds are in lean muscle tissue. On the other hand, an unathletic man with the same height, weight, and frame would be moderately overweight because his extra 14 pounds are almost all in body fat.

We know many people who can't resist weighing themselves

every day to see how they are doing. One pound gained and they are ready to quit.

The Rockport Walking Program is a lifetime plan. It's not a diet. There's no "cheating." No punishments. No crime. If you keep your weigh-ins to once a week, you'll see a steady weight loss—without the day-to-day fluctuations that can sabotage the best-laid plans.

The fact is that slight weight gains are perfectly normal. They are due to stress, water retention, body chemistry, and to the fact that many of you will be exercising for the first time in your life, and growing muscles initially add weight. When you start an exercise program, your body composition changes, your blood volume increases, and your circulation improves—all signs that you're getting into shape and all worth any slight initial weight gain. And the good news is that inches will continue to come off.

A scale does not discriminate between lean muscle weight and fat. The best way to determine how much body fat you have—and how much you are losing—is with underwater weighing. Since lean muscle tissue is heavier than water, the more lean muscle tissue in relation to fat tissue you have, the more you will weigh underwater. On the other hand, the more body fat you have, the lower the reading will be. To coin a phrase: Muscles sink and fat floats.

Fat-fold measurements are an alternative way to determine body fat but not as accurate as underwater weighing. In our lab, we use calipers to "pinch" various parts of a subject's body lightly and measure the thickness of body fat within the pinched fold. The thickness of fat folds from certain body sites can be used to estimate total body fat. In The Rockport Walking Program study, we took 30 fat-fold measurements and circumferences for each of our 80 subjects—everything from the shoulder to the ankle. Ideally, body fat should be about 15 to 18 percent in men and 20 to 25 percent in women.

Unfortunately, underwater weighing and fat-fold measurements must be performed in a laboratory setting by trained personnel. In situations where these measurements cannot be made we recommend using body mass index (BMI). BMI is a ratio of weight to height that correlates highly with amount of body fat. However, it does not distinguish body fat and muscle. You can determine your BMI from the nomogram on the next page. Criteria for "acceptable" weight and "overweight" have been developed from large population studies. You can also use the nomogram to determine an acceptable weight based on your height.

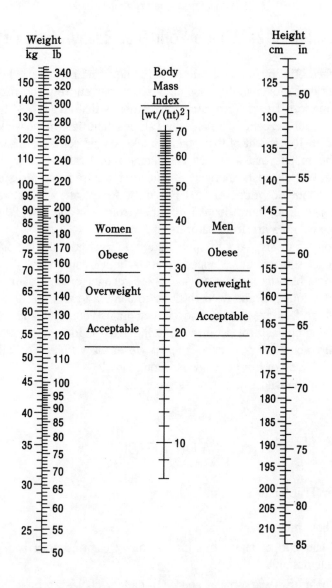

A nomogram for determining body mass index (BMI). To use this nomogram, place a ruler or other straight edge between the column for height and the column for weight connecting an individual's numbers for those two variables. Read the BMI in kg/m^2 where the straight line crosses the middle lines when the height and weight are connected. *Overweight*: BMI of 24 to 30 kg/m^2 ; *Obesity*: BMI above kg/m^2. Heights and weights are without shoes or clothes.

Source: Bray, G. A. 1985. "Obesity: Definition, diagnoses and disadvantages." *The Medical Journal of Australia* 142: S2-S8. Copyright © 1985, *The Medical Journal of Australia*, reprinted with permission.

Self-Test 2: What's Your Diet Really Made Of?

It's a fact. Americans have one of the richest and most varied diets in the world. Unfortunately, though, we also eat entirely too much fat. The American Heart Association recommends that adults hold their fat intake to 30 percent of total daily calories (and less if possible). No more than 10 percent of the total fat intake should come from saturated fat. This means that a person consuming 2,000 calories a day should only get 600 of those calories from fat. (Six hundred calories is equivalent to about 66 grams of fat.) But most Americans get between *35 and 40 percent* of their total daily calories from fat—and *15 to 20 percent* of those calories are from saturated fat.

Some fats are easy to spot: butter, margarine, cooking oil, salad dressings, sour cream, whipped cream—the list can go on.

Some high-fat foods are also easy to recognize: ice cream, French fries, potato chips, and fried chicken, to name a few.

Other fats are hidden and can sabotage your diet and increase your blood cholesterol, as discussed on page 10. In fact, studies show that only about 40 percent of the fat we eat is visible. The other 60 percent is hidden from our unsuspecting view!

Take this short quiz and test your fat I.Q.

A FAT ATTACK

Answer True or False to the following:

1. Whole milk is high in fat.
2. A half cup of sugar has just as many calories as a half cup of vegetable oil.
3. Whole eggs are a major source of dietary cholesterol.
4. A baked potato is much more fattening than a chef salad.
5. Soup is a good low-calorie choice.
6. Meat is too high in calories even to contemplate including in a weight-loss diet.
7. Spaghetti is just plain fattening.
8. Chicken—no matter how it's cooked—is a great diet food.
9. Deli tuna sandwiches make great low-calorie lunches.
10. Low-calorie cream cheese is a low-fat spread.

ANSWERS*

1. *Milk Talk.* True. Whole milk has the equivalent of 2 pats of butterfat in every 8-ounce glass and 53 percent of its 170 calories comes from fat. Even 2-percent milk, with 1 pat of butterfat per 8-ounce glass, provides 36 percent of its 125 calories from fat. Better choices would be 1-percent milk, with only ½ a pat of butterfat in every glass, or skim milk with virtually no "hidden" fat.

2. *Calorie Count.* False! A half cup of sugar has 400 calories. A half cup of flour has 200. But a half cup of oil has 1,000 calories! The plain truth: Protein and carbohydrate provide 4 calories per gram, while fat has a fattening 9 calories per gram. The bottom line is that fats are fattening; they provide twice the number of calories per gram as protein and carbohydrates.

3. *Reducing Cholesterol.* True. A large, whole egg contains about 280 milligrams of cholesterol—and all of it is found in the yolk. It's smart to eat less dietary cholesterol to keep your cholesterol level in check. In fact, the American Heart Association recommends limiting your cholesterol to less than 300 milligrams a day.

4. *Chef Know-How.* False. This was a trick question, in part. The truth is that a *plain* baked potato is low in calories. As long as you stay away from fattening toppings like butter and sour cream, you can have a delicious and nutritious large baked potato for only about 140 calories—adding only a little bit more for diet margarine or a spoonful of yogurt and chives. A chef salad, on the other hand, may contain high-fat luncheon meats, cheese, and eggs—and usually more than a dollop of fat-rich dressing.

5. *Soup Food for Thought.* True . . . if you make it yourself from scratch and control the ingredients. Otherwise, you may be getting a considerable amount of fat from chicken skin, added oil, fatty meats, or cream.

6. *Meat Rap.* False. Meat has gotten a bad reputation. Yes, certain cuts, such as porterhouse steak, contain a lot of fat. How can you tell? Just look closely at a cut of meat. If it has a lot of streaks of fat (called *marbling*) through it, the cut will be high in fat. But lean cuts such as top round beef have just over half the calories found in a porterhouse steak of the same size.

*Answers to questions 1, 2, 4, 7, 8, and 9 are adapted from Eve Lowry, R.D., Lean Life Food series, Sound/Slide Program, NUTRIVISUALS, P.O. Box 1367, Shingle Springs, CA 95682.

7. *Pasta Performance*. False! Believe it or not, you'd have to eat about 7 cups of spaghetti to equal the number of calories in a 12-ounce untrimmed porterhouse steak. Because it is a complex carbohydrate, pasta is readily turned into glycogen—which is the fuel used to work our muscles. In fact, the American Heart Association recommends that 50 to 60 percent of your total daily calories come from carbohydrate.

8. *Skin Is Not Skinny*. False. This was an easy question. Of course, *fried* chicken is higher in calories than *baked* chicken. Here are the facts on chicken as described by Eve Lowry, R.D., in her Lean Life Food series:

   • An average broiler/fryer weighing 3 pounds has about 2,625 calories
   • The meat itself weighs in at 2¼ pounds and has only 880 calories
   • The skin, at a scant ¾ pound, has all the rest—a whopping 1,745 calories!

   There's no doubt about it: Chicken skin is almost all fat; so, for maximum weight loss and maximum health, cut away the skin before you cook.

9. *Tuna Helper*. False—most likely! A tuna sandwich is an ideal food to eat when you're watching your weight—as long as you make it yourself. Deli tuna sandwiches can have up to 500 calories from the oil in which the tuna was packed, the lavish use of mayonnaise, and the bread "fillers" that are sometimes added to create that creamy texture. Tuna packed in oil has more than twice the calories of tuna packed in water.

10. *Say Cream Cheese*. Merry Yamartino, one of the registered dietitians who worked on The Rockport Walking Program study, summed up this hidden fat this way: "Putting cream cheese on a bagel is like spreading it with shortening." Even low-fat cream cheese can be deceiving, despite the product's claims. "Low-fat" can still translate into too much fat.

SCORING

If you've answered between 8 and 10 questions correctly, you have "fat savvy." If you've answered between 5 and 7 correctly, you're definitely on the "fat track"—but there are still some things you can discover. If you've answered fewer than 5 correctly, you need to pay more attention to what you eat. But don't despair. By sticking to The Rockport Walking Program, a "fat cat" can become lean and healthy.

FAT CHART OF COMMON FOODS*

	PRODUCT/AMOUNT	PAT(S) OF FAT**
Obvious Fats (100% fat; visible fat)	Butter, 1 Tbsp.	3
	Lard, 1 Tbsp.	3
	Margarine, 1 Tbsp.	3
	Mayonnaise, 1 Tbsp.	2
	Vegetable oil, 1 Tbsp.	3
	Vegetable shortening, 1 Tbsp.	3
Fats Incognito (in general, more than 50% fat; foods that are naturally high in fat; invisible fat)	Cream cheese, 2 Tbsp.	2
	Cheese (most types), 1 oz.	2
	Half & Half, 1 fl. oz.	1
	Ice cream 10% fat (supermarket), 1 cup	3
	Ice cream 16% fat (gourmet), 1 cup	5
	Sour cream, 2 Tbsp.	1
	Table cream, 1 fl. oz.	1
	2% milk, 1 cup	1
	Whipped cream, ¼ cup	2
	Whole milk, 1 cup	2
	Egg, whole, medium	1
	Avocado, ⅓ medium	2
	Nuts, ¼ cup	4
	Olives, 10 medium	1
	Peanut butter, 2 Tbsp.	3
	Salad dressing, 2 Tbsp.	3
	Seeds, 1 oz.	3
	Bacon, 3 slices	2
	Bologna, 1 oz.	2
	Cheeseburger, ¼ lb regular ground beef, cooked	6
	Frankfurter, 1 medium	3
	Hamburger, ¼ lb regular ground beef, cooked	4
	Sausage, 1 oz.	2
	Sirloin steak, 6 oz.	6
	T-bone steak, 6 oz.	8
Fats Undercover (fat added during preparation; invisible fat)	Biscuit, 1 medium	2
	Croissant, 1 medium	2
	Muffin, 1 large	2
	Corn chips/tortilla chips, 1 oz.	2
	Crackers (butter-type), 5	1
	French fries, 1 cup/15, 2"-3" long	2
	Popcorn, microwave (movie theater), 4 cups	2
	Potato chips, 1 oz./15 chips	2
	Cheese sauce, ¼ cup	2
	Gravy, homemade brown, ¼ cup	3
	White sauce, thick, ¼ cup	2
	Chicken, breaded and fried, 3 oz.	3
	Fish, breaded and fried, 3 oz.	2
	Mayonnaise-based salads (potato/ macaroni/coleslaw), ½ cup	2
	Pizza, (15" diameter), 1 slice	2
	Cookies, chocolate chip (2¼" diameter), 4	2
	Cookies, oatmeal (2 ⅝" diameter), 4	2
	Pie, any kind	3

Source: Paula Cuneo, R.D., and Merry Yamartino, R.D.

*Those foods containing fat that are most commonly used are included above. But this is *not* a complete listing of foods that contain fat. For more information on the fat content of various foods, refer to Appendix E: Fat and Cholesterol Comparison Chart.

**One pat equals 1 teaspoon or 5 grams of fat.

To see how your daily eating habits really measure up, a fat analysis of your diet is needed. That's where the second part of the "What's Your Diet Really Made Of?" self-test comes in.

"BE A FAT DETECTIVE" QUIZ

1. Complete a one-day food diary on the blank diary sheet in appendix D. Follow the format used on the examples in the appendix. Remember: There's no cheating. This is for your eyes only. Try to write down everything you eat during these 24 hours.
2. You're now ready to analyze your fat intake. You will be going through your diary three times as you examine it for high-fat foods. Use the Fat Chart of Common Foods (page 25) to determine your score.
3. The first time through your diary, you are looking for *obvious fats*—the foods that are virtually 100 percent fat and that are easy to see in our diet. Butter, margarine, and cooking oil are some examples of obvious fats. When you spot an obvious fat in your diary, circle both the food item and the amount that was used. (See the obvious-fat example in appendix D.) Compare the amount you used with the amounts on the Fat Chart. Keep track of how many "pats" you are using on a separate sheet of paper.
4. The second time around, you are looking for *fats incognito*. These are the foods that are naturally high in fat. More than 50 percent of their calories come from fat, but we're not always aware of this because we can't see the fat. Fats incognito include olives, sour cream, and frankfurters. Again, circle all of the foods on your diary that fit this description, and jot down how many "pats" you had in your diet.
5. The third and final time through your food diary you're looking for *fats undercover*. Like fats incognito, these are fats we cannot see but that have been added during the preparation of the food and have made that food high in fat. Muffins, gravy, French fries, and cookies are examples of fats undercover. Follow the same procedure as above to record how many "pats" you had.
6. Add up your three "pat" scores. You now have a total number of "pats" for the day, indicating the number of teaspoons of fat that were consumed for that day. Here are some guidelines you can follow to help you better understand what your total number means:

• If you were eating a 1,200-calorie diet with 30 percent fat (Ameri-

can Heart Association recommendation), you would not want to exceed 8 pats of fat per day.
- If you were following a 1,500-calorie diet with 30 percent fat, you would be limited to 10 pats of fat per day.
- If you were following an 1,800-calorie diet with 30 percent fat, you would be eating no more than 12 pats of fat per day.

By the end of the study, our subjects' average fat intake went from 37 percent to 25 percent of calories and saturated fat intake went from 13 percent to 8 percent of calories. Retake this test one month into the program. You'll see, like those in our study, that your diet has become healthier and wiser.

Self-Test 3: The Rockport Fitness Walking Test

Before we introduced The Rockport Fitness Walking Test in 1986, there was a real need for a simple, easy, unsupervised test to determine a person's level of fitness before starting an exercise program. After 18 months of vigorous testing, our Exercise Physiology and Nutrition Laboratory, in conjunction with our colleagues from the Department of Exercise Science at the University of Massachusetts in Amherst, designed The Rockport Fitness Walking Test—a step-by-step method of finding your level of fitness simply by walking one mile as fast as you can! The test in this book is a modification of the original Rockport Walking Test designed for different body weights. By taking this quick test, you'll also know which one of our three Walking Programs—Blue, White, or Red—will give you the best results.

What about medications? There is a class of drugs called "beta blockers" that slows the heart rate response to exercise. If you are taking a beta blocker, The Rockport Fitness Walking Test may overestimate your fitness level and you may not be able to achieve the training heart rates recommended in the exercise programs. Speak to your physician about an appropriate exercise program.

More than 1 million people have taken The Rockport Fitness Walking Test since we first presented it at the American College of Sports Medicine. It has received national attention from the media, including "Good Morning, America," "The Today Show," and USA Today. One of the most accurate tests for determining cardiovascular fitness regardless of age, weight, and sex, it proves that The Rockport Walking Program is as easy as . . . taking a walk. All you need is a watch and a pair of walking shoes!

BEFORE YOU START

1. *Take your pulse.* You need to know how to count your pulse (heart rate) during The Rockport Fitness Walking Test. If you don't already know how to take your pulse, here's an easy and accurate way to do so:

   - Put your second and third fingers together and place them on your radial artery just inside your wrist bone, or on your neck's carotid artery, on either side of your Adam's apple.
   - Walk in place for 30 seconds if you have trouble finding your pulse, then try again.
   - Using a watch with a second hand, count your pulse for 15 seconds.
   - Multiply this number by 4 in order to calculate your pulse rate per minute. The normal resting range in healthy adults is between 60 and 100 beats per minute, but rates can increase from fear, physical exercise, stress, temperature change, and pain.

2. *Find a mile-length track.* Since you'll be walking one mile as briskly as you can for The Rockport Fitness Walking Test, you'll need to determine your one-mile route before you start. Choose a route that's as flat and smooth as possible. Most high schools, colleges, and local health clubs and recreational facilities have quarter-mile tracks. If you map out one mile with your car's odometer, pick a route with the least possible amount of stoplights, crowded sidewalks, and traffic.

3. *Warm up and stretch for five minutes.* Warming up helps get the blood flowing to your muscles. Stretching your muscles will keep them from getting stiff. (You'll find some stretches in chapter 3.)

TAKING THE TEST STEP BY STEP

1. *Walk the one mile as fast as you can.*
2. *Immediately take your pulse.* Your heart rate will start to slow down almost immediately after you've completed your walk, so it's important you count your pulse as soon as you've reached your one-mile mark.
3. *Record your time to the nearest second.* It should take you anywhere between 10 and 25 minutes.
4. *That's it!* You're now ready to find out your relative fitness level—and the Walking Program that's tailor-made for you.

FINDING YOUR FITNESS LEVEL

1. *Find the relative fitness graph that best fits your age and sex.* Based on fitness norms established by the American Heart Association, it will show how your performance compares with others your age and sex.
2. *Mark the point defined by your Rockport Walking Test results.* Locate the time scale along the bottom that corresponds to your body weight. Mark your walking time on this scale. Mark your heart rate at the end of the walk on the left side of the scale. Draw a vertical line from your walk time and a horizontal line from your heart rate to the point where they intersect. The area where these two points meet shows your relative fitness level: either high, above average, average, below average, or low as compared to others in your age, sex, and weight category.

For example, a forty-two-year-old woman who weighed 180 pounds, completed the one-mile walk test in 18 minutes, 15 seconds, and had a heart rate at the end of the mile of 33 beats/15 seconds or 132 beats per minute. Her results are plotted on the next page. She fell into the below average fitness category.

FINDING YOUR INDIVIDUAL EXERCISE PROGRAM

1. *Find the exercise program that best fits your age, weight, and sex.* Mark your time and your heart rate just as you did on the relative fitness graph. The labeled area where these two points converge shows you the specific walking program that is just right for you: either Blue, White, or Red.
2. *Remember your program name.* In the next section, you'll be putting your individual walking program into practice—by starting day one of your 30-Day Rockport Walking Program!

For example, the forty-two-year-old woman described above fell into the White Exercise Program Chart and would follow the White 20-week exercise prescription (see next page).

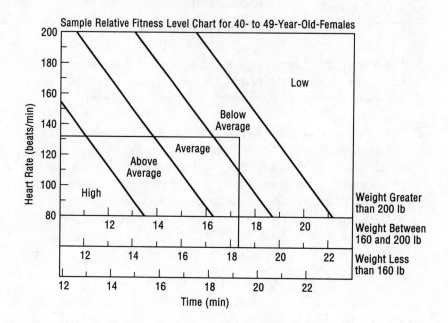

Sample Relative Fitness Level Chart for 40- to 49-Year-Old-Females

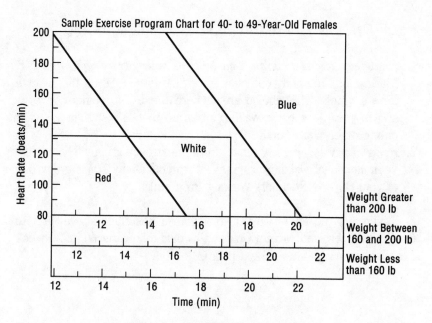

Sample Exercise Program Chart for 40- to 49-Year-Old Females

30

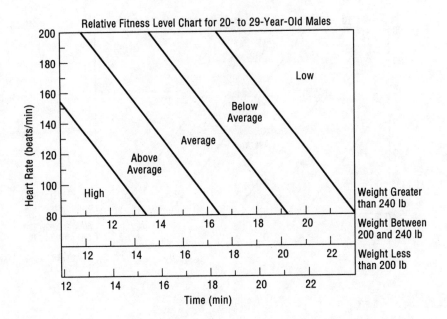

Relative Fitness Level Chart for 20- to 29-Year-Old Males

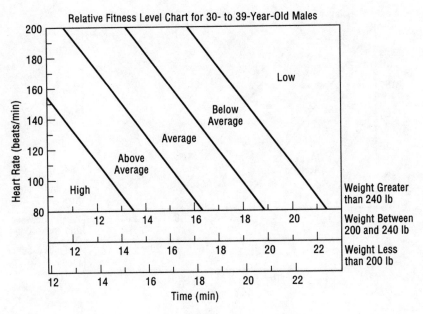

Relative Fitness Level Chart for 30- to 39-Year-Old Males

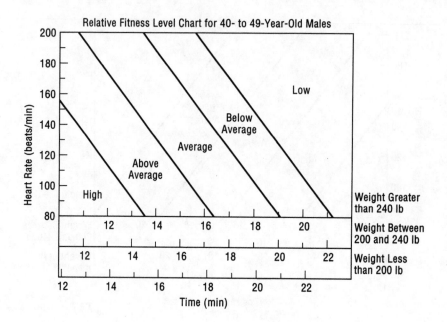

Relative Fitness Level Chart for 40- to 49-Year-Old Males

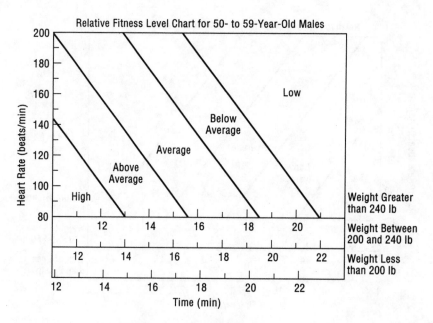

Relative Fitness Level Chart for 50- to 59-Year-Old Males

32

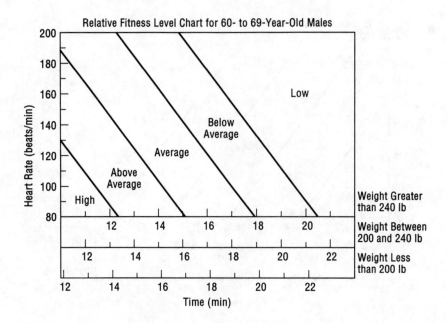

Relative Fitness Level Chart for 60- to 69-Year-Old Males

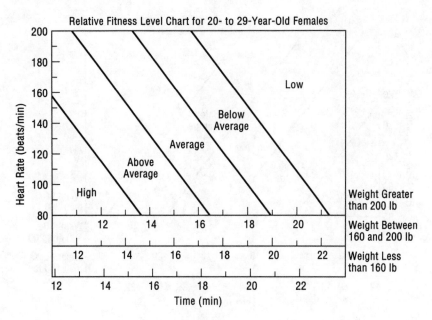

Relative Fitness Level Chart for 20- to 29-Year-Old Females

33

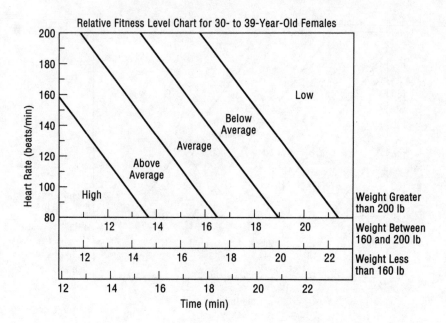

Relative Fitness Level Chart for 30- to 39-Year-Old Females

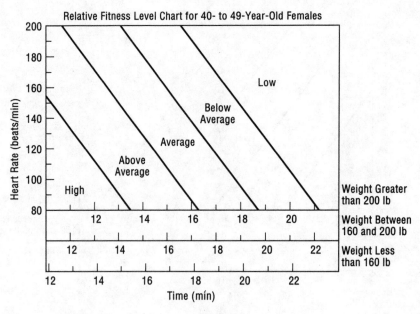

Relative Fitness Level Chart for 40- to 49-Year-Old Females

34

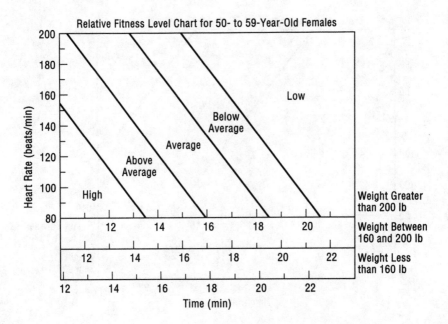

Relative Fitness Level Chart for 50- to 59-Year-Old Females

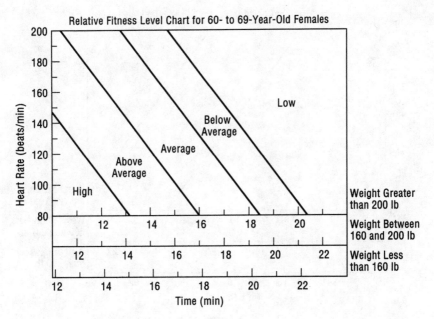

Relative Fitness Level Chart for 60- to 69-Year-Old Females

35

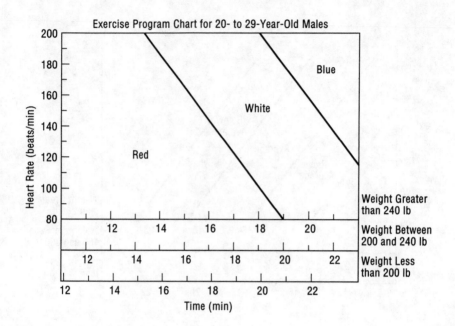

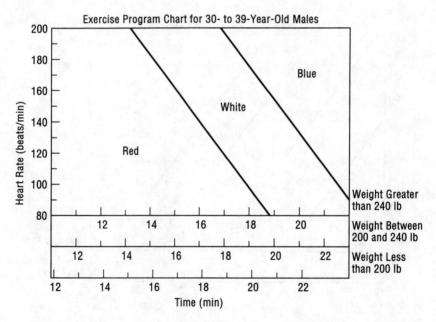

36

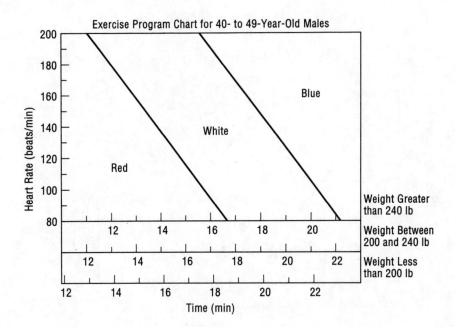

Exercise Program Chart for 40- to 49-Year-Old Males

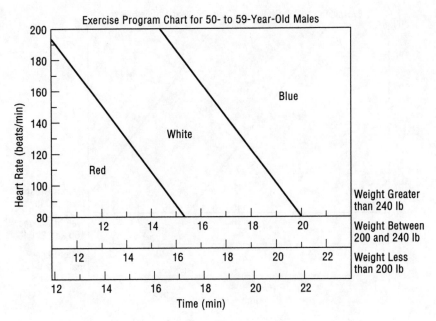

Exercise Program Chart for 50- to 59-Year-Old Males

37

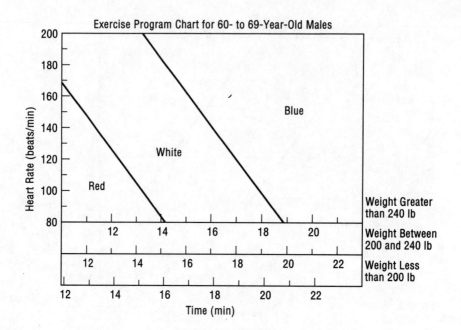

Exercise Program Chart for 60- to 69-Year-Old Males

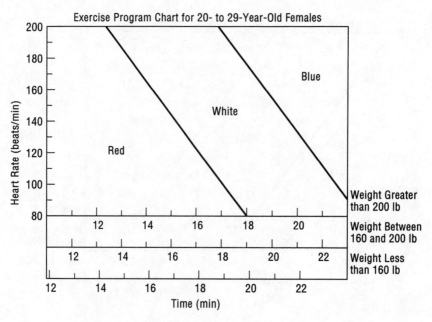

Exercise Program Chart for 20- to 29-Year-Old Females

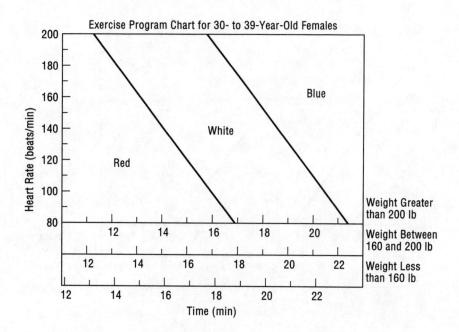

Exercise Program Chart for 30- to 39-Year-Old Females

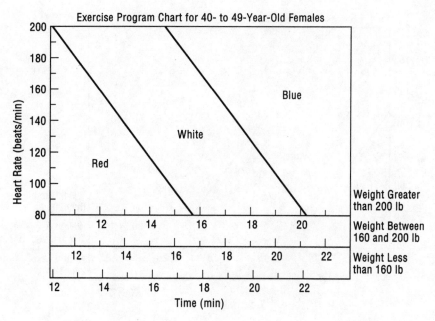

Exercise Program Chart for 40- to 49-Year-Old Females

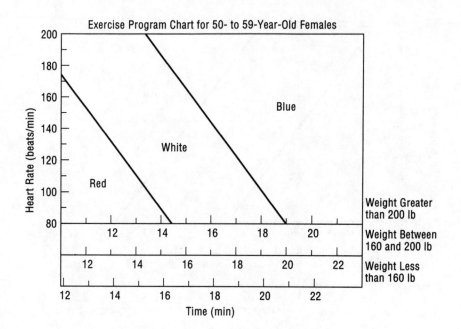

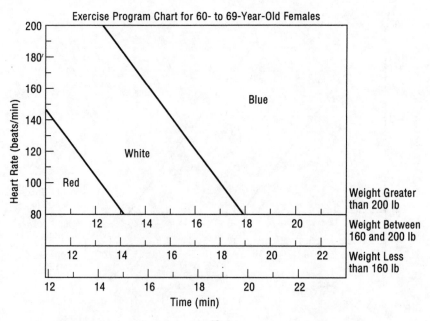

Self-Test 4: Evaluating Your Blood-Cholesterol Values

We strongly suggest you be tested for cholesterol levels before starting The Rockport Walking Program. But getting your blood tested is one
thing—and understanding what the results mean is another. This test is
meant to demystify the numbers and give you a better comprehension
of your cholesterol values, for optimal prediction and reduction of
coronary-heart-disease risk.

EVALUATING CHOLESTEROL VALUES

Answer True or False to the following statements:

1. Total cholesterol should be measured in every adult 45 years and
   older.
2. Getting your cholesterol measured every 10 years is a good rule of
   thumb.
3. A measurement below 200 milligrams per deciliter of blood is a
   "desirable blood-cholesterol" level.
4. A "borderline-high blood cholesterol" is any measurement between
   200 and 239 milligrams per deciliter of blood.
5. "High blood cholesterol" is classified as any measurement above
   240 milligrams per deciliter of blood.
6. Men are considered at a higher risk when cholesterol values are
   measured.

ANSWERS

1. *False.* Adults should start having their cholesterol tested when they
   reach their twenties.
2. *False.* The National Heart, Lung, and Blood Institute recommends
   that adults get retested for cholesterol *at least* every five years.
3. *True.* But that doesn't mean you can forget about the risks of high
   cholesterol. For the best preventive care, keep your intake of
   saturated fats low, your walking program consistent, and do get
   retested every five years.
4. *True.* If your levels are in the borderline range, we suggest you
   repeat your blood-cholesterol test to confirm the value. If you do
   not have coronary heart disease and you don't have more than two
   other risk factors (see chapter 1), your levels can be controlled by a

low-fat diet. But do have a cholesterol test taken once a year. However, if you have two or more coronary-heart-disease risk factors in addition to your high blood cholesterol, a lipoprotein analysis should be done to determine your LDL-cholesterol level. Consult your physician for the best course of action.

5. *True*. A lipoprotein analysis is recommended at this point. Medication may or may not be prescribed—depending on other coronary-heart-disease risk factors you might have. Consult your physician on drug treatment and dietary guidelines.

6. *True*. In addition to the eight risk factors for coronary heart disease discussed in chapter 1, being male is considered an additional risk.

SCORING

Knowledge is only the first step to preventive care. Whether you've answered all six questions correctly or incorrectly is not the point. The real points are: Eat a healthy, low-fat diet, participate in a consistent exercise program, listen to your physician, and have your cholesterol checked on a regular basis.

Self-Test 5: Your Blood-Pressure Readings

Along with high cholesterol and cigarette smoking, high blood pressure is a major risk factor for coronary disease. It's a silent killer with no visible symptoms that can double your risk of heart attack 10 or 15 years down the road. We recommend that you have your blood pressure taken before you start The Rockport Walking Program.

To test your knowledge of high blood pressure, see if you can answer the following questions:

1. What do the terms *systolic* and *diastolic* mean?
2. What is a mild high-blood-pressure reading?
3. How can you lower your blood pressure?
4. How often should you have your blood pressure taken?
5. What exactly is hypertension?

ANSWERS

1. *Systolic* blood pressure is the upper number of your reading, and it reflects the pressure your heart exerts when it squeezes down and contracts, pushing the blood through your arteries. *Diastolic* blood pressure is the lower number of your reading, and it reflects the pressure the arteries feel while the heart is resting between beats. A high-blood-pressure reading means that the heart is squeezing too hard to get the blood moving through your arteries (systolic), and the blood in the arteries is straining too hard to flow smoothly and evenly while the heart rests (diastolic).

2. You can be considered as having mild high blood pressure if your reading is above 140/90.

3. High blood pressure can be prevented through a regular program of diet and exercise. Remember, for every two pounds of weight you lose, you'll lose one millimeter of mercury off your blood pressure reading. Our studies at the Exercise Physiology and Nutrition Laboratory have shown that daily aerobic exercise like walking will help reduce your blood pressure—and keep it low. Medication can also help lower blood pressure. Consult your physician for specific guidelines.

4. More than 60 million Americans have high blood pressure—and between 30 and 40 percent of all Americans do not even know what their blood pressure is. Today, getting your blood pressure taken is as accessible as your corner drugstore. We suggest you have your blood pressure taken at least twice a year.

5. *Hypertension* is another name for high blood pressure. It literally means increased (*hyper*) pressure (*tension*). Hypertension can be inherited, but 90 percent of all cases are a mystery. For some reason—and nobody understands what this reason is—arterial pressure can get elevated and result in hypertension. But high blood pressure can be prevented by a regular program of weight loss and exercise like The Rockport Walking Program.

Self-Test 6: Determining Your Individual Meal Plan

We have three basic Meal Plans: 1,200 calories a day, 1,500 calories a day, and 1,800 calories a day. To determine which one is best for you, it's important to keep in mind that *slow and steady wins the race*. No, you will not lose 10 pounds in three days on The Rockport Walking Program. But we guarantee a consistent weight loss on the average of 1 to 2 pounds a week if you follow the program. This might not sound like a lot, but those "only" 1 or 2 pounds a week add up dramatically:

How weight loss adds up...

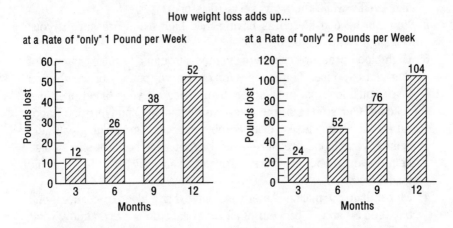

Further, a greater percentage of the pounds you lose will be body fat—not lean muscle tissue or water. And, because exercise is included, The Rockport Walking Program will help keep your setpoint low and your metabolism high. Most important, because you are not feeling deprived, you'll want to stay with it—for good!

Picking a Winning Meal Plan

First, calculate your caloric needs to maintain your present weight. How? Simply by adding a zero to your weight. For example, if you weigh 180 pounds, your daily caloric needs to maintain that weight would be 1,800.

To lose approximately one pound a week, you need to burn 3,500 calories, or 500 calories per day:

$$500 \times 7 = 3,500 = 1 \text{ pound of fat}$$

Using our example, if you want to lose one pound a week and you presently weigh 180 pounds, you'll need to subtract 500 calories a day from your present intake of 1,800 calories:

$$1,800 - 500 = 1,300 \text{ calories a day}$$

Thirteen hundred calories is certainly enough to ensure that your daily nutritional needs. But The Rockport Walking Program Meal Plans utilize both a healthy diet *and* moderate exercise to burn that pound of fat without deprivation or strain. By taking into account the calories you'll be burning by walking, you can actually eat more food—and still lose that pound a week. Here's how:

Add the calories you will burn in your daily walk. We use 200 calories a day as an average. In the above example, you'd add 200 extra calories to your 1,300-calorie diet:

$$200 \text{ "exercise" calories} + 1,300 \text{ "diet" calories} = 1,500$$

Using our example, if you weighed 180 pounds before starting The Rockport Walking Program, you'd choose the 1,500-Calorie Meal Plan to ensure a safe and steady weight loss of one pound a week.

Let's try another example, using 150 pounds as your present weight. Add the zero and you will see that you need 1,500 calories a day to maintain your 150 pounds. To lose one pound a week, subtract 500 calories from the original 1,500:

$$1,500 - 500 = 1,000 \text{ calories a day}$$

Add 200 calories for daily exercise:

$$200 \text{ "exercise" calories} + 1,000 \text{ "diet" calories} = 1,200$$

The 1,200-Calorie Meal Plan is the one you should choose to safely lose one pound a week.

But what if your results fall somewhere in between one of our three plans? Let's try one:

If you presently weigh 140 pounds, you need 1,400 calories a day to maintain that weight. Subtract 500 calories in order to lose one pound a week:

$$1,400 - 500 = 900 \text{ calories a day}$$

Add 200 calories for exercise:

$$200 \text{ "exercise" calories} + 900 \text{ "diet" calories} = 1,100$$

Your best choice would be the 1,200-Calorie Meal Plan because eating less than 1,200 calories a day can be harmful to your health. On the 1,200-Calorie Plan, you would still be consuming fewer calories than you'd need to maintain your 140 pounds—and you would safely lose weight. What's more, as you increase your walking mileage, you'll be increasing the number of calories you burn on a daily basis.

On the other hand, let's say you weigh 220 pounds and you need 2,200 calories a day to maintain that weight:

$$2,200 - 500 = 1,700 \text{ calories a day}$$

$$200 \text{ "exercise" calories} + 1,700 \text{ "diet" calories} = 1,900$$

Here, you'd choose the 1,800-Calorie Meal Plan. Chances are, anything above that and you'll be consuming too much fat for a healthy weight-loss diet.

Use the plan that best fits into the above equation. Remember, you only want to lose one to two pounds a week. Any more weight loss and you might be sacrificing your nutritional needs—and losing lean muscle instead of fat. If, in one month's time, you are not losing weight or you've reached a plateau, go to the next lower plan or increase your walking. But, again, don't go below 1,200 calories a day.

Whether 1,200, 1,500, or 1,800, remember the meal plan you choose. You're about to put it into practice in the 30-Day Rockport Walking Program—and turn what you've learned throughout this chapter into positive results. Get ready to change your life—in only one month!

II

30 DAYS TO CHANGE YOUR LIFE

3

GETTING READY TO
START YOUR
30-DAY PROGRAM

Before we go over the specifics you'll need to know for your 30-Day Rockport Walking Program, we're going to ask you to do something: Forget every diet you have ever been on.

That means forgetting the deprivation of dieting—and the "food prison" you put yourself in for weeks at a time for the "heinous" crime of overeating. That means forgetting the promises of "Lose ten pounds in three days!"—with "successful" weight reduction that comes back as quickly as you take it off. That means forgetting the misconceptions, the misguided notions, and the missed goals that come from trying to stick to impossible diet plans. In fact, I'd like you to take the word *dieting* out of your vocabulary.

Your 30-Day Meal Plan

Deprivation is a dirty word in The Rockport Walking Program plan—because it leads to feelings of discouragement that will make you quit. Depriving yourself takes enormous willpower—and can only last so long.

Instead, The Rockport Walking Program offers a pleasing alternative: a wide variety of good-tasting foods that are incorporated into three meals a day plus built-in snacks—all of which follow the American Heart Association's (AHA) guidelines:

- Keep fats down to 30 percent of total calories, with only 10 percent of these fats as saturated.
- Raise your carbohydrate intake to 50 or 60 percent of your total daily calories.
- Limit your cholesterol intake to less than 300 milligrams per day.
- Limit your salt intake.

Exchanging Calories for Exchanges

The American Heart Association guidelines are a national standard and a good outline to use, but they only give you broad brushstrokes. The American Diabetes Association and The American Dietetic Association diet guidelines consist of low-fat, balanced meal plans based on an exchange system. They give more detailed and more specific information —which is why Research Nutritionist Diane Morris, and Registered Dietitians Merry Yamartino and Paula Cuneo merged both the AHA and the ADA/ADA guidelines to design The Rockport Walking Program.

Some of you are already familiar with an exchange system. For those of you who are not, an exchange is pretty much what it sounds like. Within a food category, one food can be "exchanged" or swapped for another. An apple can be swapped for a nectarine on the exchange system—as long as the portion sizes always equal the amount we list per serving. We've divided your food groups into six exchange lists:

1. Starch/Bread
2. Meat
3. Vegetable
4. Fruit
5. Milk
6. Fat

Calorie counting can be tedious and time-consuming. The secret to changing your eating habits successfully is ease; a diet plan should not be a burden. "In my experience, people who want to lose weight need some structure because they feel out of control," says Dr. Morris. "Using easy-to-follow exchanges will help people gain control in an area where they feel they have little control. Once people understand the exchange system, they will become more relaxed and their thinking will become more automatic. Within a few weeks, they can say, 'Oh, I have one more fruit to go today,' or 'I've got a big dinner party tonight, so I'll save most of my starches and fats for later.' "

Each day, you will eat a certain amount of food from each of these six exchange categories. To give you a head start, we've planned your menus for the next 30 days. For your first month, you'll find three daily meals plus snacks for the 1,200-, 1,500-, and 1,800-Calorie Meal Plans. Each day, you only have to look at your Meal Plan (which you chose in chapter 2) to see what you'll be eating.

In chapter 5, you'll discover the array of foods available to help you to keep up a steady weight loss after you've completed your 30-Day Program. And, in the back of this book (see "The Rockport Recipes"), you'll find delicious recipes that are used in the 30-Day Program. Because each recipe lists the exchanges per serving, you can also use and reuse them after your first month is finished and you are on your own (for information on your exchange lists see chapter 5).

Measuring Your Foods for Maximum Results

When you look over the 30-Day Meal Plans, you'll see that portion sizes are designated. It's important to keep to the portions we suggest—and that means *measuring* your foods.

Accurate measurements are crucial for maximum weight loss—at least in the beginning. In time, you'll find that you can determine a portion size by eye, but for now, keep your measuring spoons and cups nearby.

But your Meal Plan is only half of your 30-Day Program. The other half is exercise—where you put your individual Walking Program into action.

Your 30-Day Walking Program

Walking requires no special skills. It needs no expensive equipment or training. It doesn't take a health-club membership or a mail-order video to do. It's a completely portable exercise. And, because you determined your individual Walking Program in chapter 2, you'll be assured of starting out at a level that will help you burn calories and improve your aerobic capabilities without overexertion.

But before you turn to Day One in our 30-Day Program, you need to understand your daily exercise program. You need to get ready with:

- An accurate target heart-rate zone
- A good pair of walking shoes
- Proper clothing
- Warm-ups, cool-downs, and stretches

Let's go over each of these items.

Fitness First: Walking in Your Target Heart-Rate Zone

The percentage of maximum heart rate that achieves the best results for you—without strain—is called your *target heart-rate zone*. Reaching your target heart-rate zone when you exercise will ensure that you're reaping the optimal cardiovascular benefits.

To determine your maximum heart rate, subtract your age from 220 heartbeats per minute. For example, a man or a woman who is 40 years old would have a maximum heart rate of 180 (220 − 40 = 180).

To calculate your target heart-rate zone, simply take the percentage of your maximum heart rate indicated in the 30-Day Plan.

TARGET HEART-RATE ZONE (BEATS/MIN)

AGE (YRS)	TARGET ZONE (BEATS/MIN)				AVERAGE MAX HR (100%)
	50%	60%	70%	80%	
20	100	120	140	170	200
25	98	117	137	166	195
30	95	114	133	162	190
35	93	111	130	157	185
40	90	108	126	153	180
45	88	105	123	149	175
50	85	102	119	145	170
55	83	99	116	140	165
60	80	96	112	136	160
65	78	93	109	132	155
70	75	90	105	128	150

Source: Adapted with permission from *Starting Your Personal Fitness Walking Program.* Ann Ward, Ph.D., and James M. Rippe, M.D. Philadelphia: J. B. Lippincott Co., 10.

The usual heart-rate recommendation for improving cardiovascular fitness is 70 to 85 percent of maximum heart rate (corresponding, by the way, to 60 to 80 percent of VO_2max). This ensures that you are working hard enough to get fit but not so hard that you will have to stop after only a few minutes. However, in The Rockport Walking Program, we use 50- to 60-percent maximum heart rate to get you started. We want you to enjoy your walk, limit your chances of injury, and, because you can walk longer at this lower intensity without getting tired, maximize your caloric expenditure.

As the weeks go by, we will be gradually increasing your percentages of maximum heart rate—and thereby increasing the intensity of your workout and your target heart-rate zone. You'll find out more about this in chapter 6, after you've completed your 30-Day Plan.

For now, simply follow the instructions for your daily walking goal, and you will be assured of reaching your target-heart-rate zone.

The Walking Shoe: The Best Equipment for the Best Walk

"Come on, you don't need a special shoe for walking."

"I've been walking around in my street shoes forever."

"Running shoes or sneakers will work just as well."

You've probably heard these arguments time and time again. In fact, you might even have said these things yourself. But it's time to separate fact from misconception. The unequivocal truth is that, yes, you need a good walking shoe for a safer, better, and more enjoyable workout.

Over the past few years, a new scientific discipline called *biomechanics* has taken the sports world by storm. Literally translated as "the mechanics of biological motion," biomechanics is the study of the smallest, most precise increments of movement made when someone runs, plays tennis, skis, walks—or practices virtually any other sport.

Thanks to the development of sophisticated high-speed filming techniques that enable 50 to 100 snapshots to be taken per second, as well as the proliferation of computers, scientists can analyze movements that, in the past, went by almost unseen. They can determine how techniques and equipment can be improved for better performance and less risk of injury. Today, top athletes have biomechanic analyses done as a matter of course and, within every sports corporation, you'll find at least one biomechanic scientist.

Because of the work done in this field, modern ski boots have replaced leather lace-up models for skiing, modern running shoes have replaced tennis sneakers for jogging, and walking shoes have replaced running shoes for walking.

At the Exercise Physiology and Nutrition Laboratory, we have studied the biomechanics of walking versus running intensely. We have proved beyond doubt that *walking is not slow running*—and that it requires a different type of shoe.

When people run, they literally leap off the ground with every step, and they hit the ground with an impact of three to four times their body weight. When people walk, one foot is always in contact with the ground, and they hit the ground with an impact of only one to one and a half times their body weight. Walkers land on the outside of their heels and slowly roll their weight forward to the ball of the foot. This is a completely different biomechanical motion than running.

Biomechanical scientists have found that a good athletic shoe must serve two purposes: It must cushion the impact when the foot hits the ground, and it must control the excessive side-to-side motion of the foot known as *pronation*.

Pronation is a natural breaking motion that is necessary to stop your body's forward motion as you take a stride. In 95 percent of the people who walk, the foot lands on the outside of the heel and rolls to the inside in a natural pronation. But too much pronation creates a twisting motion that moves up to the ankles, knees, and hips—and can lead to injuries in the weakest of these joints.

Now these two goals are somewhat at cross-purposes: Soft materials used to cushion impact do not necessarily supply the support needed to control pronation. When we compared a shoe specifically designed for walking with court sneakers, running shoes, aerobic sneakers, and cross-training shoes, we found that the walking shoe was at least as good in controlling impact and *much better* at controlling pronation during walking.

Ask yourself these eight questions before you select your walking shoe:

1. *Is it lightweight?* Any excess weight in the shoe translates into extra weight that you will have to lift with each step.
2. *Is it made of a durable material?* We favor shoes made of leather or leather and mesh for durability. A good walking shoe must be

durable to support your foot muscles during your walk. Think about the last time you wore canvas sneakers all day long. Weren't your feet tired at the end of the day? With a durable leather walking shoe, you'll have less foot fatigue.

3. *Does it cushion the heel adequately?* Even though walking is a low-stress activity, the heel does continuously hit the ground—and you need extra cushioning to avoid major heel stress. In our studies at the Exercise Physiology and Nutrition Laboratory, we have discovered that women and men walk differently. Women actually land with more force on their heels, making a well-cushioned heel even more crucial if you are a woman. Look for a thick Vibram sole and a well-cushioned heel that's supported somewhat higher than the rest of the foot.

4. *Does the shoe have pronation control?* A good walking shoe will try to control excessive motion when your heel hits the ground with a heel counter—a part of the shoe's heel design that literally "grabs" your heel and keeps it stable.

5. *Does the sole's design accommodate the rolling motion of the walking stride?* When you walk, your weight "rolls" from the heel to the ball of the foot. At the Exercise Physiology and Nutrition Laboratory, our studies have shown that a good walking shoe needs something that allows this roll to occur. We call it a *rocker profile*—a shoe with a sole that is designed to rock from back to front.

ProWalker™ 9000-2300 Series (Courtesy The Rockport Company)

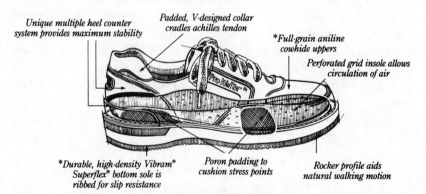

Unique multiple heel counter system provides maximum stability

Padded, V-designed collar cradles achilles tendon

*Full-grain aniline cowhide uppers

Perforated grid insole allows circulation of air

*Durable, high-density Vibram® Superflex® bottom sole is ribbed for slip resistance

Poron padding to cushion stress points

Rocker profile aids natural walking motion

* Available in some styles

6. *Is the shoe slightly stiff?* A good walking shoe doesn't need as much sole flexibility as a running shoe. In fact, a little stiffness and support is advantageous during the rolling walking motion.

7. *Is the arch well supported?* Look inside the shoe. Feel the inside bottom to see if it is well cushioned and whether there are strong internal arch supports.

8. *Does it have an ample toe box?* Your toes naturally spread out when you walk. To avoid cramping, you need a roomy toe box. Your toes should not feel "tight" against the front or sides. A hint: Purchase your shoes in the afternoon because your feet swell during the day.

Add socks that fit without bagging or pulling in a breathable fabric like cotton or an Orlon/cotton blend and you'll feel like you're "walking on air" as you do your fitness walk.

Cold-Weather Walking

Walking is one of the great outdoor exercises. Getting out there in the warm sun, feeling the slight breeze, listening to the sounds of nature. . . . But one of its most positive aspects can turn into a real negative one when the weather gets bad. Here are some suggestions to make walking a year-round exercise even in cold weather:

- Remember that walking warms you up. So when the weather gets cold, don't start reaching for the down coat and heavy wool sweater. Instead, dress in layers that you can take off as you warm up.
- Between two-thirds and three-quarters of our body heat is released through our heads, so wear a hat that covers your ears.
- Keep your hands warm with lightweight wool mittens or gloves. Keep your legs toasty with leg warmers over sweat pants.
- If it's windy, start your walk against the wind and return with it. And, a nylon suit will keep the wind-chill factor at bay.
- For those really frigid, icy days, investigate indoor tracks at local schools or health clubs. Today, many shopping malls provide areas and times for fitness walking; many of them have calculated the mileage for you. Check your local American Heart and Lung Associations for information.
- Motorized treadmills you can operate at home are a good choice when it's too cold to even open the door.

Hot Summer Walking

Any loose-fitting T-shirt and shorts will do when the weather sizzles. But make sure you add sun screen to your exposed areas. A visor will keep away glare and sunglasses will protect your eyes from the sun. On really hot days, add a protective hat and don't push yourself. Try walking in the early morning or evening when the weather is cooler. Dehydration and heat stress are very real problems in the hot summer sun. To avoid any problems, drink plenty of water: six to eight ounces before you start and at twenty- or thirty-minute intervals during your walk. If you start feeling any signs of heat stress—dizziness, headache, stomach cramps, or lack of perspiration—stop and do your walk another day.

Clothes Make the Walk

You can wear almost anything when you walk. Shorts, sweat pants, jeans, and T-shirt—whatever feels right. There are no special uniforms for walking, but there is one essential rule to remember when you're getting dressed: comfort. Choose loose, comfortable clothes that won't hamper your stride. Wearing a breathable fiber like cotton, wool, or treated nylon will allow sweat to evaporate. You'll stay warm, dry, and comfortable. And never overdress. Your body will stay warm during your walk—even when it's cold outside.

Warm-Ups and Cool-Downs

Warming up before aerobic activity and cooling down afterwards is crucial in any exercise program—and walking is no exception. People think that cutting out warm-ups and cool-downs will keep their walk time down, but that's ultimately a big mistake. Just as a car needs to "warm up" before you start it on cool days, your body needs to prepare itself before moving up to your target heart-rate zone. Similarly, in the same way you slow your car down before you park it, your body needs to come down gradually from its target heart-rate zone. Including five minutes of "revving up" and five minutes of "slowing down" in your daily walk will:

- Loosen muscles
- Aid flexibility
- Help prevent soreness
- Avoid unnecessary cardiac strain
- Enhance performance
- Avoid the risk of injury
- Mentally prepare you for your walk

Stretching is not the same thing as warming up and cooling down. Contrary to popular opinion, stretching can't take the place of walking at a slow pace for five minutes. But it can supplement your warm-up and cool-down time. The best prescription is the following:

- Walk at a slow pace for five minutes to get your blood flowing to your muscles.
- Then stretch for five minutes to increase your flexibility. Stretching is easier and more beneficial after your muscles have had a chance to warm up.

The following are a series of simple stretches you can use after both the warm-up and the cool-down. They are also great exercises for relieving stress and increasing your flexibility throughout the day. Take a break and do them in your office, while watching television, or when you're doing your household chores.

Perform these stretches slowly and smoothly. *Do not bounce.* You should feel a "pull" or stretch in the muscle—but no pain. Hold each stretch for approximately 10 to 15 seconds.

Stretching Program

---

1. *Calf (back of lower leg)*
   a. Straight knee—start with the leg to be stretched approximately three feet from the wall and the opposite leg one step forward. Lean toward wall, keeping heels down and foot turned in slightly.
   b. Bent knee—start same as above, but move approximately one foot closer to the wall and bend knee of back leg to be stretched.
   c. Repeat using other leg.

2. *Iliotibial Band (outside of hip)*
   a. Start with leg to be stretched one step back and behind opposite foot. Move hips sideways toward side being stretched. Keep upper body away from wall and do not bend forward.
   b. Repeat using other leg.
3. *Lower Back, Hips, Groin, and Hamstrings*
   Stand with feet about shoulder-width apart and pointed straight ahead. Slowly bend forward from the hips. Always keep knees slightly bent. Go to the point where you feel a slight stretch in the back of your legs.
4. *Side Bends*
   a. Stand with your feet about shoulder-width apart and toes pointed straight ahead. Keep your knees slightly bent, one hand on your hip; extend your other arm up and over your head. Slowly bend at your waist to the side, toward the hand on your hip.
   b. Extend both arms overhead. Hold your right hand with your left hand and bend slowly to the left, using your left arm to pull the right arm gently over the head and down toward the ground.
   c. Repeat with other side.
5. *Quadriceps (front of thigh)*
   a. Lying on your stomach, pull heel toward buttocks with opposite hand. Keep thigh in close to other leg.
   b. The same stretch can be done standing. Do not allow thigh to come in front of you and do not bend forward at the waist.
   c. Do this exercise twice—once for each leg.
6. *Groin (inside of thigh)*
   a. Sit on floor with soles of feet together. Gently push knees down toward floor with elbows.
   b. Stand with feet three to four feet apart and turned out slightly. Keep knee of leg to be stretched straight, and bend opposite knee as you move your body toward the bent leg. Keep toes pointed forward.
   c. Repeat using other leg.
7. *Hamstrings (back of thigh)*
   a. Sit with one knee bent and leg to be stretched out straight. Reach for toes of straight leg with right hand and then left hand.
   b. Repeat with other leg.
8. *Gluteus (back of hip)*
   a. Lie on your back. Pull one knee up to chest while keeping opposite leg down on the floor with knee straight.
   b. The same may be done standing.
   c. Repeat with other leg.

9. *Anterior Tibialis (front of shin)*
   a. Stand with all of your weight on one leg. Extend opposite leg forward and flex and point at the ankle.
   b. Repeat using the other leg.

That's all there is to it: wearing the right shoes and clothing, warming up and stretching, and reaching your target heart-rate zone. Add your food exchanges and your food measurements and you're ready to begin.

On your mark. Get set. And go—to the 30-Day Rockport Walking Program.

4

THE 30-DAY PROGRAM
CALENDAR

This section is designed to take you step by step through your program and guide you through a month of Sundays—and every other day of the week!

For each day, you'll find your daily exercise goal, an inspiring message to keep your motivation strong, and sample menus that fit your diet plan. Dishes in your Meal Plan's daily menus that require recipes are indicated by uppercase letters (e.g., Oat Bran Muffin). You'll find these recipes in the section entitled "The Rockport Recipes" at the back of the book.

Exchange Lists and Weight Loss

Chapter 5 will go into detail on how to use exchange lists to vary your diet. For now, here are the number of food exchanges you'll need to eat every day to lose weight healthfully:

1,200-CALORIE-A-DAY MEAL PLAN

Starch/Bread	4
Meat	5
Vegetable	4
Fruit	3
Milk	2
Fat	3

1,500-CALORIE-A-DAY MEAL PLAN

Starch/Bread	6
Meat	6
Vegetable	4
Fruit	4
Milk	2
Fat	4

1,800-CALORIE-A-DAY MEAL PLAN

Starch/Bread	8
Meat	7
Vegetable	5
Fruit	4
Milk	2
Fat	5

And, because not everyone has the time or the inclination to cook and plan each day's menu, we've added a special bonus: hints and suggestions for dining out, holiday meals, brown-bag lunches, at-home entertainment, and much more—all specifically designed to make your transition into the "real" world of food smooth and hassle-free.

Get ready to change your life—in only one month!

Day 1

"When you say you're going to do it, say you're doing it for yourself. That's the key. I am not doing it for someone else, or because my doctor told me, or whatever. I am doing it for me because I want it. I made the choice."

—Joyce Danielson
Rockport Walking Program subject

For Each Exercise Program: 5 to 7 minutes of warm-ups

BLUE: Walk 1.5 miles today at 50 percent of your maximum heart rate.

WHITE: Walk 2.0 miles today at 60 percent of your maximum heart rate.

RED: Walk 3.0 miles today at 60 percent of your maximum heart rate.

For Each Exercise Program: 5 to 7 minutes of cool-downs

1,200-CALORIE DIET   DAY 1

| 4 Starch/Bread | 4 Vegetable | 2 Milk |
| 5 Meat | 3 Fruit | 3 Fat |

BREAKFAST
½ cup oatmeal
½ grapefruit
1 cup milk (skim or 1-percent)
Coffee or tea (optional)

LUNCH
Sandwich with:
    2 slices whole-wheat bread
    2 ounces low-fat Cheddar cheese
    Lettuce leaves
1 cup Delicious Gold and Red Coleslaw (p. 244)
1 tomato, sliced
½ tablespoon reduced-calorie mayonnaise
1 small apple
Noncaloric beverage

DINNER
1 cup garden salad with:
    2 tablespoons reduced-calorie salad dressing
3 ounces cooked chicken breast
⅓ cup brown rice
1 cup cooked carrots
1 teaspoon margarine
Noncaloric beverage

SNACK
½ cup low-fat frozen yogurt with:
    ½ banana, sliced
Noncaloric beverage

1,500-CALORIE DIET   DAY 1

6 Starch/Bread	4 Vegetable	2 Milk
6 Meat	4 Fruit	4 Fat

BREAKFAST
1½ cups whole-grain cold cereal
½ grapefruit
1 cup milk (skim or 1-percent)
Coffee or tea (optional)

LUNCH
Sandwich with:
  2 slices whole-wheat bread
  2 ounces low-fat Cheddar cheese
  Lettuce leaves
1 cup Delicious Gold and Red Coleslaw (p. 244)
1 tomato, sliced
½ tablespoon reduced-calorie mayonnaise
1 small apple
Noncaloric beverage

SNACK
1 Oatmeal-Raisin Bar (p. 330)
Noncaloric beverage

DINNER
1 cup garden salad with:
  2 tablespoons reduced-calorie salad dressing
4 ounces cooked chicken breast
⅓ cup brown rice
1 cup cooked carrots
1 teaspoon margarine
1¼ cups watermelon cubes
Noncaloric beverage

SNACK
½ cup low-fat frozen yogurt with:
  ½ banana, sliced
  1 tablespoon chopped nuts
Noncaloric beverage

1,800-CALORIE DIET   DAY 1

8 Starch/Bread	5 Vegetable	2 Milk
7 Meat	4 Fruit	5 Fat

BREAKFAST
1½ cups whole-grain cold cereal
½ grapefruit
1 cup milk (skim or 1-percent)
Coffee or tea (optional)

SNACK
1 Oatmeal-Raisin Bar (p. 330)
Noncaloric beverage

LUNCH
Sandwich with:
   2 slices whole-wheat bread
   1 ounce 95% fat-free ham
   2 ounces low-fat Cheddar cheese
   Lettuce leaves
1 cup Delicious Gold and Red Coleslaw (p. 244)
1 tomato, sliced
1 tablespoon reduced-calorie mayonnaise
1 small apple
Noncaloric beverage

SNACK
¾ ounce pretzels
Noncaloric beverage

DINNER
2 cups garden salad with:
   3 tablespoons reduced-calorie salad dressing
4 ounces cooked chicken breast
⅔ cup brown rice
1 cup Sliced Carrots with Snow Peas (p. 287)
1¼ cups watermelon cubes
Noncaloric beverage

SNACK
½ cup low-fat frozen yogurt with:
   ½ banana, sliced
   1 tablespoon chopped nuts
Noncaloric beverage

Day 2

"Walking makes for a long life."

—Hindu proverb

For Each Exercise Program: 5 to 7 minutes of warm-ups

BLUE: Walk 1.5 miles today at 50 percent of your maximum heart rate.

WHITE: Walk 2.0 miles today at 60 percent of your maximum heart rate.

RED: Walk 3.0 miles today at 60 percent of your maximum heart rate.

For Each Exercise Program: 5 to 7 minutes of cool-downs

1,200-CALORIE DIET   DAY 2

4 Starch/Bread	4 Vegetable	2 Milk
5 Meat	3 Fruit	3 Fat

BREAKFAST   ½ cup bran flakes with:
½ banana, sliced
1 cup milk (skim or 1-percent)
Coffee or tea (optional)

LUNCH   Sandwich with:
2 slices whole-wheat bread
2 tablespoons peanut butter*
1 cup carrot sticks
1 small apple
Noncaloric beverage

DINNER   1 cup garden salad with:
2 tablespoons reduced-calorie dressing
3 ounces Poached Salmon (p. 258) with:
Cucumber Sauce (p. 305)
1 small baked potato (3 ounces)
1 cup Petite Vegetables in Lemon Sauce (p. 299)
1 teaspoon margarine
Noncaloric beverage

SNACK   1 cup plain nonfat yogurt with:
2 tablespoons raisins

*In moderation, peanut butter is an acceptable food for a low-fat, low-calorie diet. If used frequently, we recommend "natural" or "old-fashioned" peanut butter, which is lower in saturated fat.

1,500-CALORIE DIET   DAY 2

| 6 Starch/Bread | 4 Vegetable | 2 Milk |
| 6 Meat | 4 Fruit | 4 Fat |

BREAKFAST
1 cup bran flakes with:
 ½ banana, sliced
1 cup milk (skim or 1-percent)
Coffee or tea (optional)

LUNCH
Sandwich with:
 2 slices whole-wheat bread
 2 tablespoons peanut butter*
1 cup carrot sticks
1 small apple
Noncaloric beverage

SNACK
3 graham-cracker squares
½ cup grapefruit juice

DINNER
1 cup garden salad with:
 2 tablespoons reduced-calorie dressing
4 ounces Poached Salmon (p. 258) with:
 Cucumber Sauce (p. 305)
1 small baked potato (3 ounces)
1 cup Petite Vegetables in Lemon Sauce (p. 299)
2 teaspoons margarine
Noncaloric beverage

SNACK
1 cup plain nonfat yogurt with:
 2 tablespoons raisins

*In moderation, peanut butter is an acceptable food for a low-fat, low-calorie diet. If used frequently, we recommend "natural" or "old-fashioned" peanut butter, which is lower in saturated fat.

1,800-CALORIE DIET   DAY 2

8 Starch/Bread	5 Vegetable	2 Milk
7 Meat	4 Fruit	5 Fat

BREAKFAST
1 cup bran flakes with:
  ½ banana, sliced
1 slice whole-grain toast
1 teaspoon margarine
1 cup milk (skim or 1-percent)
Coffee or tea (optional)

SNACK
½ cup grapefruit juice

LUNCH
Sandwich with:
  2 slices whole-wheat bread
  2 tablespoons peanut butter*
1 cup carrot sticks
1 small apple
Noncaloric beverage

SNACK
4 rye wafers
1 ounce part-skim Mozzarella cheese
Noncaloric beverage

DINNER
2 cups garden salad with:
  2 tablespoons reduced-calorie dressing
4 ounces Poached Salmon (p. 258) with:
  Cucumber Sauce (p. 305)
1 large baked potato (6 ounces)
1 cup Petite Vegetables in Lemon Sauce (p. 299)
2 teaspoons margarine
Noncaloric beverage

SNACK
1 cup plain nonfat yogurt with:
  2 tablespoons raisins

*In moderation, peanut butter is an acceptable food for a low-fat low-calorie diet. If used frequently, we recommend "natural" or "old-fashioned" peanut butter, which is lower in saturated fat.

Day 3

"I don't feel like it's a diet. And it doesn't really feel like exercise either. We're just doing what we should be doing— what the rest of the world should be doing. It's a way of life."

—Ceile Burgess
Rockport Walking Program subject

For Each Exercise Program: 5 to 7 minutes of warm-ups

BLUE: Walk 1.5 miles today at 50 percent of your maximum heart rate.

WHITE: Walk 2.0 miles today at 60 percent of your maximum heart rate.

RED: Walk 3.0 miles today at 60 percent of your maximum heart rate.

For Each Exercise Program: 5 to 7 minutes of cool-downs

1,200-CALORIE DIET   DAY 3

4 Starch/Bread	4 Vegetable	2 Milk
5 Meat	3 Fruit	3 Fat

BREAKFAST ½ English muffin with:
   2 tablespoons Yogurt Cheese (optional) (p. 313)
   ½ cup milk (skim or 1-percent)
   1 orange

LUNCH Grilled open-face hamburger with:
   2 ounces extra-lean ground beef
   ½ hamburger bun
   Grilled onion and mushroom slices
   Fresh tomato slices and lettuce leaves
   1 cup melon cubes
   ½ cup low-fat frozen yogurt
   Noncaloric beverage

DINNER 1 cup spinach salad with:
   2 tablespoons reduced-calorie dressing
   3 ounces Cornish Game Hen (p. 272)
   1 serving Savory Almond Rice (p. 296)
   ½ cup steamed broccoli and cauliflower
   1 teaspoon margarine
   ¾ cup fresh pineapple
   Noncaloric beverage

SNACK 1 cup carrot sticks with:
   2 tablespoons reduced-calorie dressing
   Noncaloric beverage

1,500-CALORIE DIET   DAY 3

| 6 Starch/Bread | 4 Vegetable | 2 Milk |
| 6 Meat | 4 Fruit | 4 Fat |

BREAKFAST   ½ English muffin with:
    2 tablespoons Yogurt Cheese (p. 313)
½ cup milk (skim or 1-percent)
1 orange

LUNCH   Grilled hamburger with:
    3 ounces extra-lean ground beef
    1 hamburger bun
    Grilled onion and mushroom slices
    Fresh tomato slices and lettuce leaves
1 cup melon cubes
½ cup low-fat frozen yogurt
Noncaloric beverage

SNACK   1 Oatmeal-Raisin Bar (p. 330)
Noncaloric beverage

DINNER   1 cup spinach salad with:
    2 tablespoons reduced-calorie dressing
3 ounces Cornish Game Hen (p. 272)
1 serving Savory Almond Rice (p. 296)
1 cup steamed broccoli and cauliflower
2 teaspoons margarine
¾ cup fresh pineapple
Noncaloric beverage

SNACK   1 cup carrot sticks with:
    2 tablespoons reduced-calorie dressing
½ cup grapefruit juice

1,800-CALORIE DIET DAY 3

| 8 Starch/Bread | 5 Vegetable | 2 Milk |
| 7 Meat | 4 Fruit | 5 Fat |

BREAKFAST
1 English muffin with:
    2 teaspoons margarine
1 serving Fortified Hot Chocolate (p. 334)
1 orange

SNACK
1 Oatmeal-Raisin Bar (p. 330)
Noncaloric beverage

LUNCH
Grilled hamburger with:
    3 ounces extra-lean ground beef
    1 hamburger bun
    Grilled onion and mushroom slices
    Fresh tomato slices and lettuce leaves
1 cup melon cubes
½ cup low-fat frozen yogurt
Noncaloric beverage

SNACK
5 Melba toast crackers
1 ounce low-fat cheese
Noncaloric beverage

DINNER
1 cup spinach salad with:
    2 tablespoons reduced-calorie dressing
3 ounces Cornish Game Hen (p. 272)
1 serving Savory Almond Rice (p. 296)
1 cup steamed broccoli and cauliflower
1 teaspoon margarine
¾ cup fresh pineapple
Noncaloric beverage

SNACK
1 cup carrot sticks with:
    2 tablespoons reduced-calorie dressing
½ cup grapefruit juice

Day 4

"The chief goal is to combine diet and exercise to find a weight you can permanently maintain without feeling deprived. After nine weeks, I'm 12 pounds closer to such discovery. Now there's a D word that won't let you down."
—Brad Ketchum
Editor, *The Walking Magazine*

For Each Exercise Program: 5 to 7 minutes of warm-ups

BLUE: Walk 1.5 miles today at 50 percent of your maximum heart rate.

WHITE: Walk 2.0 miles today at 60 percent of your maximum heart rate.

RED: Walk 3.0 miles today at 60 percent of your maximum heart rate.

For Each Exercise Program: 5 to 7 minutes of cool-downs

1,200-CALORIE DIET   DAY 4

4 Starch/Bread	4 Vegetable	2 Milk
5 Meat	3 Fruit	3 Fat

BREAKFAST   1 cup Tofu Breakfast Shake (p. 334)

LUNCH
2 cups mixed vegetable salad with:
    2 ounces sliced turkey
    2 tablespoons reduced-calorie dressing
2 rye wafers
1 cup plain nonfat yogurt with:
    1 cup cantaloupe cubes
Noncaloric beverage

DINNER
1 serving Hearty Caesar Salad (p. 245)
1 serving Fettuccine with Tomatoes and Basil (p. 264)
½ cup steamed zucchini
1 cup milk (skim or 1-percent)
Noncaloric beverage

SNACK
¾ ounce whole-wheat crackers
1½ ounces low-fat cheese
Noncaloric beverage

1,500-CALORIE DIET   DAY 4

6 Starch/Bread	4 Vegetable	2 Milk
6 Meat	4 Fruit	4 Fat

BREAKFAST   1 cup Tofu Breakfast Shake (p. 334)
½ cup oatmeal

LUNCH   2 cups mixed vegetable salad with:
3 ounces sliced turkey
2 tablespoons reduced-calorie dressing
2 rye wafers
1 cup plain nonfat yogurt with:
1 cup cantaloupe cubes
Noncaloric beverage

SNACK   1 small fresh pear
Noncaloric beverage

DINNER   1 serving Hearty Caesar Salad (p. 245)
1 serving Fettuccine with Tomatoes and Basil (p. 264)
1 slice Garlic Bread (p. 320)
½ cup steamed zucchini
1 cup milk (skim or 1-percent)
Noncaloric beverage

SNACK   ¾ ounce whole-wheat crackers
1½ ounces low-fat cheese
Noncaloric beverage

1,800-CALORIE DIET   DAY 4

| 8 Starch/Bread | 5 Vegetable | 2 Milk |
| 7 Meat | 4 Fruit | 5 Fat |

BREAKFAST
1 cup Tofu Breakfast Shake (p. 334)
1 cup oatmeal

SNACK
1 small bran muffin
Noncaloric beverage

LUNCH
2 cups mixed vegetable salad with:
  3½ ounces sliced turkey
  2 tablespoons reduced-calorie dressing
2 rye wafers
1 cup plain nonfat yogurt with:
  1 cup cantaloupe cubes
Noncaloric beverage

SNACK
1 small fresh pear
Noncaloric beverage

DINNER
1 serving Hearty Caesar Salad (p. 245)
1 serving Fettuccine with Tomatoes and Basil (p. 264)
1 slice Garlic Bread (p. 320)
1 cup steamed zucchini
1 cup milk (skim or 1-percent)
Noncaloric beverage

SNACK
¾ ounce whole-wheat crackers
2 ounces low-fat cheese
Noncaloric beverage

Day 5

When you diet alone, a fat person is always lurking inside. But when you combine dieting and exercising your body image actually changes—and you become a thin person who . . .

- *Doesn't live to eat*
- *Has control over his or her eating habits*
- *Fits exercise into his or her daily routine*
- *Maintains weight loss*
- *Feels confident and physically more alive!*

For Each Exercise Program: 5 to 7 minutes of warm-ups

BLUE: Walk 1.5 miles today at 50 percent of your maximum heart rate.

WHITE: Walk 2.0 miles today at 60 percent of your maximum heart rate.

RED: Walk 3.0 miles today at 60 percent of your maximum heart rate.

For Each Exercise Program: 5 to 7 minutes of cool-downs

1,200-CALORIE DIET   DAY 5

4 Starch/Bread	4 Vegetable	2 Milk
5 Meat	3 Fruit	3 Fat

BREAKFAST
1 slice whole-wheat toast
1 teaspoon margarine
1 cup honeydew melon cubes
1 cup milk (skim or 1-percent)

LUNCH
1 large (6 inches across) pita bread filled with:
  ½ cup Tuna Salad (p. 250)
  Tomato and onion slices and lettuce leaves
1 cup carrot sticks and green pepper slices
1 fresh orange
Noncaloric beverage

DINNER
1 cup garden salad with:
  2 tablespoons no-oil dressing (free exchange)
3 ounces Priscilla's Teriyaki Steak (p. 252) or lean broiled steak
⅓ cup white rice
½ cup steamed asparagus*
1 teaspoon margarine
Noncaloric beverage

SNACK
½ cup ice milk
¾ cup fresh blueberries
Noncaloric beverage

*Cook extra for Day 6 lunch.

1,500-CALORIE DIET   DAY 5

| 6 Starch/Bread | 4 Vegetable | 2 Milk |
| 6 Meat | 4 Fruit | 4 Fat |

BREAKFAST
1 slice whole-wheat toast
1 teaspoon margarine
1 cup honeydew melon cubes
1 cup milk (skim or 1-percent)

LUNCH
1 large (6 inches across) pita bread filled with:
  ½ cup Tuna Salad (p. 250)
  Tomato and onion slices and lettuce leaves
1 cup carrot sticks and green pepper slices
1 fresh orange
Noncaloric beverage

SNACK
3 cups plain air-popped popcorn
½ cup grapefruit juice

DINNER
1 cup garden salad with:
  2 tablespoons reduced-calorie dressing
4 ounces Priscilla's Teriyaki Steak (p. 252) or lean broiled steak
⅔ cup white rice
½ cup steamed asparagus*
1 teaspoon margarine
Noncaloric beverage

SNACK
½ cup ice milk
¾ cup fresh blueberries
Noncaloric beverage

*Cook extra for Day 6 lunch.

1,800-CALORIE DIET   DAY 5

8 Starch/Bread	5 Vegetable	2 Milk
7 Meat	4 Fruit	5 Fat

BREAKFAST
1 egg, cooked any style without fat
2 slices whole-wheat toast
1 teaspoon margarine
1 cup honeydew melon cubes
1 cup milk (skim or 1-percent)

SNACK
½ cup grapefruit juice

LUNCH
1 large (6 inches across) pita bread filled with:
    ½ cup Tuna Salad (p. 250)
    Tomato and onion slices and lettuce leaves
1 cup carrot sticks and green pepper slices
1 fresh orange
Noncaloric beverage

SNACK
3 cups plain air-popped popcorn
Noncaloric beverage

DINNER
1 cup garden salad with:
    2 tablespoons reduced-calorie dressing
4 ounces Priscilla's Teriyaki Steak (p. 252) or lean
    broiled steak
1 cup white rice
1 cup steamed asparagus*
1 teaspoon margarine
Noncaloric beverage

SNACK
½ cup ice milk
¾ cup fresh blueberries
Noncaloric beverage

*Cook extra for Day 6 lunch.

Day 6

"Sometimes when you diet you feel like you are denying yourself, but with exercise you are giving yourself something. Something that you can keep on doing day after day."

—Kathy Madden
Rockport Walking Program subject

For Each Exercise Program: 5 to 7 minutes of warm-ups

BLUE: Walk 1.5 miles today at 50 percent of your maximum heart rate.

WHITE: Walk 2.0 miles today at 60 percent of your maximum heart rate.

RED: Walk 3.0 miles today at 60 percent of your maximum heart rate.

For Each Exercise Program: 5 to 7 minutes of cool-downs

1,200-CALORIE DIET   DAY 6

4 Starch/Bread	4 Vegetable	2 Milk
5 Meat	3 Fruit	3 Fat

BREAKFAST
½ cup Shredded Wheat
1½ dried figs, chopped
1 cup milk (skim or 1-percent)
Coffee or tea (optional)

LUNCH
1 serving Turkey-Asparagus Roll-Ups (pps. 272–73)
1 1-ounce roll
1 teaspoon margarine
1 fresh peach
Noncaloric beverage

DINNER
2 cups garden salad with:
    2 tablespoons reduced-calorie dressing
2 slices Nouvelle Pizza (p. 280) or other thin-crust pizza
    with vegetables
1 cup milk (skim or 1-percent)
Noncaloric beverage

SNACK
¼ cup low-fat cottage cheese
⅓ cup canned pineapple (in its own juice)
Noncaloric beverage

1,500-CALORIE DIET   DAY 6

| 6 Starch/Bread | 4 Vegetable | 2 Milk |
| 6 Meat | 4 Fruit | 4 Fat |

BREAKFAST
½ cup Shredded Wheat
1½ dried figs, chopped
1 slice whole-wheat toast
1 teaspoon margarine
1 cup milk (skim or 1-percent)
Coffee or tea (optional)

LUNCH
1 serving Turkey-Asparagus Roll-Ups (pps. 272–73)
1 1-ounce roll
1 teaspoon margarine
1 fresh peach
Noncaloric beverage

SNACK
1 small bran muffin
Noncaloric beverage

DINNER
2 cups garden salad with:
    2 tablespoons low-calorie dressing
2 slices Nouvelle Pizza (p. 280) or other thin-crust pizza
    with vegetables
1 cup milk (skim or 1-percent)
Noncaloric beverage

SNACK
½ cup low-fat cottage cheese
⅔ cup canned pineapple (in its own juice)
Noncaloric beverage

1,800-CALORIE DIET   DAY 6

8 Starch/Bread	5 Vegetable	2 Milk
7 Meat	4 Fruit	5 Fat

BREAKFAST
½ cup Shredded Wheat
1½ dried figs, chopped
1 slice whole-wheat toast
1 teaspoon margarine
1 cup milk (skim or 1-percent)
Coffee or tea (optional)

SNACK
3 graham-cracker squares
Noncaloric beverage

LUNCH
1 serving Turkey-Asparagus Roll-Ups (pps. 272–73)
1 1-ounce roll
1½ teaspoons margarine
1 fresh peach
½ cup vegetable juice

SNACK
1 small bran muffin
Noncaloric beverage

DINNER
2 cups garden salad with:
    2 tablespoons low-calorie dressing
3 slices Nouvelle Pizza (p. 280) or other thin-crust pizza
    with vegetables
1 cup milk (skim or 1-percent)
Noncaloric beverage

SNACK
½ cup low-fat cottage cheese
⅔ cup canned pineapple (in its own juice)
Noncaloric beverage

Day 7

"One of the basic things I have learned is how to eat right. I have never, ever eaten right in my life. But I've learned to eat three balanced meals a day right now and I feel fantastic!"

—George Maloney
Rockport Walking Program subject

For Each Exercise Program: 5 to 7 minutes of warm-ups

BLUE: Walk 1.5 miles today at 50 percent of your maximum heart rate.

WHITE: Walk 2.0 miles today at 60 percent of your maximum heart rate.

RED: Walk 3.0 miles today at 60 percent of your maximum heart rate.

For Each Exercise Program: 5 to 7 minutes of cool-downs

1,200-CALORIE DIET   DAY 7

4 Starch/Bread	4 Vegetable	2 Milk
5 Meat	3 Fruit	3 Fat

BREAKFAST
½ cup oatmeal
½ cup grapefruit juice
1 cup milk (skim or 1-percent)
Coffee or tea (optional)

LUNCH
Sandwich with:
  2 slices whole-wheat bread
  2 ounces low-fat cheese
  Tomato and onion slices and lettuce leaves
  1 tablespoon reduced-calorie mayonnaise
1 small apple
1 cup milk (skim or 1-percent)

DINNER
Salad d'Amour (p. 250)
3 ounces Beef Tenderloin with Capers (p. 251)
1 1-ounce French roll
1 cup steamed broccoli
Noncaloric beverage

SNACK
1 small fresh pear
Noncaloric beverage

1,500-CALORIE DIET   DAY 7

6 Starch/Bread	4 Vegetable	2 Milk
6 Meat	4 Fruit	4 Fat

BREAKFAST
½ cup oatmeal
½ cup grapefruit juice
1 cup milk (skim or 1-percent)
Coffee or tea (optional)

LUNCH
Sandwich with:
    2 slices whole-wheat bread
    2 ounces low-fat cheese
    Tomato and onion slices and lettuce leaves
    1 tablespoon reduced-calorie mayonnaise
1 small apple
1 cup milk (skim or 1-percent)

SNACK
5 vanilla wafers
Noncaloric beverage

DINNER
Salad d'Amour (p. 250)
4 ounces Beef Tenderloin with Capers (p. 251)
⅓ cup rice
1 cup steamed broccoli
1 1-ounce French roll
1 teaspoon margarine
½ cup fruit salad
Noncaloric beverage

SNACK
1 small fresh pear
Noncaloric beverage

1,800-CALORIE DIET   DAY 7

8 Starch/Bread	5 Vegetable	2 Milk
7 Meat	4 Fruit	5 Fat

BREAKFAST
1 Oat Bran Muffin (p. 315)
¾ cup whole-grain cold cereal
½ cup grapefruit juice
1 cup milk (skim or 1-percent)
Coffee or tea (optional)

SNACK
2 tangerines

LUNCH
Sandwich with:
  2 slices whole-wheat bread
  1 ounce sliced turkey
  2 ounces low-fat cheese
  Tomato and onion slices and lettuce leaves
  1 tablespoon reduced-calorie mayonnaise
1 cup cucumber slices
1 small apple
1 cup milk (skim or 1-percent)

SNACK
5 vanilla wafers
Noncaloric beverage

DINNER
Salad d'Amour (p. 250)
4 ounces Beef Tenderloin with Capers (p. 251)
½ cup rice
1 cup steamed broccoli
½ cup cooked carrots
1 1-ounce French roll
1 teaspoon margarine
Noncaloric beverage

SNACK
1 small fresh pear
Noncaloric beverage

Day 8

"The high part of my day is getting out, doing the walking, getting the exercise, and coming back and taking a shower. Walking helps me accomplish a day's work by noon."
—Victor Manno

For Each Exercise Program: 5 to 7 minutes of warm-ups

BLUE: Walk 1.5 miles today at 50 percent of your maximum heart rate.

WHITE: Walk 2.0 miles today at 60 percent of your maximum heart rate.

RED: Walk 3.0 miles today at 60 percent of your maximum heart rate.

For Each Exercise Program: 5 to 7 minutes of cool-downs

1,200-CALORIE DIET   DAY 8

4 Starch/Bread	4 Vegetable	2 Milk
5 Meat	3 Fruit	3 Fat

BREAKFAST
½ cup bran flakes
1 cup milk (skim or 1-percent)
Coffee or tea (optional)

BRUNCH
½ cup orange juice
1 serving Eastern Omelette (p. 278)
1 serving Tropical Puff Pancake (p. 316)
Noncaloric beverage

DINNER
2 cups mixed vegetable salad with:
    2 tablespoons reduced-calorie dressing
1 serving Grilled Pork with Raspberry Sauce (p. 266)
⅓ cup brown rice
1 cup steamed snow peas
Noncaloric beverage

SNACK
½ cup milk (skim or 1-percent)
1 Oatmeal-Raisin Bar (p. 330)

1,500-CALORIE DIET   DAY 8

| 6 Starch/Bread | 4 Vegetable | 2 Milk |
| 6 Meat | 4 Fruit | 4 Fat |

BREAKFAST   ½ cup bran flakes
1 cup milk (skim or 1-percent)
1¼ cups whole fresh strawberries
Coffee or tea (optional)

BRUNCH   ½ cup orange juice
1 serving Eastern Omelette (p. 278)
1 serving Tropical Puff Pancake (p. 316)
½ (1 ounce) bagel with:
   1 teaspoon margarine
Noncaloric beverage

DINNER   2 cups mixed vegetable salad with:
   2 tablespoons reduced-calorie dressing
   ½ ounce low-fat cheese
1 serving Grilled Pork with Raspberry Sauce (p. 266)
⅔ cup brown rice
1 cup steamed snow peas
Noncaloric beverage

SNACK   ½ cup milk (skim or 1-percent)
1 Oatmeal-Raisin Bar (p. 330)

1,800-CALORIE DIET   DAY 8

8 Starch/Bread	5 Vegetable	2 Milk
7 Meat	4 Fruit	5 Fat

BREAKFAST
1 cup bran flakes
1 cup milk (skim or 1-percent)
1¼ cups whole fresh strawberries
Coffee or tea (optional)

BRUNCH
½ cup orange juice
1 serving Eastern Omelette (p. 278)
1 serving Tropical Puff Pancake (p. 316)
1 (2 ounces) bagel with:
    2 teaspoons margarine
Coffee or tea (optional)

DINNER
2 cups mixed vegetable salad with:
    2 tablespoons reduced-calorie dressing
    1½ ounces low-fat cheese
1 serving Grilled Pork with Raspberry Sauce (p. 266)
⅔ cup brown rice
1 cup steamed snow peas
½ cup cooked carrots
Noncaloric beverage

SNACK
½ cup milk (skim or 1-percent)
1 Oatmeal-Raisin Bar (p. 330)

Day 9

"Even my wife says I look sexy now! She loved me before, but she sees other women's heads turning now when we go out. It's true. I'm getting different looks now."
—Nick Rioux
Rockport Walking Program subject

For Each Exercise Program: 5 to 7 minutes of warm-ups

BLUE: Walk 1.5 miles today at 50 percent of your maximum heart rate.

WHITE: Walk 2.0 miles today at 60 percent of your maximum heart rate.

RED: Walk 3.0 miles today at 60 percent of your maximum heart rate.

For Each Exercise Program: 5 to 7 minutes of cool-downs

1,200-CALORIE DIET   DAY 9

| 4 Starch/Bread | 4 Vegetable | 2 Milk |
| 5 Meat | 3 Fruit | 3 Fat |

BREAKFAST   ½ (1 ounce) bagel with:
    2 tablespoons Yogurt Cheese (p. 313)
½ banana
Coffee or tea (optional)

LUNCH   Sandwich with:
    2 slices light oat bread (40 calories per slice)
    2 ounces lean roast beef
    Tomato and onion slices and lettuce leaves
    1 tablespoon reduced-calorie mayonnaise
1 cup sliced green pepper
1 fresh orange
½ cup milk (skim or 1-percent)

DINNER   1 serving Belgian Salad with Raspberry Dressing (p. 241)
3 ounces baked or broiled fish
1 small seasoned boiled potato (3 ounces)
1 cup green beans
1 cup cubed melon
Noncaloric beverage

SNACK   1 cup milk (skim or 1-percent)
3 graham-cracker squares

1,500-CALORIE DIET   DAY 9

| 6 Starch/Bread | 4 Vegetable | 2 Milk |
| 6 Meat | 4 Fruit | 4 Fat |

BREAKFAST
    1 (2 ounces) bagel with:
        2 tablespoons Yogurt Cheese (p. 313)
    ½ banana
    Coffee or tea (optional)

LUNCH
    Sandwich with:
        2 slices oat bread
        2 ounces lean roast beef
        Tomato and onion slices and lettuce leaves
        1 tablespoon reduced-calorie mayonnaise
    1 cup jicama, julienned
    1 fresh orange
    ½ cup milk (skim or 1-percent)
    Noncaloric beverage

SNACK
    1 fresh nectarine
    Noncaloric beverage

DINNER
    1 serving Belgian Salad with Raspberry Dressing (p. 241)
    4 ounces baked or broiled fish
    1 small seasoned boiled potato (3 ounces)
    1 cup green beans
    1 teaspoon margarine
    1 cup cubed melon
    Noncaloric beverage

SNACK
    1 cup milk (skim or 1-percent)
    3 graham-cracker squares

1,800-CALORIE DIET DAY 9

8 Starch/Bread	5 Vegetable	2 Milk
7 Meat	4 Fruit	5 Fat

BREAKFAST
1 (2 ounces) bagel with:
   2 tablespoons Yogurt Cheese (p. 313)
½ banana
Coffee or tea (optional)

SNACK
1 fresh nectarine

LUNCH
Sandwich with:
   2 slices oat bread
   2 ounces lean roast beef
   Tomato and onion slices and lettuce leaves
   1 tablespoon reduced-calorie mayonnaise
1 cup sliced green pepper
1 cup cauliflower flowerets
1 fresh orange
½ cup milk (skim or 1-percent)
Noncaloric beverage

SNACK
1 slice whole-wheat bread with:
   1 tablespoon peanut butter*
Noncaloric beverage

DINNER
1 serving Belgian Salad with Raspberry Dressing (p. 241)
4 ounces baked or broiled fish
1 small seasoned boiled potato (3 ounces)
1 cup green beans
1 1-ounce sourdough roll
2 teaspoons margarine
1 cup cubed melon
Noncaloric beverage

SNACK
1 cup milk (skim or 1-percent)
3 graham-cracker squares

---

*In moderation, peanut butter is an acceptable food for a low-fat, low-calorie diet. If used frequently, we recommend "natural" or "old-fashioned" peanut butter, which is lower in saturated fat.

Day 10

*Subject George Maloney dropped two strokes off his golf
game as he lost weight. Plus he has so much energy, he's
out tending his garden early in the morning. He's asked us
to change the name of The Rockport Walking Program to
the "Lawn-Golf Weight-Loss Program."*

For Each Exercise Program: 5 to 7 minutes of warm-ups

BLUE: Walk 1.5 miles today at 50 percent of your maximum heart rate.

WHITE: Walk 2.0 miles today at 60 percent of your maximum heart rate.

RED: Walk 3.0 miles today at 60 percent of your maximum heart rate.

For Each Exercise Program: 5 to 7 minutes of cool-downs

1,200-CALORIE DIET   DAY 10

4 Starch/Bread	4 Vegetable	2 Milk
5 Meat	3 Fruit	3 Fat

BREAKFAST
1 egg, cooked any style without fat
1 slice whole-grain toast
1 teaspoon margarine
1 orange
1 cup milk (skim or 1-percent)
Coffee or tea (optional)

LUNCH
½ cup Two-Bean Salad (p. 243) on:
   1½ cups salad greens with 2 tablespoons no-oil dressing
    (free exchange)
¼ cup low-fat cottage cheese with:
   1 peach, sliced
Noncaloric beverage

DINNER
2 cups garden salad with:
   2 tablespoons reduced-calorie dressing
3 ounces Dijon Chicken (p. 267) on:
   ½ cup fettuccine mixed with 1 teaspoon olive oil
1 cup cooked carrots
1 kiwi, sliced
Noncaloric beverage

SNACK
1 package sugar-free hot cocoa
3 gingersnaps

1,500-CALORIE DIET   DAY 10

6 Starch/Bread	4 Vegetable	2 Milk
6 Meat	4 Fruit	4 Fat

BREAKFAST	1 egg, cooked any style without fat
	1 slice whole-grain toast
	1 teaspoon margarine
	1 orange
	1 cup milk (skim or 1-percent)
	Coffee or tea (optional)
LUNCH	½ cup Two-Bean Salad (p. 243) on:
	1½ cups salad greens with 2 tablespoons reduced-calorie dressing
	¼ cup low-fat cottage cheese with:
	1 peach, sliced
	Noncaloric beverage
SNACK	½ (1 ounce) toasted bagel
	½ cup apple juice
DINNER	2 cups garden salad with:
	2 tablespoons reduced-calorie dressing
	4 ounces Dijon Chicken (p. 267) on:
	1 cup fettuccine mixed with 1 teaspoon olive oil
	1 cup cooked carrots
	1 kiwi, sliced
	Noncaloric beverage
SNACK	1 package sugar-free hot cocoa
	3 gingersnaps

1,800-CALORIE DIET   DAY 10

8 Starch/Bread	5 Vegetable	2 Milk
7 Meat	4 Fruit	5 Fat

BREAKFAST
1 egg, cooked any style without fat
2 slices whole-grain toast
1 teaspoon margarine
1 orange
1 cup milk (skim or 1-percent)
Coffee or tea (optional)

SNACK
4 rye wafers
Noncaloric beverage

LUNCH
½ cup Two-Bean Salad (p. 243) on:
   1½ cups salad greens with 2 tablespoons reduced-calorie dressing
½ cup low-fat cottage cheese with:
   1 peach, sliced
Noncaloric beverage

SNACK
½ (1 ounce) toasted bagel
1 teaspoon margarine
½ cup apple juice

DINNER
2 cups garden salad with:
   2 tablespoons reduced-calorie dressing
4 ounces Dijon Chicken (p. 267) on:
   1 cup fettuccine mixed with 1 teaspoon olive oil
1 cup cooked carrots
½ cup cooked broccoli
1 kiwi, sliced
Noncaloric beverage

SNACK
1 package sugar-free hot cocoa
3 gingersnaps

Day 11

If you walk four times a week, you will lose 15 pounds in one year without even trying!

For Each Exercise Program: 5 to 7 minutes of warm-ups

BLUE: Walk 1.5 miles today at 50 percent of your maximum heart rate.

WHITE: Walk 2.0 miles today at 60 percent of your maximum heart rate.

RED: Walk 3.0 miles today at 60 percent of your maximum heart rate.

For Each Exercise Program: 5 to 7 minutes of cool-downs

1,200-CALORIE DIET   DAY 11

| 4 Starch/Bread | 4 Vegetable | 2 Milk |
| 5 Meat | 3 Fruit | 3 Fat |

BREAKFAST   ½ cup Shredded Wheat with:
   3 medium pitted prunes
   1 cup milk (skim or 1-percent)
   Coffee or tea (optional)

LUNCH   1 Tostada Grande (p. 283) (or similar-size tostada)
   1 small apple
   Noncaloric beverage

DINNER   1 serving Grilled Albacore with Herbs (p. 254)
   1 small baked potato (3 ounces)
   ½ cup summer squash
   1 cup brussels sprouts
   Noncaloric beverage

SNACK   1 cup plain nonfat yogurt with:
   1¼ cups whole fresh strawberries
   Noncaloric beverage

1,500-CALORIE DIET   DAY 11

| 6 Starch/Bread | 4 Vegetable | 2 Milk |
| 6 Meat | 4 Fruit | 4 Fat |

BREAKFAST   1 cup Shredded Wheat with:
3 medium pitted prunes
1 cup milk (skim or 1-percent)
Coffee or tea (optional)

LUNCH   1 Tostada Grande (p. 283) (or similar-size tostada)
1 small apple
Noncaloric beverage

SNACK   1 Oatmeal-Raisin Bar (p. 330)
Noncaloric beverage

DINNER   1 serving Grilled Albacore with Herbs (p. 254)
1 small baked potato (3 ounces)
½ cup summer squash
1 cup brussels sprouts
1 teaspoon margarine
12 cherries
Noncaloric beverage

SNACK   1 cup plain nonfat yogurt with:
1¼ cups whole fresh strawberries
Noncaloric beverage

1,800-CALORIE DIET   DAY 11

8 Starch/Bread	5 Vegetable	2 Milk
7 Meat	4 Fruit	5 Fat

BREAKFAST
1 cup Shredded Wheat with:
   3 medium pitted prunes
1 cup milk (skim or 1-percent)
½ cup carrot juice
Coffee or tea (optional)

SNACK
2 Oatmeal-Raisin Bars (p. 330)

LUNCH .
1 Tostada Grande (p. 283) (or similar-size tostada)
1 small apple
Noncaloric beverage

SNACK
5 Melba toast crackers
1 ounce low-fat cheese
Noncaloric beverage

DINNER
1 serving Grilled Albacore with Herbs (p. 254)
1 small (3 ounces) baked potato with:
   1 ounce shredded low-fat cheese
½ cup summer squash
1 cup brussels sprouts
2 teaspoons margarine
12 cherries
Noncaloric beverage

SNACK
1 cup plain nonfat yogurt with:
   1¼ cups whole fresh strawberries
Noncaloric beverage

Day 12

MOTIVATION DOS

- *Do practice being honest with yourself.*
- *Do decide that you don't "want to" because you would rather have the benefits of weight loss.*
- *Do expect to reach plateaus.*
- *Do take one day at a time.*
- *Do keep a positive attitude.*
- *Do lose weight for yourself.*

For Each Exercise Program: 5 to 7 minutes of warm-ups

BLUE: Walk 1.5 miles today at 50 percent of your maximum heart rate.

WHITE: Walk 2.0 miles today at 60 percent of your maximum heart rate.

RED: Walk 3.0 miles today at 60 percent of your maximum heart rate.

For Each Exercise Program: 5 to 7 minutes of cool-downs

1,200-CALORIE DIET   DAY 12

4 Starch/Bread	4 Vegetable	2 Milk
5 Meat	3 Fruit	3 Fat

BREAKFAST
1 Oat Bran Muffin (p. 315)
1 cup melon cubes
1 cup milk (skim or 1-percent)
Coffee or tea (optional)

LUNCH
Grilled sandwich with:
    2 slices light rye bread (40 calories per slice)
    1 ounce 95% fat-free boiled ham
    1 ounce low-fat Swiss cheese
    1 teaspoon mustard (optional)
1 tomato, sliced
1 cup green pepper slices
1 tangerine
1 cup milk (skim or 1-percent)

DINNER
1 serving Cucumber Salad (p. 242)
3 ounces baked chicken*
½ cup green peas
1 cup beets
1 teaspoon margarine
1 plum
Noncaloric beverage

SNACK
1½ cups plain air-popped popcorn with:
    1 teaspoon margarine
1 serving Sparkling Fruit Juice (p. 335)

*Bake extra chicken for Day 13 lunch.

1,500-CALORIE DIET   DAY 12

| 6 Starch/Bread | 4 Vegetable | 2 Milk |
| 6 Meat | 4 Fruit | 4 Fat |

BREAKFAST
1 Oat Bran Muffin (p. 315)
1 cup melon cubes
1 cup milk (skim or 1-percent)
Coffee or tea (optional)

LUNCH
Grilled sandwich with:
  2 slices rye bread
  1 ounce 95% fat-free boiled ham
  1 ounce low-fat Swiss cheese
  1 teaspoon mustard (optional)
1 tomato, sliced
1 cup green pepper slices
1 tangerine
1 cup milk (skim or 1-percent)

SNACK
½ (1 ounce) toasted bagel
1 teaspoon margarine
½ cup apple juice

DINNER
1 serving Cucumber Salad (p. 242)
4 ounces baked chicken*
½ cup green peas
1 cup beets
1 teaspoon margarine
1 plum
Noncaloric beverage

SNACK
1½ cups plain air-popped popcorn with:
  1 teaspoon margarine
1 serving Sparkling Fruit Juice (p. 335)

*Bake extra chicken for Day 13 lunch.

1,800-CALORIE DIET   DAY 12

8 Starch/Bread	5 Vegetable	2 Milk
7 Meat	4 Fruit	5 Fat

BREAKFAST
1 Oat Bran Muffin (p. 315)
¾ cup whole-grain cold cereal
1 cup melon cubes
1 cup milk (skim or 1-percent)
Coffee or tea (optional)

SNACK
1 small apple
Noncaloric beverage

LUNCH
Grilled sandwich with:
    2 slices rye bread
    2 ounces 95% fat-free boiled ham
    1 ounce low-fat Swiss cheese
    1 teaspoon mustard (optional)
1 tomato, sliced
1 cup green pepper slices
2 tablespoons reduced-calorie dressing
1 tangerine
1 cup milk (skim or 1-percent)

SNACK
½ toasted bagel
1 teaspoon margarine
½ cup vegetable oil
Noncaloric beverage

DINNER
1 serving Cucumber Salad (p. 242)
4 ounces baked chicken*
3 ounces boiled new potatoes
½ cup green peas
1 cup beets
1 teaspoon margarine
1 plum
Noncaloric beverage

SNACK
1½ cups plain air-popped popcorn with:
    1 teaspoon margarine
1 serving Sparkling Fruit Juice (p. 335)

*Bake extra chicken for Day 13 lunch.

Day 13

President Harry Truman made his "evening constitutional" famous, walking so briskly that he left many a Secret Service agent—not to mention reporters—breathless. His prescription? "Walk as if you have someplace to go."

For Each Exercise Program: 5 to 7 minutes of warm-ups

BLUE: Walk 1.5 miles today at 50 percent of your maximum heart rate.

WHITE: Walk 2.0 miles today at 60 percent of your maximum heart rate.

RED: Walk 3.0 miles today at 60 percent of your maximum heart rate.

For Each Exercise Program: 5 to 7 minutes of cool-downs

1,200-CALORIE DIET   DAY 13

4 Starch/Bread	4 Vegetable	2 Milk
5 Meat	3 Fruit	3 Fat

BREAKFAST
1½ cups puffed-wheat cereal
½ grapefruit
1 cup milk (skim or 1-percent)
Coffee or tea (optional)

LUNCH
2 ounces cooked, chopped chicken breast mixed with 1
    tablespoon reduced-calorie mayonnaise on:
    2 cups garden salad with 2 tablespoons reduced-calorie
    dressing
½ of 6-inch pita pocket
1 small apple
Noncaloric beverage

DINNER
1 steamed artichoke with:
    Fresh lemon wedges
1 serving Capellini with Clam Sauce (p. 263)
½ cup broccoli, cauliflower, and carrot medley
1 fudge bar or low-fat frozen yogurt bar
Noncaloric beverage

SNACK
¼ cup low-fat cottage cheese
2 canned peach halves (in their own juice)
Noncaloric beverage

1,500-CALORIE DIET   DAY 13

| 6 Starch/Bread | 4 Vegetable | 2 Milk |
| 6 Meat | 4 Fruit | 4 Fat |

BREAKFAST
1 cup oatmeal
½ grapefruit
1 cup milk (skim or 1-percent)
Coffee or tea (optional)

LUNCH
2 ounces cooked, chopped chicken breast mixed with 1
   tablespoon reduced-calorie mayonnaise on:
   2 cups garden salad with 2 tablespoons reduced-calorie
      dressing
½ of 6-inch pita pocket
1 small apple
Noncaloric beverage

SNACK
½ (1 ounce) bagel
1 ounce low-fat Jack cheese
½ cup orange juice

DINNER
1 steamed artichoke with:
   Fresh lemon wedges
   1 tablespoon reduced-calorie mayonnaise
1 serving Capellini with Clam Sauce (p. 263)
½ cup broccoli, cauliflower, and carrot medley
1 fudge bar or low-fat frozen yogurt bar
Noncaloric beverage

SNACK
¼ cup low-fat cottage cheese
2 canned peach halves (in their own juice)
Noncaloric beverage

1,800-CALORIE DIET   DAY 13

8 Starch/Bread	5 Vegetable	2 Milk
7 Meat	4 Fruit	5 Fat

BREAKFAST	1 cup oatmeal ½ grapefruit 1 cup milk Coffee or tea (optional)
SNACK	½ cup tomato juice
LUNCH	2 ounces cooked, chopped chicken breast mixed with 1 tablespoon reduced-calorie mayonnaise on: 2 cups garden salad with 1 tablespoon reduced-calorie dressing 4 rye wafers 1 small apple Noncaloric beverage
SNACK	½ (1 ounce) bagel 1 ounce low-fat Jack cheese ½ cup orange juice
DINNER	1 steamed artichoke with: Fresh lemon wedges 1 tablespoon reduced-calorie mayonnaise 1½ servings Capellini with Clam Sauce (p. 263) ½ cup broccoli, cauliflower, and carrot medley 1 slice Italian bread ½ tablespoon diet margarine 1 fudge bar or low-fat frozen yogurt bar Noncaloric beverage
SNACK	¼ cup low-fat cottage cheese 2 canned peach halves (in their own juice) Noncaloric beverage

Day 14

"When I first started using my exchange lists, I had to look up everything. Now it's a piece of (nonfattening) cake. I'm eating to live—not living to eat. And all it took was a desire to change—and a few weeks to see it through."
—Katie Allen
Rockport Walking Program subject

For Each Exercise Program: 5 to 7 minutes of warm-ups

BLUE: Walk 1.5 miles today at 50 percent of your maximum heart rate.

WHITE: Walk 2.0 miles today at 60 percent of your maximum heart rate.

RED: Walk 3.0 miles today at 60 percent of your maximum heart rate.

For Each Exercise Program: 5 to 7 minutes of cool-downs

1,200-CALORIE DIET   DAY 14

4 Starch/Bread	4 Vegetable	2 Milk
5 Meat	3 Fruit	3 Fat

BREAKFAST
1 ounce Canadian bacon
1 slice whole-wheat toast
1 teaspoon margarine
1 cup cantaloupe cubes
Coffee or tea (optional)

LUNCH
Sandwich with:
  1 (2 ounces) bagel, sliced
  2 ounces chicken luncheon meat
  Lettuce leaves, tomato slice
  1 tablespoon reduced-calorie mayonnaise
1 nectarine
1 cup milk (skim or 1-percent)

DINNER
1 serving Eggplant Parmesan (p. 279)
1 slice Garlic Bread (p. 320)
½ cup green beans
1 cup milk (skim or 1-percent)

SNACK
12 fresh cherries
Noncaloric beverage

1,500-CALORIE DIET   DAY 14

6 Starch/Bread	4 Vegetable	2 Milk
6 Meat	4 Fruit	4 Fat

BREAKFAST
1 ounce Canadian bacon
2 slices whole-wheat toast
1 tablespoon diet margarine
1 cup cantaloupe cubes
Coffee or tea (optional)

LUNCH
Sandwich with:
  1 (2 ounces) bagel, sliced
  3 ounces chicken luncheon meat
  Lettuce leaves, tomato slice
  1 tablespoon reduced-calorie mayonnaise
1 nectarine
1 cup milk (skim or 1-percent)

SNACK
1 small blueberry muffin
Noncaloric beverage

DINNER
1 serving Eggplant Parmesan (p. 279)
1 slice Garlic Bread (p. 320)
½ cup green beans
2 plums
1 cup milk (skim or 1-percent)

SNACK
12 fresh cherries
Noncaloric beverage

1,800-CALORIE DIET   DAY 14

8 Starch/Bread	5 Vegetable	2 Milk
7 Meat	4 Fruit	5 Fat

BREAKFAST
1 ounce Canadian bacon
2 slices whole-wheat toast
1 tablespoon diet margarine
1 cup cantaloupe cubes
Coffee or tea (optional)

SNACK
6 saltine-type crackers
½ cup grapefruit juice

LUNCH
Sandwich with:
  1 (2 ounces) bagel, sliced
  3 ounces chicken luncheon meat
  Lettuce leaves, tomato slice
  1 tablespoon reduced-calorie mayonnaise
1 nectarine
1 cup milk (skim or 1-percent)

SNACK
1 cup celery sticks with:
  1 tablespoon peanut butter*
Noncaloric beverage

DINNER
1 serving Eggplant Parmesan (p. 279)
2 slices Garlic Bread (p. 320)
1 cup green beans
2 plums
1 cup milk (skim or 1-percent)

SNACK
3 cups air-popped popcorn with:
  1 tablespoon diet margarine
Noncaloric beverage

---

*In moderation, peanut butter is an acceptable food for a low-fat, low-calorie diet. If used frequently, we recommend "natural" or "old-fashioned" peanut butter, which is lower in saturated fat.

Day 15

"Walking, man's oldest form of transportation, is also a constantly self-renewing source of pleasure. Think about it for a moment. On vacation, it is when you are done with airports, train stations, cars, and highways—when you start walking around the holiday place—that the fun begins. It is on foot that we discover the wonders of this world whether at home or abroad. Indeed sometimes a walk nearby can be more rejuvenating and pleasurable than traveling to faraway places."

—Margot Patterson Doss

author and walking columnist for the *San Francisco Chronicle*

For Each Exercise Program: 5 to 7 minutes of warm-ups

BLUE: Walk 2.0 miles today at 50 percent of your maximum heart rate.

WHITE: Walk 2.5 miles today at 60 percent of your maximum heart rate.

RED: Walk 3.5 miles today at 60 percent of your maximum heart rate.

For Each Exercise Program: 5 to 7 minutes of cool-downs

1,200-CALORIE DIET   DAY 15

| 4 Starch/Bread | 4 Vegetable | 2 Milk |
| 5 Meat | 3 Fruit | 3 Fat |

BREAKFAST   ½ cup oat bran with:
    ½ banana, sliced
1 cup milk (skim or 1-percent)
Coffee or tea (optional)

LUNCH   Sandwich with:
    2 slices rye bread
    2 tablespoons peanut butter*
1 cup carrot sticks
1 orange
Noncaloric beverage

DINNER   1 cup garden salad with:
    2 tablespoons reduced-calorie salad dressing
3 ounces Priscilla's Teriyaki Chicken (p. 252)
⅓ cup white rice
1 cup summer squash
½ cup cooked spinach
2 teaspoons margarine
Noncaloric beverage

SNACK   ¾ cup plain low-fat yogurt with:
    ½ banana, sliced
Noncaloric beverage

*In moderation, peanut butter is an acceptable food for a low-fat, low-calorie diet. If used frequently, we recommend "natural" or "old-fashioned" peanut butter, which is lower in saturated fat.

1,500-CALORIE DIET   DAY 15

6 Starch/Bread	4 Vegetable	2 Milk
6 Meat	4 Fruit	4 Fat

BREAKFAST
½ cup oat bran with:
  ½ banana, sliced
1 slice whole-wheat toast
1 teaspoon margarine
1 cup milk (skim or 1-percent)
Coffee or tea (optional)

LUNCH
Sandwich with:
  2 slices rye bread
  2 tablespoons peanut butter*
1 cup carrot sticks
1 orange
Noncaloric beverage

SNACK
1 Oatmeal-Raisin Bar (p. 330)
Noncaloric beverage

DINNER
1 cup garden salad with:
  3 tablespoons reduced-calorie salad dressing
4 ounces Priscilla's Teriyaki Chicken (p. 252)
⅓ cup white rice
1 cup summer squash
½ cup cooked spinach
2 teaspoons margarine
1¼ cups watermelon cubes
Noncaloric beverage

SNACK
¾ cup plain low-fat yogurt with:
  ½ banana, sliced
Noncaloric beverage

*In moderation, peanut butter is an acceptable food for a low-fat, low-calorie diet. If used frequently, we recommend "natural" or "old-fashioned" peanut butter, which is lower in saturated fat.

1,800-CALORIE DIET   DAY 15

| 8 Starch/Bread | 5 Vegetable | 2 Milk |
| 7 Meat | 4 Fruit | 5 Fat |

BREAKFAST
½ cup oat bran with:
   ½ banana, sliced
1 slice whole-wheat toast
1 teaspoon margarine
1 cup milk (skim or 1-percent)
Coffee or tea (optional)

SNACK
2 Oatmeal-Raisin Bars (p. 330)
Noncaloric beverage

LUNCH
Sandwich with:
   2 slices rye bread
   2 tablespoons peanut butter*
1 cup carrot sticks
1 orange
Noncaloric beverage

SNACK
1 ounce low-fat cheese
1 cup cherry tomatoes
Noncaloric beverage

DINNER
1 cup garden salad with:
   2 tablespoons reduced-calorie salad dressing
4 ounces Priscilla's Teriyaki Chicken (p. 252)
⅔ cup white rice
1 cup summer squash
½ cup cooked spinach
2 teaspoons margarine
1 cup melon cubes
Noncaloric beverage

SNACK
¾ cup plain low-fat yogurt with:
   ½ banana, sliced
Noncaloric beverage

*In moderation, peanut butter is an acceptable food for a low-fat, low-calorie diet. If used frequently, we recommend "natural" or "old-fashioned" peanut butter, which is lower in saturated fat.

Day 16

"If someone told me a year ago that I wouldn't think twice about walking five miles, I would have told them they were crazy. I wish I had found this ten years ago!"
—Gee Mahassel
Rockport Walking Program subject

For Each Exercise Program: 5 to 7 minutes of warm-ups

BLUE: Walk 2.0 miles today at 50 percent of your maximum heart rate.

WHITE: Walk 2.5 miles today at 60 percent of your maximum heart rate.

RED: Walk 3.5 miles today at 60 percent of your maximum heart rate.

For Each Exercise Program: 5 to 7 minutes of cool-downs

1,200-CALORIE DIET   DAY 16

4 Starch/Bread	4 Vegetable	2 Milk
5 Meat	3 Fruit	3 Fat

BREAKFAST
½ cup bran flakes
½ grapefruit
1 cup milk (skim or 1-percent)
Coffee or tea (optional)

LUNCH
Sandwich with:
    2 slices whole-wheat bread
    3 ounces sliced turkey breast
    Fresh tomato slices and lettuce leaves
    1 tablespoon reduced-calorie mayonnaise
1 cup carrot sticks
1 small apple
Noncaloric beverage

DINNER
1 cup garden salad with:
    2 tablespoons reduced-calorie dressing
1 serving Summertime Seafood Kabobs (p. 260)
1 small baked potato (3 ounces)
1 teaspoon margarine
½ cup mixed fresh fruit
Noncaloric beverage

SNACK
½ cup sugar-free pudding (made with skim milk)
Noncaloric beverage

1,500-CALORIE DIET   DAY 16

6 Starch/Bread	4 Vegetable	2 Milk
6 Meat	4 Fruit	4 Fat

BREAKFAST
1 hard-boiled egg
½ cup bran flakes
½ grapefruit
1 cup milk (skim or 1-percent)
Coffee or tea (optional)

LUNCH
Sandwich with:
   2 slices whole-wheat bread
   3 ounces sliced turkey breast
   Fresh tomato slices and lettuce leaves
   1 tablespoon reduced-calorie mayonnaise
1 cup carrot sticks
1 small apple
Noncaloric beverage

SNACK
3 graham-cracker squares
½ cup pineapple juice

DINNER
1 cup garden salad with:
   2 tablespoons low-calorie dressing
1 serving Summertime Seafood Kabobs (p. 260)
1 large baked potato (6 ounces)
2 teaspoons margarine
½ cup mixed fresh fruit
Noncaloric beverage

SNACK
½ cup sugar-free pudding (made with skim milk)
Noncaloric beverage

1,800-CALORIE DIET DAY 16

8 Starch/Bread	5 Vegetable	2 Milk
7 Meat	4 Fruit	5 Fat

BREAKFAST
1 hard-boiled egg
1 cup bran flakes
½ grapefruit
1 cup milk (skim or 1-percent)
Coffee or tea (optional)

SNACK
1 Oatmeal-Raisin Bar (p. 330)
Noncaloric beverage

LUNCH
Sandwich with:
    2 slices whole-wheat bread
    3 ounces sliced turkey breast
    Fresh tomato slices and lettuce leaves
    1 tablespoon reduced-calorie mayonnaise
1 cup carrot sticks
1 small pear
Noncaloric beverage

SNACK
1 slice whole-wheat toast
1 teaspoon margarine
½ cup apple juice
Noncaloric beverage

DINNER
1 cup garden salad with:
    2 tablespoons reduced-calorie dressing
1½ servings Summertime Seafood Kabobs (p. 260)
1 large baked potato (6 ounces)
2 teaspoons margarine
½ cup mixed fresh fruit
Noncaloric beverage

SNACK
½ cup sugar-free pudding (made with skim milk)
Noncaloric beverage

Day 17

THE "3 M" PLEDGE:

1. *I will keep my* motivation *high with rewards and reach-able goals.*
2. *I will have a visual* measurement *of success by retaking my "Body Fat" (Self-Test 1, pps. 19–22) and "What Shape Are You In?" (Self-Test 3, pps. 27–40) tests and keeping my exercise log.*
3. *I will* maintain *my weight loss because it feels too good to stop.*

For Each Exercise Program: 5 to 7 minutes of warm-ups

BLUE: Walk 2.0 miles today at 50 percent of your maximum heart rate.

WHITE: Walk 2.5 miles today at 60 percent of your maximum heart rate.

RED: Walk 3.5 miles today at 60 percent of your maximum heart rate.

For Each Exercise Program: 5 to 7 minutes of cool-downs

1,200-CALORIE DIET   DAY 17

4 Starch/Bread	4 Vegetable	2 Milk
5 Meat	3 Fruit	3 Fat

BREAKFAST ½ English muffin with:
  1 tablespoon diet margarine
1 orange
1 cup milk (skim or 1-percent)

LUNCH Grilled open-face hamburger with:
  2 ounces extra-lean ground beef
  ½ hamburger bun
  Grilled onion slices
  Fresh tomato slices and lettuce leaves
1 serving pineapple, ¾ cup fresh or ⅓ cup canned
Noncaloric beverage

DINNER 1 cup garden salad with:
  2 tablespoons reduced-calorie dressing
1 serving Chicken Fajitas* (p. 269)
15 grapes
Noncaloric beverage

SNACK ½ cup ice milk
Noncaloric beverage

*Cook extra chicken for Day 18 dinner.

1,500-CALORIE DIET   DAY 17

6 Starch/Bread	4 Vegetable	2 Milk
6 Meat	4 Fruit	4 Fat

BREAKFAST   1 Oat Bran Muffin (p. 315) with:
    2 tablespoons Yogurt Cheese (p. 313)
1 orange
1 cup milk (skim or 1-percent)

LUNCH   Grilled hamburger with:
    3 ounces extra-lean ground beef
    1 hamburger bun
    Grilled onion slices
    Fresh tomato slices and lettuce leaves
1 serving pineapple, ¾ cup fresh or ⅓ cup canned
Noncaloric beverage

SNACK   1 small apple
Noncaloric beverage

DINNER   1 cup garden salad with:
    2 tablespoons reduced-calorie dressing
1 serving Chicken Fajitas* (p. 269)
½ cup ice milk with:
    ¾ cup fresh blueberries
Noncaloric beverage

SNACK   1½ cups plain air-popped popcorn with:
    1 teaspoon margarine
Noncaloric beverage

*Cook extra chicken for Day 18 dinner.

1,800-CALORIE DIET   DAY 17

8 Starch/Bread	5 Vegetable	2 Milk
7 Meat	4 Fruit	5 Fat

BREAKFAST

1 Oat Bran Muffin (p. 315) with:
   2 tablespoons Yogurt Cheese (p. 313)
1 orange
½ cup milk (skim or 1-percent)
Coffee or tea (optional)

SNACK

5 Melba toast crackers
1 ounce low-fat cheese
Noncaloric beverage

LUNCH

Grilled hamburger with:
   3 ounces extra-lean ground beef
   1 hamburger bun
   Grilled onion slices
   Fresh tomato slices and lettuce leaves
1 serving pineapple, ¾ cup fresh or ⅓ cup canned
Noncaloric beverage

SNACK

1 small apple
Noncaloric beverage

DINNER

1 cup garden salad with:
   2 tablespoons reduced-calorie dressing
1 serving Chicken Fajitas* (p. 269)
1 serving Spanish-Style Rice (p. 295)
½ cup ice milk with:
   ¾ cup fresh blueberries
Noncaloric beverage

SNACK

1½ cups plain air-popped popcorn with:
   2 teaspoons margarine
Non-caloric beverage

*Cook extra chicken for Day 18 dinner.

Day 18

"If you exercise and maintain temperance throughout your life, you can carry much of the strength of your youth into old age."

—Cicero

first century B.C.

For Each Exercise Program: 5 to 7 minutes of warm-ups

BLUE: Walk 2.0 miles today at 50 percent of your maximum heart rate.

WHITE: Walk 2.5 miles today at 60 percent of your maximum heart rate.

RED: Walk 3.5 miles today at 60 percent of your maximum heart rate.

For Each Exercise Program: 5 to 7 minutes of cool-downs

1,200-CALORIE DIET   DAY 18

| 4 Starch/Bread | 4 Vegetable | 2 Milk |
| 5 Meat | 3 Fruit | 3 Fat |

BREAKFAST   ½ cup cream of wheat with:
          2 tablespoons raisins
     1 cup milk (skim or 1-percent)
     Coffee or tea (optional)

LUNCH   2 cups mixed vegetable salad with:
          1 ounce sliced turkey
          1½ ounces sliced lean ham
          2 tablespoons reduced-calorie dressing
     24 oyster crackers
     ½ cup milk (skim or 1-percent)
     Noncaloric beverage

DINNER   1 serving Hearty Caesar Salad (p. 245)
     1 serving Chicken Pasta Primavera (p. 270)
     1 orange, sliced
     Noncaloric beverage

SNACK   1 cup cantaloupe cubes

1,500-CALORIE DIET   DAY 18

| 6 Starch/Bread | 4 Vegetable | 2 Milk |
| 6 Meat | 4 Fruit | 4 Fat |

BREAKFAST	1 cup cream of wheat with:
	2 tablespoons raisins
	1 cup milk (skim or 1-percent)
	Coffee or tea (optional)

LUNCH	2 cups mixed vegetable salad with:
	2 ounces sliced turkey
	1½ ounces sliced lean ham
	2 tablespoons reduced-calorie dressing
	24 oyster crackers
	½ cup milk (skim or 1-percent)
	Noncaloric beverage

SNACK	1 small pear
	Noncaloric beverage

DINNER	1 serving Hearty Caesar Salad (p. 245)
	1 serving Chicken Pasta Primavera (p. 270)
	1 slice Garlic Bread (p. 320)
	1 orange, sliced
	Noncaloric beverage

SNACK	1 cup cantaloupe cubes

1,800-CALORIE DIET   DAY 18

8 Starch/Bread	5 Vegetable	2 Milk
7 Meat	4 Fruit	5 Fat

BREAKFAST
1 cup cream of wheat with:
    2 tablespoons raisins
1 cup milk (skim or 1-percent)
Coffee or tea (optional)

SNACK
1 cup celery sticks with:
    1 tablespoon peanut butter*
Noncaloric beverage

LUNCH
Sandwich with:
    2 slices bread
    2 ounces sliced turkey
    1½ ounces sliced lean ham
    1 tablespoon reduced-calorie mayonnaise
2 cups mixed vegetable salad with:
    2 tablespoons reduced-calorie dressing
1 cup cantaloupe cubes
Noncaloric beverage

SNACK
1 small pear
Noncaloric beverage

DINNER
1 serving Hearty Caesar Salad (p. 245)
1 serving Chicken Pasta Primavera (p. 270)
1 slice Garlic Bread (p. 320)
1 orange, sliced
Noncaloric beverage

SNACK
½ cup milk (skim or 1-percent)
3 graham-cracker squares

*In moderation, peanut butter is an acceptable food for a low-fat, low-calorie diet. If used frequently, we recommend "natural" or "old-fashioned" peanut butter, which is lower in saturated fat.

Day 19

"This time belongs to me!"

—Katie Allen
Rockport Walking Program subject

For Each Exercise Program: 5 to 7 minutes of warm-ups

BLUE: Walk 2.0 miles today at 50 percent of your maximum heart rate.

WHITE: Walk 2.5 miles today at 60 percent of your maximum heart rate.

RED: Walk 3.5 miles today at 60 percent of your maximum heart rate.

For Each Exercise Program: 5 to 7 minutes of cool-downs

1,200-CALORIE DIET   DAY 19

| 4 Starch/Bread | 4 Vegetable | 2 Milk |
| 5 Meat | 3 Fruit | 3 Fat |

BREAKFAST
1 slice whole-wheat toast
1 teaspoon margarine
½ cup grapefruit juice
1 serving Fortified Hot Chocolate (p. 334)

LUNCH
½ large (6 inches across) pita bread filled with:
   ½ cup Tuna Salad (p. 250)
   Tomato and onion slices and lettuce leaves
1 small peach
Noncaloric beverage

DINNER
1 cup spinach salad with:
   2 tablespoons reduced-calorie dressing
1 serving Peppered Pork with Black Beans (p. 268)
⅓ cup white rice
½ cup cooked zucchini
1 cup honeydew melon cubes
Noncaloric beverage

SNACK
½ cup ice milk
Noncaloric beverage

1,500-CALORIE DIET   DAY 19

| 6 Starch/Bread | 4 Vegetable | 2 Milk |
| 6 Meat | 4 Fruit | 4 Fat |

BREAKFAST
2 slices whole-wheat toast
2 teaspoons margarine
½ cup grapefruit juice
1 serving Fortified Hot Chocolate (p. 334)

LUNCH
Sandwich with:
    1 large (6 inches across) pita bread
    ½ cup Tuna Salad (p. 250)
    1 ounce low-fat cheese
    Tomato and onion slices and lettuce leaves
1 small peach
Noncaloric beverage

SNACK
½ cup unsweetened applesauce
Noncaloric beverage

DINNER
1 cup spinach salad with:
    2 tablespoons reduced-calorie dressing
1 serving Peppered Pork with Black Beans (p. 268)
⅓ cup white rice
½ cup cooked zucchini
1 cup honeydew melon cubes
Noncaloric beverage

SNACK
½ cup ice milk
Noncaloric beverage

1,800-CALORIE DIET   DAY 19

| 8 Starch/Bread | 5 Vegetable | 2 Milk |
| 7 Meat | 4 Fruit | 5 Fat |

BREAKFAST
1 egg, cooked any style without fat
2 slices whole-wheat toast
2 teaspoons margarine
½ cup grapefruit juice
Coffee or tea (optional)

SNACK
1 serving Fortified Hot Chocolate (p. 334)

LUNCH
Sandwich with:
    1 large (6 inches across) pita bread
    ½ cup Tuna Salad (p. 250)
    1 ounce low-fat cheese
    Tomato and onion slices and lettuce leaves
1 cup green pepper slices
1 small peach
Noncaloric beverage

SNACK
½ English muffin, toasted
1 teaspoon margarine
½ cup pineapple juice

DINNER
1 cup spinach salad with:
    2 tablespoons reduced-calorie dressing
1 serving Peppered Pork with Black Beans (p. 268)
⅔ cup white rice
½ cup cooked zucchini
1 cup honeydew melon cubes
Noncaloric beverage

SNACK
½ cup ice milk
Noncaloric beverage

Day 20

"I perceive this as a change that I am planning to incorporate. I would like to be a tall, straight, slim, healthy, sharp old lady someday, and I see this as something I can do to bring that about. I want to be healthy till I drop!"

—Ceile Burgess
Rockport Walking Program subject

For Each Exercise Program: 5 to 7 minutes of warm-ups

BLUE: Walk 2.0 miles today at 50 percent of your maximum heart rate.

WHITE: Walk 2.5 miles today at 60 percent of your maximum heart rate.

RED: Walk 3.5 miles today at 60 percent of your maximum heart rate.

For Each Exercise Program: 5 to 7 minutes of cool-downs

1,200-CALORIE DIET   DAY 20

4 Starch/Bread	4 Vegetable	2 Milk
5 Meat	3 Fruit	3 Fat

BREAKFAST ½ (1 ounce) bagel with:
　　　　1 tablespoon diet margarine
　　1 serving sugar-free shake mix (70 calories) blended with:
　　　　½ banana
　　Coffee or tea (optional)

LUNCH Sandwich with:
　　　　1 large pita bread (6 inches across)
　　　　2 ounces lean roast beef
　　　　Tomato and onion slices and lettuce leaves
　　　　1 tablespoon reduced-calorie mayonnaise
　　1 cup green pepper slices
　　1 fresh orange
　　Noncaloric beverage

DINNER 1 serving Cucumber Salad (p. 242)
　　3 ounces baked fish
　　1 serving Potatoes Mediterranean (p. 292)
　　1 cup cooked carrots
　　Noncaloric beverage

SNACK ¾ cup plain low-fat yogurt with:
　　　　¾ cup blueberries
　　Noncaloric beverage

1,500-CALORIE DIET   DAY 20

6 Starch/Bread	4 Vegetable	2 Milk
6 Meat	4 Fruit	4 Fat

BREAKFAST

1 (2 ounces) bagel with:
    1 tablespoon diet margarine
1 serving sugar-free shake mix (70 calories) blended with:
    ½ banana
Coffee or tea (optional)

LUNCH

Sandwich with:
    1 large pita bread (6 inches across)
    2 ounces lean roast beef
    Tomato and onion slices and lettuce leaves
    1 tablespoon reduced-calorie mayonnaise
1 cup green pepper slices
1 fresh orange
Noncaloric beverage

SNACK

1 Oatmeal-Raisin Bar (p. 330)
Noncaloric beverage

DINNER

1 serving Cucumber Salad (p. 242)
4 ounces baked fish
1 serving Potatoes Mediterranean (p. 292)
1 cup cooked carrots
1 teaspoon margarine
½ cup mixed fresh fruit
Noncaloric beverage

SNACK

¾ cup plain low-fat yogurt with:
    ¾ cup blueberries
Noncaloric beverage

1,800-CALORIE DIET   DAY 20

8 Starch/Bread	5 Vegetable	2 Milk
7 Meat	4 Fruit	5 Fat

BREAKFAST 1 (2 ounces) bagel with:
　　　　　　　　1 tablespoon diet margarine
　　　　　　　1 serving sugar-free shake mix (70 calories) blended with:
　　　　　　　　½ banana
　　　　　　　Coffee or tea (optional)

SNACK 1 Oatmeal-Raisin Bar (p. 330)
　　　　　Noncaloric beverage

LUNCH Sandwich with:
　　　　　　1 large pita bread (6 inches across)
　　　　　　3 ounces lean roast beef
　　　　　　Tomato and onion slices and lettuce leaves
　　　　　　1 tablespoon reduced-calorie mayonnaise
　　　　　1 fresh orange
　　　　　½ cup vegetable juice

SNACK 2 rice cakes
　　　　　½ cup tomato juice

DINNER 1 serving Cucumber Salad (p. 242)
　　　　　4 ounces baked fish
　　　　　2 servings Potatoes Mediterranean (p. 292)
　　　　　1 cup cooked carrots
　　　　　1 teaspoon margarine
　　　　　½ cup mixed fresh fruit
　　　　　Noncaloric beverage

SNACK ¾ cup plain low-fat yogurt with:
　　　　　　¾ cup blueberries
　　　　　Noncaloric beverage

Day 21

MOTIVATION DON'TS

- Don't *look back and feel guilty if you go off your weight-loss plan.*
- Don't *tell yourself that you "can't" eat certain foods.*
- Don't *think of this as a "diet."*
- Don't *expect to get support from relatives and friends— but enjoy it if you do.*
- Don't *concentrate on the scale.*
- Don't *discount your achievements—whether it be one pound lost or one pound not gained.*
- Don't give up!

For Each Exercise Program: 5 to 7 minutes of warm-ups

BLUE: Walk 2.0 miles today at 50 percent of your maximum heart rate.

WHITE: Walk 2.5 miles today at 60 percent of your maximum heart rate.

RED: Walk 3.5 miles today at 60 percent of your maximum heart rate.

For Each Exercise Program: 5 to 7 minutes of cool-downs

1,200-CALORIE DIET   DAY 21

4 Starch/Bread	4 Vegetable	2 Milk
5 Meat	3 Fruit	3 Fat

BREAKFAST
½ cup oatmeal
½ grapefruit
1 cup milk (skim or 1-percent)
Coffee or tea (optional)

LUNCH
Sandwich with:
　　2 slices whole-wheat bread
　　2 ounces low-fat cheese
　　Tomato and onion slices and lettuce leaves
　　1 tablespoon reduced-calorie mayonnaise
1 small apple
½ cup low-fat frozen yogurt
Noncaloric beverage

DINNER
Belgian Salad with Raspberry Dressing (p. 241)
3 ounces broiled round steak
1 1-ounce French roll
1 cup steamed broccoli
½ cup steamed cauliflower
Noncaloric beverage

SNACK
1 small pear
Noncaloric beverage

1,500-CALORIE DIET   DAY 21

| 6 Starch/Bread | 4 Vegetable | 2 Milk |
| 6 Meat | 4 Fruit | 4 Fat |

BREAKFAST
1 cup oatmeal
½ grapefruit
1 cup milk (skim or 1-percent)
Coffee or tea (optional)

LUNCH:
Sandwich with:
    2 slices whole-wheat bread
    2 ounces low-fat cheese
    Tomato and onion slices and lettuce leaves
    1 tablespoon reduced-calorie mayonnaise
1 small apple
½ cup low-fat frozen yogurt
Noncaloric beverage

SNACK
1 nectarine
Noncaloric beverage

DINNER
Belgian Salad with Raspberry Dressing (p. 241)
4 ounces broiled round steak
1 small baked potato (3 ounces)
1 1-ounce French roll
1 cup steamed broccoli
½ cup steamed cauliflower
1 teaspoon margarine
Noncaloric beverage

SNACK
1 small pear
Noncaloric beverage

1,800-CALORIE DIET   DAY 21

8 Starch/Bread	5 Vegetable	2 Milk
7 Meat	4 Fruit	5 Fat

BREAKFAST
1 cup oatmeal
½ grapefruit
1 cup milk (skim or 1-percent)
Coffee or tea (optional)

SNACK
1 nectarine
Noncaloric beverage

LUNCH
Sandwich with:
  2 slices whole-wheat bread
  2 ounces low-fat cheese
  Tomato and onion slices and lettuce leaves
  1 tablespoon reduced-calorie mayonnaise
1 cup carrot sticks
1 small apple
½ cup low-fat frozen yogurt
Noncaloric beverage

SNACK
1 slice bread with:
  1 tablespoon peanut butter*
Noncaloric beverage

DINNER
Belgian Salad with Raspberry Dressing (p. 241)
4 ounces broiled steak
1 large baked potato (6 ounces)
1 1-ounce French roll
1 cup steamed broccoli
½ cup steamed cauliflower
2 teaspoons margarine
Noncaloric beverage

SNACK
1 small pear
Noncaloric beverage

*In moderation, peanut butter is an acceptable food for a low-fat, low-calorie diet. If used frequently, we recommend "natural" or "old-fashioned" peanut butter, which is lower in saturated fat.

Day 22

*An easy diet strategy: Steer clear of "hidden" fat. It trans-
lates into a weight loss of ten pounds a year—effortlessly!*

For Each Exercise Program: 5 to 7 minutes of warm-ups

BLUE: Walk 2.0 miles today at 50 percent of your maximum heart rate.

WHITE: Walk 2.5 miles today at 60 percent of your maximum heart rate.

RED: Walk 3.5 miles today at 60 percent of your maximum heart rate.

For Each Exercise Program: 5 to 7 minutes of cool-downs

1,200-CALORIE DIET   DAY 22

| 4 Starch/Bread | 4 Vegetable | 2 Milk |
| 5 Meat | 3 Fruit | 3 Fat |

BREAKFAST
1 ounce Canadian bacon
1 slice whole-wheat toast
1 teaspoon margarine
1 cup cantaloupe cubes
½ cup milk (skim or 1-percent)
Coffee or tea (optional)

BRUNCH
1 serving Cheesy Turkey-Ham Bake (p. 273)
1 tomato, sliced with:
   1 tablespoon reduced-calorie mayonnaise
15 grapes
Noncaloric beverage

DINNER
2 cups mixed vegetable salad with:
   2 tablespoons reduced-calorie dressing
   1 ounce shredded low-fat cheese
1 serving Pasta and Bean Soup (p. 265)
½ cup unsweetened applesauce
Noncaloric beverage

SNACK
½ cup low-fat frozen yogurt

1,500-CALORIE DIET   DAY 22

6 Starch/Bread	4 Vegetable	2 Milk
6 Meat	4 Fruit	4 Fat

BREAKFAST
1 ounce Canadian bacon
2 slices whole-wheat toast
1 tablespoon diet margarine
1 cup cantaloupe cubes
½ cup milk (skim or 1-percent)
Coffee or tea (optional)

BRUNCH
1 serving Cheesy Turkey-Ham Bake (p. 273)
1 tomato, sliced with:
   1 tablespoon reduced-calorie mayonnaise
15 grapes
Noncaloric beverage

SNACK
1 tablespoon peanut butter*
1 small apple
Noncaloric beverage

DINNER
2 cups mixed vegetable salad with:
   2 tablespoons reduced-calorie dressing
   1 ounce shredded low-fat cheese
1 serving Pasta and Bean Soup (p. 265)
1 slice bread
1 teaspoon margarine
Noncaloric beverage

SNACK
½ cup low-fat frozen yogurt with:
   1 cup raspberries

*In moderation, peanut butter is an acceptable food for a low-fat, low-calorie diet. If used frequently, we recommend "natural" or "old-fashioned" peanut butter, which is lower in saturated fat.

1,800-CALORIE DIET   DAY 22

| 8 Starch/Bread | 5 Vegetable | 2 Milk |
| 7 Meat | 4 Fruit | 5 Fat |

BREAKFAST
1 ounce Canadian bacon
2 slices whole-wheat toast
2 teaspoons margarine
1 cup cantaloupe cubes
½ cup milk (skim or 1-percent)
Coffee or tea (optional)

BRUNCH
1 serving Cheesy Turkey-Ham Bake (p. 273)
1 tomato, sliced with:
    1 tablespoon reduced-calorie mayonnaise
5 vanilla wafers
½ cup orange juice
Noncaloric beverage

SNACK
1 tablespoon peanut butter*
1 small apple
Noncaloric beverage

DINNER
2 cups mixed vegetable salad with:
    2 tablespoons reduced-calorie dressing
    1 ounce shredded low-fat cheese
2 servings Pasta and Bean Soup (p. 265)
1 slice bread
1 teaspoon margarine
Noncaloric beverage

SNACK
½ cup low-fat frozen yogurt with:
    1 cup raspberries
Noncaloric beverage

---

*In moderation, peanut butter is an acceptable food for a low-fat, low-calorie diet. If used frequently, we recommend "natural" or "old-fashioned" peanut butter, which is lower in saturated fat.

Day 23

"I took all my clothes when I first started this diet and put them in a locker in the garage. I went out the other day to try some of them on. Two of us could have fit in them. I couldn't believe it!"

—George Maloney
Rockport Walking Program subject

For Each Exercise Program: 5 to 7 minutes of warm-ups

BLUE: Walk 2.0 miles today at 50 percent of your maximum heart rate.

WHITE: Walk 2.5 miles today at 60 percent of your maximum heart rate.

RED: Walk 3.5 miles today at 60 percent of your maximum heart rate.

For Each Exercise Program: 5 to 7 minutes of cool-downs

1,200-CALORIE DIET   DAY 23

4 Starch/Bread	4 Vegetable	2 Milk
5 Meat	3 Fruit	3 Fat

BREAKFAST
½ cup Shredded Wheat with:
    1½ dried figs, chopped
1 cup milk (skim or 1-percent)
Coffee or tea (optional)

LUNCH
1 serving Turkey-Asparagus Roll-Ups (pps. 272–73)
1 tomato, sliced
1 1-ounce roll
1 teaspoon margarine
2 tangerines
Noncaloric beverage

DINNER
½ steamed artichoke with:
    1 tablespoon reduced-calorie mayonnaise
1 serving Shrimp Curry (p. 261) with:
    1 tablespoon chopped peanuts
½ cup green beans
Noncaloric beverage

SNACK
½ cup milk (skim or 1-percent)
1 small pear
1 ounce low-fat Cheddar cheese

1,500-CALORIE DIET   DAY 23

6 Starch/Bread	4 Vegetable	2 Milk
6 Meat	4 Fruit	4 Fat

BREAKFAST
1 cup Shredded Wheat with:
  1½ dried figs, chopped
1 cup milk (skim or 1-percent)
Coffee or tea (optional)

LUNCH
1 serving Turkey-Asparagus Roll-Ups (pps. 272–73)
1 tomato, sliced, with:
  1 tablespoon reduced-calorie mayonnaise
1 1-ounce roll
1 teaspoon margarine
2 tangerines
Noncaloric beverage

SNACK
½ cup low-fat cottage cheese
1 small pear, sliced

DINNER
½ steamed artichoke with:
  1 tablespoon reduced-calorie mayonnaise
1 serving Shrimp Curry (p. 261) with:
  1 tablespoon chopped peanuts
½ cup green beans
1 serving pineapple, ¾ cup fresh or ⅓ cup canned
Noncaloric beverage

SNACK
½ cup milk (skim or 1-percent)
3 graham-cracker squares

1,800-CALORIE DIET   DAY 23

8 Starch/Bread	5 Vegetable	2 Milk
7 Meat	4 Fruit	5 Fat

BREAKFAST
1 cup Shredded Wheat with:
   1½ dried figs, chopped
1 cup milk (skim or 1-percent)
Coffee or tea (optional)

SNACK
1 small pear
1 ounce low-fat Cheddar cheese
Noncaloric beverage

LUNCH
2 servings Turkey-Asparagus Roll-Ups (pps. 272–73)
1 1-ounce roll
1 teaspoon margarine
2 tangerines
Noncaloric beverage

SNACK
2 Country Classic Cookies (p. 321)
Noncaloric beverage

DINNER
1 steamed artichoke with:
   2 tablespoons reduced-calorie mayonnaise
1 serving Shrimp Curry (p. 261) with:
   1 tablespoon chopped peanuts
½ cup green beans
1 serving pineapple, ¾ cup fresh or ⅓ cup canned
Noncaloric beverage

SNACK
½ cup milk (skim or 1-percent)
3 graham-cracker squares

Day 24

"Yesterday when I went for my walk, I passed a few other walkers. We waved and smiled at each other. It was a communal thing, an instant camaraderie and understanding. For that brief moment of time, I felt at peace with the world."

—Moire Johnson
Rockport Walking Program subject

For Each Exercise Program: 5 to 7 minutes of warm-ups

BLUE: Walk 2.0 miles today at 50 percent of your maximum heart rate.

WHITE: Walk 2.5 miles today at 60 percent of your maximum heart rate.

RED: Walk 3.5 miles today at 60 percent of your maximum heart rate.

For Each Exercise Program: 5 to 7 minutes of cool-downs

1,200-CALORIE DIET   DAY 24

4 Starch/Bread	4 Vegetable	2 Milk
5 Meat	3 Fruit	3 Fat

BREAKFAST
1 egg, cooked any style without fat
1 slice whole-wheat toast
1 teaspoon margarine
1 orange
1 cup milk (skim or 1-percent)
Coffee or tea (optional)

LUNCH
Sandwich with:
   2 slices light oat bread (40 calories/slice)
   2 ounces lean honey ham
   Tomato slices and lettuce leaves
   1 tablespoon reduced-calorie mayonnaise
1 small apple
½ cup vegetable juice

DINNER
1 cup vegetable salad with:
   2 tablespoons no-oil dressing (free exchange)
   1 serving Spinach Quesadillas with Black Bean Sauce
   (p. 282)
½ cup low-fat frozen yogurt with:
   1 peach, sliced
Noncaloric beverage

SNACK
1 slice 40-calorie bread
1 tablespoon peanut butter*
Noncaloric beverage

*In moderation, peanut butter is an acceptable food for a low-fat, low-calorie diet. If used frequently, we recommend "natural" or "old-fashioned" peanut butter, which is lower in saturated fat.

1,500-CALORIE DIET   DAY 24

6 Starch/Bread	4 Vegetable	2 Milk
6 Meat	4 Fruit	4 Fat

BREAKFAST
1 egg, cooked any style without fat
1 slice whole-wheat toast
1 teaspoon margarine
1 orange
1 cup milk (skim or 1-percent)
Coffee or tea (optional)

LUNCH
Sandwich with:
    2 slices oat bread
    3 ounces lean honey ham
    Tomato slices and lettuce leaves
    1 tablespoon reduced-calorie mayonnaise
1 fresh peach
Noncaloric beverage

SNACK
1 cup cantaloupe cubes
Noncaloric beverage

DINNER
1 cup vegetable salad with:
    2 tablespoons no-oil dressing (free exchange)
2 servings Spinach Quesadillas with Black Bean Sauce
    (p. 282)
1 small apple
Noncaloric beverage

SNACK
½ cup low-fat frozen yogurt
Noncaloric beverage

1,800-CALORIE DIET   DAY 24

8 Starch/Bread	5 Vegetable	2 Milk
7 Meat	4 Fruit	5 Fat

BREAKFAST
1 egg, cooked any style without fat
2 slices whole-wheat toast
2 teaspoons margarine
½ cup orange juice
1 cup milk (skim or 1-percent)
Coffee or tea (optional)

SNACK
2 rice cakes
Noncaloric beverage

LUNCH
Sandwich with:
  2 slices oat bread
  3 ounces lean honey ham
  Tomato slices and lettuce leaves
  1 tablespoon reduced-calorie mayonnaise
1 fresh peach
½ cup vegetable juice

SNACK
¼ cup low-fat cottage cheese
1 cup cantaloupe cubes
Noncaloric beverage

DINNER
1 cup vegetable salad with:
  2 tablespoons no-oil dressing (free exchange)
2 servings Spinach Quesadillas with Black Bean Sauce
  (p. 282)
1 small apple
Noncaloric beverage

SNACK
½ cup low-fat frozen yogurt
Noncaloric beverage

Day 25

"Today I have grown taller from walking with the trees."
—Karle Wilson Baker
1878, *Good Company*

For Each Exercise Program: 5 to 7 minutes of warm-ups

BLUE: Walk 2.0 miles today at 50 percent of your maximum heart rate.

WHITE: Walk 2.5 miles today at 60 percent of your maximum heart rate.

RED: Walk 3.5 miles today at 60 percent of your maximum heart rate.

For Each Exercise Program: 5 to 7 minutes of cool-downs

1,200-CALORIE DIET   DAY 25

| 4 Starch/Bread | 4 Vegetable | 2 Milk |
| 5 Meat | 3 Fruit | 3 Fat |

BREAKFAST
½ cup Shredded Wheat with:
  ½ banana, sliced
1 cup milk (skim or 1-percent)
Coffee or tea (optional)

LUNCH
Grilled sandwich with:
  2 slices rye bread
  1 ounce lean ham
  1 ounce low-fat Swiss cheese
  1 teaspoon mustard (optional)
1 tomato, sliced
1 cup green pepper slices
2 tablespoons reduced-calorie dressing
1 cup honeydew melon cubes
Noncaloric beverage

DINNER
3 ounces baked chicken* basted with:
  1 tablespoon reduced-calorie Italian dressing
⅓ cup sweet potato
1 serving Broccoli with Mustard Sauce (p. 286)
1 teaspoon margarine
1 kiwi, sliced
Noncaloric beverage

SNACK
½ cup sugar-free pudding (made with skim milk)

*Bake extra chicken breast for Day 26 lunch.

1,500-CALORIE DIET　　　　　DAY 25

6 Starch/Bread	4 Vegetable	2 Milk
6 Meat	4 Fruit	4 Fat

BREAKFAST

1 cup Shredded Wheat with:
　½ banana, sliced
1 cup milk (skim or 1-percent)
Coffee or tea (optional)

LUNCH

Grilled sandwich with:
　2 slices rye bread
　1 ounce lean ham
　1 ounce low-fat Swiss cheese
　1 teaspoon mustard (optional)
　1 teaspoon margarine (for grilling)
1 tomato, sliced
1 cup green pepper slices
2 tablespoons reduced-calorie dressing
1 cup honeydew melon cubes
Noncaloric beverage

SNACK

2 tangerines
Noncaloric beverage

DINNER

4 ounces baked chicken* basted with:
　1 tablespoon reduced-calorie Italian dressing
⅔ cup sweet potato
1 serving Broccoli with Mustard Sauce (p. 286)
1 teaspoon margarine
1 kiwi, sliced
Noncaloric beverage

SNACK

½ cup sugar-free pudding (made with skim milk)
Noncaloric beverage

*Bake extra chicken breast for Day 26 lunch.

1,800-CALORIE DIET   DAY 25

8 Starch/Bread	5 Vegetable	2 Milk
7 Meat	4 Fruit	5 Fat

BREAKFAST
1 cup Shredded Wheat with:
  ½ banana, sliced
1 cup milk (skim or 1-percent)
Coffee or tea (optional)

SNACK
2 tangerines
Noncaloric beverage

LUNCH
Grilled sandwich with:
  2 slices rye bread
  1½ ounces lean ham
  1½ ounces low-fat Swiss Cheese
  1 teaspoon mustard (optional)
  1 teaspoon margarine (for grilling)
1 tomato, sliced
1 cup green pepper slices
2 tablespoons reduced-calorie dressing
1 cup honeydew melon cubes
Noncaloric beverage

SNACK
2 Country Classic Cookies (p. 321)
Noncaloric beverage

DINNER
1 cup vegetable salad with:
  2 tablespoons no-oil dressing (free exchange)
4 ounces baked chicken* basted with:
  1 tablespoon reduced-calorie Italian dressing
⅔ cup sweet potato
1 serving Broccoli with Mustard Sauce (p. 286)
1 teaspoon margarine
1 kiwi, sliced
Noncaloric beverage

SNACK
½ cup sugar-free pudding (made with skim milk)
Noncaloric beverage

*Bake extra chicken breast for Day 26 lunch.

Day 26

"I can be very intense and have a lot of things on my mind. But when I come in from my walk, it is like I feel I can put my thoughts where I want them. My head clears. I make good decisions when I'm on my walk. I can go out when I'm upset, and I can come back and handle some things a lot better than I would have before."

—Kathy Madden
Rockport Walking Program subject

For Each Exercise Program: 5 to 7 minutes of warm-ups

BLUE: Walk 2.0 miles today at 50 percent of your maximum heart rate.

WHITE: Walk 2.5 miles today at 60 percent of your maximum heart rate.

RED: Walk 3.5 miles today at 60 percent of your maximum heart rate.

For Each Exercise Program: 5 to 7 minutes of cool-downs

1,200-CALORIE DIET   DAY 26

4 Starch/Bread	4 Vegetable	2 Milk
5 Meat	3 Fruit	3 Fat

BREAKFAST
1 Oat Bran Muffin (p. 315)
1 cup melon cubes
1 cup milk (skim or 1-percent)
Coffee or tea (optional)

LUNCH
2 cups garden salad with:
    2 ounces cooked, chopped chicken breast
    3 tablespoons no-oil dressing (free exchange)
4 rye wafers
1 nectarine
Noncaloric beverage

DINNER
1 serving Veal Marsala (p. 275)
1 1-ounce whole-grain roll
½ cup summer squash
½ cup brussels sprouts
1 teaspoon margarine
½ cup ice milk
Noncaloric beverage

SNACK
1¼ cups whole fresh strawberries
Noncaloric beverage

1,500-CALORIE DIET   DAY 26

| 6 Starch/Bread | 4 Vegetable | 2 Milk |
| 6 Meat | 4 Fruit | 4 Fat |

BREAKFAST
1 Oat Bran Muffin (p. 315)
1 cup melon cubes
1 cup milk (skim or 1-percent)
Coffee or tea (optional)

LUNCH
2 cups garden salad with:
    2 ounces cooked, chopped chicken breast
    3 tablespoons no-oil dressing (free exchange)
1 1-ounce whole-grain roll
1 teaspoon margarine
1 nectarine
5 vanilla wafers
Noncaloric beverage

SNACK
1 cup celery sticks with:
    1 tablespoon peanut butter*
Noncaloric beverage

DINNER
1 serving Veal Marsala (p. 275)
1 large baked potato (6 ounces)
½ cup brussels sprouts
1 teaspoon margarine
½ cup mixed fresh fruit
Noncaloric beverage

SNACK
½ cup ice milk with:
    1¼ cups whole fresh strawberries
Noncaloric beverage

---

*In moderation, peanut butter is an acceptable food for a low-fat, low-calorie diet. If used frequently, we recommend "natural" or "old-fashioned" peanut butter, which is lower in saturated fat.

1,800-CALORIE DIET   DAY 26

8 Starch/Bread	5 Vegetable	2 Milk
7 Meat	4 Fruit	5 Fat

BREAKFAST
1 Oat Bran Muffin (p. 315)
1 cup melon cubes
1 cup milk (skim or 1-percent)
Coffee or tea (optional)

SNACK
2 rice cakes
½ cup apple juice

LUNCH
Sandwich with:
   2 slices whole-wheat bread
   3 ounces cooked, chopped chicken breast mixed with
      2 tablespoons reduced-calorie mayonnaise
2 cups garden salad with:
   2 tablespoons no-oil dressing (free exchange)
5 vanilla wafers
Noncaloric beverage

SNACK
1 cup celery sticks with:
   1 tablespoon peanut butter*
Noncaloric beverage

DINNER
1 serving Veal Marsala (p. 275)
1 large baked potato (6 ounces)
½ cup brussels sprouts
½ cup summer squash
1 teaspoon margarine
½ cup mixed fresh fruit
Noncaloric beverage

SNACK
½ cup ice milk with:
   1¼ cups whole fresh strawberries
Noncaloric beverage

*In moderation, peanut butter is an acceptable food for a low-fat, low-calorie diet. If used frequently, we recommend "natural" or "old-fashioned" peanut butter, which is lower in saturated fat.

Day 27

"For the first time in my life, I am at peace with food."
—Katie Allen
Rockport Walking Program subject

For Each Exercise Program: 5 to 7 minutes of warm-ups

BLUE: Walk 2.0 miles today at 50 percent of your maximum heart rate.

WHITE: Walk 2.5 miles today at 60 percent of your maximum heart rate.

RED: Walk 3.5 miles today at 60 percent of your maximum heart rate.

For Each Exercise Program: 5 to 7 minutes of cool-downs

1,200-CALORIE DIET   DAY 27

4 Starch/Bread	4 Vegetable	2 Milk
5 Meat	3 Fruit	3 Fat

BREAKFAST

1½ cups puffed-wheat cereal
½ grapefruit
1 cup milk (skim or 1-percent)
Coffee or tea (optional)

LUNCH

1 Tostada Grande (p. 283) (or similar-size tostada)
1 orange
Noncaloric beverage

DINNER

1 cup vegetable salad with:
   2 tablespoons low-calorie dressing (free exchange)
1 serving Steamed Sea Bass, Chinese Style (p. 259)
⅓ cup white rice
1 cup asparagus
1 serving pineapple, ¾ cup fresh or ⅓ cup canned
Noncaloric beverage

SNACK

½ cup low-fat frozen yogurt
Noncaloric beverage

1,500-CALORIE DIET   DAY 27

| 6 Starch/Bread | 4 Vegetable | 2 Milk |
| 6 Meat | 4 Fruit | 4 Fat |

BREAKFAST	1½ cups puffed-wheat cereal ½ grapefruit 1 cup milk (skim or 1-percent) Coffee or tea (optional)
LUNCH	1 Tostada Grande (p. 283) (or similar-size tostada) 1 orange Noncaloric beverage
SNACK	6 saltine-type crackers ¼ cup low-fat cottage cheese Noncaloric beverage
DINNER	1 cup vegetable salad with: 2 tablespoons reduced-calorie dressing 1 serving Steamed Sea Bass, Chinese Style (p. 259) ⅔ cup white rice 1 cup asparagus 1 serving pineapple, ¾ cup fresh or ⅓ cup canned Noncaloric beverage
SNACK	½ cup low-fat frozen yogurt with: 1 kiwi, sliced Noncaloric beverage

1,800-CALORIE DIET   DAY 27

8 Starch/Bread	5 Vegetable	2 Milk
7 Meat	4 Fruit	5 Fat

BREAKFAST	1½ cups puffed-wheat cereal 1 slice whole-grain toast 1 teaspoon margarine ½ grapefruit 1 cup milk (skim or 1-percent) Coffee or tea (optional)
SNACK	1 kiwi Noncaloric beverage
LUNCH	1 Tostada Grande (p. 283) (or similar-size tostada) 1 quesadilla (1 6-inch tortilla with 1 ounce low-fat cheese, heated) 1 nectarine Noncaloric beverage
SNACK	6 saltine-type crackers ¼ cup low-fat cottage cheese Noncaloric beverage
DINNER	2 cups vegetable salad with: 2 tablespoons reduced-calorie dressing 1 serving Steamed Sea Bass, Chinese Style (p. 259) ⅔ cup white rice 1 cup asparagus 1 serving pineapple, ¾ cup fresh or ⅓ cup canned Noncaloric beverage
SNACK	½ cup low-fat frozen yogurt Noncaloric beverage

Day 28

"That's the nice part of being in this: You really want to keep the weight off. You can fall off the wagon anytime, but you can get right back up again and just keep going."
—Nick Rioux
Rockport Walking Program subject

For Each Exercise Program: 5 to 7 minutes of warm-ups

BLUE: Walk 2.0 miles today at 50 percent of your maximum heart rate.

WHITE: Walk 2.5 miles today at 60 percent of your maximum heart rate.

RED: Walk 3.5 miles today at 60 percent of your maximum heart rate.

For Each Exercise Program: 5 to 7 minutes of cool-downs

1,200-CALORIE DIET   DAY 28

4 Starch/Bread	4 Vegetable	2 Milk
5 Meat	3 Fruit	3 Fat

BREAKFAST
½ cup bran flakes
½ cup orange juice
1 cup milk (skim or 1-percent)
Coffee or tea (optional)

LUNCH
Sandwich with:
    1 (2 ounces) bagel, sliced
    2 ounces sliced chicken
    Tomato slices and lettuce leaves
    1 tablespoon reduced-calorie mayonnaise
1 nectarine
1 cup milk

DINNER
2 cups spinach salad with:
    2 tablespoons low-calorie dressing
1 serving Steak Jardinière (p. 253)
1 small boiled potato (3 ounces)
1 teaspoon margarine
½ cup sugar-free gelatin dessert
Noncaloric beverage

SNACK
1 cup melon cubes
Noncaloric beverage

1,500-CALORIE DIET   DAY 28

6 Starch/Bread	4 Vegetable	2 Milk
6 Meat	4 Fruit	4 Fat

BREAKFAST
½ cup bran flakes
1 slice whole-wheat toast
1 teaspoon margarine
½ cup orange juice
1 cup milk (skim or 1-percent)
Coffee or tea (optional)

LUNCH
Sandwich with:
   1 (2 ounces) bagel, sliced
   2 ounces sliced chicken
   Tomato slices and lettuce leaves
   1 tablespoon reduced-calorie mayonnaise
1 nectarine
1 cup milk (skim or 1-percent)

SNACK
¼ cup low-fat cottage cheese
12 cherries
Noncaloric beverage

DINNER
2 cups mixed vegetable salad with:
   2 tablespoons reduced-calorie dressing
1 serving Steak Jardinière (p. 253)
2 small boiled potatoes
1 teaspoon margarine
½ cup sugar-free gelatin dessert
Noncaloric beverage

SNACK
1 cup melon cubes
Noncaloric beverage

1,800-CALORIE DIET
DAY 28

8 Starch/Bread	5 Vegetable	2 Milk
7 Meat	4 Fruit	5 Fat

BREAKFAST
½ cup bran flakes
1 slice whole-wheat toast
1 teaspoon margarine
½ cup orange juice
1 cup milk (skim or 1-percent)
Coffee or tea (optional)

SNACK
1 cup melon cubes
Noncaloric beverage

LUNCH
Sandwich with:
  1 (2 ounces) bagel, sliced
  3 ounces sliced chicken
  Tomato slices and lettuce leaves
  1 tablespoon reduced-calorie mayonnaise
1 cup carrot sticks
5 vanilla wafers
1 cup milk (skim or 1-percent)

SNACK
¼ cup low-fat cottage cheese
12 cherries
Noncaloric beverage

DINNER
2 cups mixed vegetable salad with:
  2 tablespoons reduced-calorie dressing
1 serving Steak Jardinière (p. 253)
2 small boiled potatoes
1 teaspoon margarine
½ cup sugar-free gelatin dessert with:
  ½ cup fruit
Noncaloric beverage

SNACK
3 cups air-popped popcorn made with:
  1 teaspoon margarine
Noncaloric beverage

Day 29

"Trust yourself. You know more than you think you do."
—Dr. Benjamin Spock

For Each Exercise Program: 5 to 7 minutes of warm-ups

BLUE: Walk 2.5 miles today at 50 percent of your maximum heart rate.

WHITE: Walk 3.0 miles today at 60 percent of your maximum heart rate.

RED: Walk 4.0 miles today at 60 percent of your maximum heart rate.

For Each Exercise Program: 5 to 7 minutes of cool-downs

1,200-CALORIE DIET   DAY 29

4 Starch/Bread	4 Vegetable	2 Milk
5 Meat	3 Fruit	3 Fat

BREAKFAST
½ cup Shredded Wheat
2 peach halves
1 cup milk (skim or 1-percent)
Coffee or tea (optional)

LUNCH
1 serving Turkey-Asparagus Roll-Ups (pps. 272–73)
6 dry-roasted almonds
1 1-ounce roll
1 teaspoon margarine
1 small apple
½ cup milk (skim or 1-percent)

DINNER
1 serving Shrimp Curry (p. 261)
1½ cups steamed broccoli, cauliflower, and zucchini
(½ cup each)
1 teaspoon margarine
Noncaloric beverage

SNACK
⅓ cup canned pineapple (in its own juice)
¼ cup low-fat cottage cheese
Noncaloric beverage

1,500-CALORIE DIET   DAY 29

6 Starch/Bread	4 Vegetable	2 Milk
6 Meat	4 Fruit	4 Fat

BREAKFAST
½ cup Shredded Wheat
2 peach halves
1 slice whole-wheat toast
1 teaspoon margarine
1 cup milk (skim or 1-percent)
Coffee or tea (optional)

LUNCH
1 serving Turkey-Asparagus Roll-Ups (pps. 272–73)
1 1-ounce roll
1 teaspoon margarine
1 small apple
½ cup milk (skim or 1-percent)

SNACK
1 small bran muffin
Noncaloric beverage

DINNER
1½ cups steamed broccoli, cauliflower, and zucchini (½ cup each)
1 teaspoon margarine
1 serving Shrimp Curry (p. 261)
½ cup orange sections
Noncaloric beverage

SNACK
½ cup low-fat cottage cheese
⅓ cup canned pineapple (in its own juice)
Noncaloric beverage

1,800-CALORIE DIET   DAY 29

| 8 Starch/Bread | 5 Vegetable | 2 Milk |
| 7 Meat | 4 Fruit | 5 Fat |

BREAKFAST
½ cup Shredded Wheat
2 peach halves
2 slices whole-wheat toast
2 teaspoons margarine
1 cup milk (skim or 1-percent)
Coffee or tea (optional)

SNACK
3 graham-cracker squares
Noncaloric beverage

LUNCH
1½ servings Turkey-Asparagus Roll-Ups (pps. 272–73)
½ cup cooked carrots
1 1-ounce roll
1 teaspoon margarine
1 small apple
½ cup milk (skim or 1-percent)

SNACK
1 small bran muffin
Noncaloric beverage

DINNER
1½ cups steamed broccoli, cauliflower, and zucchini (½ cup each)
1 teaspoon margarine
1 serving Shrimp Curry (p. 261)
½ cup orange sections
Noncaloric beverage

SNACK
½ cup low-fat cottage cheese
⅓ cup canned pineapple (in its own juice)
Noncaloric beverage

Day 30

"I feel, and will maintain, that this is probably the best and most well-thought-out program out of all of them because it's a life-style change. It doesn't have a beginning and an end . . . I think it can easily become a forever."
—Joyce Danielson
Rockport Walking Program subject

For Each Exercise Program: 5 to 7 minutes of warm-ups

BLUE: Walk 2.5 miles today at 50 percent of your maximum heart rate.

WHITE: Walk 3.0 miles today at 60 percent of your maximum heart rate.

RED: Walk 4.0 miles today at 60 percent of your maximum heart rate.

For Each Exercise Program: 5 to 7 minutes of cool-downs

1,200-CALORIE DIET   DAY 30

| 4 Starch/Bread | 4 Vegetable | 2 Milk |
| 5 Meat | 3 Fruit | 3 Fat |

BREAKFAST
1 egg, cooked any style without fat
1 slice whole-grain toast
1 teaspoon margarine
½ grapefruit
1 cup milk (skim or 1-percent)
Coffee or tea (optional)

LUNCH
1 serving Two-Bean Salad (p. 243) on:
    2 cups garden salad with 2 tablespoons reduced-calorie
        dressing
⅓ cup pineapple (in its own juice)
¼ cup low-fat cottage cheese
Noncaloric beverage

DINNER
3 ounces Dijon Chicken (p. 267) on:
    ½ cup fettuccine mixed with 1 teaspoon olive oil
½ cup cooked broccoli
1 tomato
1 pear
Noncaloric beverage

SNACK
1 package sugar-free hot cocoa
3 gingersnaps

1,500-CALORIE DIET   DAY 30

| 6 Starch/Bread | 4 Vegetable | 2 Milk |
| 6 Meat | 4 Fruit | 4 Fat |

BREAKFAST
1 egg, cooked any style without fat
1 slice whole-grain toast
1 teaspoon margarine
½ grapefruit
1 cup milk (skim or 1-percent)
Coffee or tea (optional)

LUNCH
½ cup Two-Bean Salad (p. 243) on:
    2 cups garden salad with 2 tablespoons reduced-calorie
      dressing
⅓ cup pineapple (in its own juice)
¼ cup low-fat cottage cheese
Noncaloric beverage

SNACK
5 Melba toast crackers
½ cup apple juice

DINNER
4 ounces Dijon Chicken (p. 267) on:
    1 cup fettuccine mixed with 2 teaspoons olive oil
½ cup cooked broccoli
1 tomato
1 pear
Noncaloric beverage

SNACK
1 package sugar-free hot cocoa
4 gingersnaps

1,800-CALORIE DIET   DAY 30

8 Starch/Bread	5 Vegetable	2 Milk
7 Meat	4 Fruit	5 Fat

BREAKFAST
1 egg, cooked any style without fat
2 slices whole-grain toast
2 teaspoons margarine
½ cup grapefruit
1 cup milk (skim or 1-percent)
Coffee or tea (optional)

SNACK
5 Melba toast crackers
Noncaloric beverage

LUNCH
½ cup Two-Bean Salad (p. 243) on:
  2 cups garden salad with 2 tablespoons reduced-calorie
    dressing
⅓ cup pineapple (in its own juice)
¼ cup low-fat cottage cheese
Noncaloric beverage

SNACK
½ (1 ounce) bagel
1 ounce low-fat Jack cheese
½ cup orange juice

DINNER
4 ounces Dijon Chicken (p. 267) on:
  1 cup fettuccine mixed with 2 teaspoons olive oil
1 cup cooked broccoli
1 tomato
1 pear
Noncaloric beverage

SNACK
1 package sugar-free hot cocoa
3 gingersnaps

Dining Out

A CHINESE RESTAURANT

Overheard in a Chinese restaurant: "Chinese food is the meaning of life." That might be overstating it, but there's no reason why you can't enjoy a take-out meal or a Saturday-night feast—as long as you choose wisely. It's a matter of ordering from Column A—and avoiding the foods in Column B:

COLUMN A
Steamed white or brown rice
Steamed dumplings
Stir-fried shrimp, chicken, beef, or pork with Chinese vegetables
Beef with broccoli, served with sauce on the side
Moo Shoo pork with two pancakes
Steamed or poached fish
Low-calorie steamed dishes served with white rice and sauce on the side
Chinese noodles, as indicated on your exchange list
Steamed vegetables
Szechuan chicken, with the sauce served on the side
Chow mein

COLUMN B
Deep-fried shrimp
Sweet 'n sour dishes
Fried rice
Egg rolls
Breaded or "golden" chicken dishes
Chicken or shrimp cashew entrées
Egg Foo Yung—it's high in cholesterol
Dishes made with lobster sauce—they're prepared with egg yolks
Sautéed dishes

A STEAK-AND-SEAFOOD HOUSE

Sometimes nothing less than a hearty "meat-and-potatoes" dinner will do. Here are some hints to keep your cholesterol and fat in check:

- Most entrées are cooked to order. That means you can specifically ask for your meat, poultry, or seafood to be broiled *without* butter.
- *Hearty* usually means big portions. Eat half and take the rest home.
- Ask for salad dressing on the side to control the amount used.
- Order your salad without the croutons. They add calories and fat!
- To moisten a baked potato, try substituting a few drops of milk and pepper to taste for butter. If you do indulge, keep your butter within exchange limits. Remember: It's a saturated fat.
- Try squeezing lemon juice on a steamed lobster. If the lobster is cooked properly, it will be moist and succulent.
- Trim the excess fat off meat and the skin from chicken.

Some meal suggestions to satisfy the heartiest of appetites:

APPETIZERS	Shrimp cocktail
	Oysters or clams on the half-shell
	Melon
ENTRÉES	London broil
	Flank steak
	Lean top round beef
	Filet mignon (Tenderloin)
	Charcoal-broiled chicken
	Broiled shrimp
	Steamed lobster
	Fish broiled in lemon, with the sauce on the side
SIDE DISHES	Steamed vegetables
	Salad, with the dressing on the side
	Baked potato
	Rice
DESSERTS	Fresh fruit
	Angel food cake
	Sorbet

MEXICAN STYLE

Believe it or not, a Mexican dinner can be a healthy and delicious choice—as long as you know the low-calorie customs south-of-the-border. Here are our recommendations:

- Corn tortillas are an excellent source of whole grains—as long as they are baked instead of fried.
- Steer clear of chimichangas. They're packed with lard and fried.
- Ask for your cheese, guacamole, and sour cream on the side. A little can go a long way.
- Refried beans are just what they sound like: fried twice—and cooked with lard. Use them in moderation.
- Keep the nacho chips on the far side of the table. Order a salad that you can munch while the others dip their chips.

A MEXICAN MEAL WITH A FESTIVE FLAIR	Salsa A tomato, avocado, and onion salad with fresh-squeezed lemon Seviche (spicy marinated fish) Chicken tostados Rice Fresh fruit

ITALIAN

Red-checkered tablecloths. The smell of simmering sauces. Candlelight and Chianti. Italian meals are romantic—not to mention delicious. Now you can satisfy your cravings without adding calories. Mange!

PASTA PLEASURES	Linguine with white or red clam sauce Spaghetti with marinara sauce Pasta primavera Hint: Order side-order portions. You won't be tempted to eat more than your daily exchange!
PIZZA PIZZAZZ	Two slices of plain or vegetable pizza

PIZZA (continued)	Hint: Ask if you can have your pizza with less cheese—and more mushrooms, onions, or peppers.
DELECTABLE DISHES	Chicken cacciatore Fish broiled with lemon Veal or chicken marsala with sauce on the side Hint: Avoid *parmigiana,* which means cheese, *piccata,* which means butter, and *scampi,* which means oil. Be assertive! Ask for your sauces on the side. Request broiled foods. Your waiter is there to serve you.
DESSERTS	Fresh fruit Italian ice or sorbet Espresso Hint: Add a salad with dressing on the side and a slice of Italian bread without butter—and you can use your fat exchanges for a glass of red wine (see p. 211).

A JAPANESE DINNER

A Japanese dinner has it all: elegance, good taste, and very little fat. It's a perfect choice for your new life-style. But do watch out for sodium. Japanese soups are packed with salt. And, though tempura starts out with fresh vegetables, it ends up a calorie-laden deep-fried choice. Here are some honorable ways to keep your diet plans intact:

- Pickled vegetables
- Sashimi (raw fish)
- Sushi (raw fish and rice wrapped in seaweed)
- Nabemono (a casserole)
- Chicken, shrimp, or beef teriyaki (broiled in a light sauce)
- Chicken, shrimp, or beef yakimono (broiled)
- Steamed rice
- Tofu dishes
- Sliced melon
- Japanese tea

A COFFEE-SHOP LUNCH

A diner or a neighborhood coffee shop is a great place to "get away" from the office for an hour or two. Inexpensive and fast, diners can also be surprisingly good. But avoid the fast-food "traps" that can sabotage your diet plans. Stick to basics—but low-calorie and low-fat ones. Here are some samples:

- Pickles are low in calories. So dip into the pickle bowl if you choose, but keep in mind that they are high in salt.
- Try a turkey, ham, or roast beef sandwich. Hold the mayo!
- Always order dry toast. Coffee shops are notorious for brushing butter on their bread before they toast it.
- Order fruit salad or half a grapefruit for dessert. Or save the crackers that often come with entrées to have with your coffee.
- Ask for skim or 1-percent milk. Many coffee shops and diners serve it today.
- Greek diners usually have souvlaki on their menu. It's a pita filled with broiled lamb, onions, and tomato. Souvlaki makes a good lunch— but ask that yours be made without oil or butter.

If you select luncheon salads (tuna, chicken, or seafood) be sure to save up your fat exchanges. One scoop of salad can contain 1 to 2 tablespoons of mayonnaise.

Special Occasions

THE HOLIDAYS

Christmas and Thanksgiving. The time of the year when we overstuff, overeat, and oversleep—and resolve to start a diet tomorrow. But the holidays do not have to be the "horror" days. You can celebrate without adding calories. Here are two sample menus that are low in fat and low in calories. You'll find recipes for the foods in uppercase letters (e.g., Ginger Dip) in the section entitled "The Rockport Recipes." Happy holidays!

A THANKSGIVING MEAL	Crudités in a Basket
	Ginger Dip
	Stuffed Endive Stars
	Sweet Dumpling Squash Bisque
	Delicious Gold and Red Coleslaw
	Roast turkey (without skin)
	Oven-roasted potatoes
	Cranberry sauce made with artificial sweetener
	Skillet Turnips
	Steamed string beans and pearl onions
	Old-Fashioned Apple Crisp

A CHRISTMAS FEAST	Golden Trees
	Party Meatballs
	Boston Clam Chowder
	Baked lean ham
	Cornish Game Hens
	Cheddar Potatoes
	Sweet Rutabagas
	Steamed broccoli
	Easy Plum-and-Honey Bake
	Banana Custard with Chocolate Leaves

BOUNTIFUL BREAKFASTS

Juice. Cereal. Milk. It's the most popular breakfast around, and with good reason: It's fast, convenient, and low in calories. But day in and day out, this tasty trio can get monotonous. Here are some delicious and different suggestions for both leisurely mornings and breakfasts on the go:

- For a scrumptious Sunday brunch, top two waffles with nonfat plain yogurt, artificial sweetener to taste, and fresh strawberries. Add freshly brewed coffee and enjoy!
- Other brunch suggestions: our Hawaiian Toast or Tropical Puff Pancake. They're a perfect—and elegant—way to start your day.
- Add fresh blueberries to your pancake batter. The taste is so delicious you won't want to add more than a drop of syrup.
- No time? Try spreading some peanut butter on a toasted bagel. Add

a glass of juice and you have a fast, nutritious—and different—breakfast repast.

- There's bread—and then there's bread. Perk up your mornings with whole-wheat bread, raisin bread, oat bread, date-nut bread, pumpernickel bread, seven-grain bread . . . The list goes on!
- Smoked salmon doesn't always need cream cheese. Try thin slices of salmon on a lightly buttered bagel (use diet margarine). Top with a slice of onion, a slice of tomato, and some capers. A great taste treat—with half the calories of its cream-cheese counterpart.
- Sometimes just substituting a different juice can bring variety to your mornings. Try one of the new combination juices—or make your own!
- Diet tip: Drinking vegetable juice counts as a vegetable exchange. Have yours in the morning and you can save your fruits for later in the day.
- Fresh fruit is more filling than juice. Take advantage of the summer harvest with ripe melon, fresh berries, and delectable citrus fruit. Better yet, make a fruit salad. Add low-fat cottage cheese or low-fat yogurt and sprinkle on some Grapenuts cereal. Delicious!
- Try one of our bread recipes: Mom's Applesauce Cake (p. 331), Oat Bran Muffins (p. 315), Multi-Grain Bread (p. 317), or Chi Chi Banana Muffins (p. 318). Make them the night before and you'll have breakfast ready and waiting.

COMPANY'S COMING

You're planning an elegant dinner for two—or twelve. Festive fare doesn't have to mean fattening—or boring. And low-calorie fare is much appreciated in today's weight-conscious world. Here are some company meals that are guaranteed to satisfy the most discriminating palates. You'll find the recipes for these dishes in the section entitled "The Rockport Recipes."

COMPANY MEAL 1   Vichyssoise
Red-and-White Salad
Chicken Pasta Primavera
Poached Pears

COMPANY MEAL 2	Clam-Stuffed Artichokes
	Summertime Seafood Kabobs
	Steamed rice
	Blueberry Swirl

COMPANY MEAL 3	Stuffed Endive Stars
	Sweet Dumpling Squash Bisque
	Beef Tenderloin with Capers
	Broccoli with Mustard Sauce
	Potatoes Mediterranean
	Fresh strawberries with Orange Sauce

COMPANY MEAL 4	Creamy Spinach Soup
	Belgian Salad with Raspberry Dressing
	Jane's Chicken Piccata
	Delicate Angel Pasta
	Kiwi Cups

COMPANY MEAL 5	Spinach Salad with Slivered Almonds
	Cioppino
	Garlic Bread
	Orange Sorbet

THE WEDDING PARTY

Weddings, bar mitzvahs, golden and silver anniversaries, even gala New Year's Eve events—all are cause for great celebration. Double your fun by keeping your calories down— and your spirits up. Here's how:

- Plan for the occasion before the big event arrives. Get your walking in. If you go over your daily number of exchanges, don't get discouraged. Get right back on track the next day.
- By saving up your fat exchanges (see p. 211), you can enjoy the champagne—and drink it too!
- Relish the fact that you no longer have to say, "There's a wedding in a few weeks and I have to lose weight fast!" You've already slimmed down, and it's time to show off.
- Buy a dress or a suit that displays the new you to maximum effect. A silver belt. A tapered tux. A strapless gown in a sizzling color. Your

friends and relatives will be so busy giving you compliments, you won't have time to think about food.

- If the party is a buffet, use "The Cocktail Party" hints: Don't be first in line, keep to plainer fare, steer away from the cheese and the dips, and think crudités, shrimp, and lean cuts of meat.
- A sit-down dinner usually comes with a choice of entrée. Choose the leaner of the two, and ask for your salad dressing on the side.
- You don't have to desert dessert. One bite of wedding cake will not add pounds—and a taste can go a long way.
- Burn those calories before you eat or drink them. Dance the night away!

THE COCKTAIL PARTY

A celebration can truly be a "happy hour" if you follow these tips:

- Concentrate on how great you look—and how much better you feel. Invest in clothes that show you at your "fashionable" best—no matter what time you show up. Looking elegant and being sociable will keep your food cravings at bay.
- Eat some vegetables or a low-fat yogurt before you go. You won't feel as hungry.
- Order your drinks mixed with seltzer or water. A spritzer has half the calories of a glass of wine! Sip them slowly so they will last longer.
- Keep your distance from the buffet table. Mingle at the other side of the room.
- Stick with cold hors d'oeuvres. Chances are, they'll have a lot less calories than hot ones. Avoid "stuffed," "fried," and "pastry" tidbits.
- Don't say "cheese!" Six small cubes of Cheddar have more than 400 calories.
- Crudités are a perfect choice—but don't "dip in" to the dip. You'll add at least 15 calories per dip!
- Never say "never." Nibble on nuts if you like, but don't forget your fat exchanges for the day. A better choice is pretzels—a bread exchange without any fat!
- Wait until everyone else has been to the buffet table. As the platters get depleted, they lose their appeal.

GUESS WHO'S COMING FOR DINNER

You're invited to a friend's house for dinner. You can either (a) say nothing and feel miserable after you've eaten too much fat and too many calories; (b) say nothing and not eat certain foods—and possibly insult your host or hostess; (c) plan ahead.

Right. The answer is *c*. Calling up a few days before the party can make all the difference between having a disastrous time—or an enjoyable evening out. Close friends will already know you're on The Rockport Walking Program. Chances are, they will let you know what they're serving before you even ask!

Once you know the menu, you can make some choices. You can decide to:

- Eat what is being served because it is reasonably low in calories.
- Ask if you can bring some crudités that you can nibble on while the others are deep in their dip.
- Find out if it would be too much trouble for your host or hostess to have some low-calorie foods ready for you: seltzer, crudités, salad without dressing, and fresh fruit.
- Eat less during the day and save up your exchanges for that night's dining and drinking.
- Keep your eating to a minimum. Only taste the desserts. Stay away from seconds. Merely nibble the hors d'oeuvres.
- Concentrate on the conversation. A good time with good friends is worth a lot more than an extra helping of chocolate cake.

Miscellaneous Menus

COUCH POTATOES OF THE WORLD UNITE!

You've taken up knitting. You've done your nails. You've polished your shoes, and you've folded laundry for the last three days. You've even walked a mile on your treadmill. And you still want to lie on the couch, watch television, and have some snacks. For those times when nothing else will do but the tube and the tray, here's some low-cal, low-fat food for thought:

COUCH POTATO 1	Air-popped popcorn topped with a drizzle of melted diet margarine Diet soda
COUCH POTATO 2	Fresh crudités Ginger Dip White-wine spritzer
COUCH POTATO 3	Baked Wonton Chips Mixed green salad with reduced-calorie dressing V-8 juice
COUCH POTATO 4	Bananas and cottage cheese with artificial sweetener to taste Slice of rye toast spread with all-fruit preserves Seltzer with a wedge of lime
COUCH POTATO 5	Celery sticks Apple slices Melba toast, or rye crisps Cheddar Cheese Spread Sugar-free fruit drink
COUCH POTATO 6	Sugar-free pudding made with skim milk Fat-Free Whipped Topping 3 graham squares Skim milk

BROWN-BAG LUNCHES WITH PANACHE

Lunchtime doesn't have to mean celery, carrots, and cot-
tage cheese day in and day out. Turn your noontime rou-
tine into luncheon delights with these delicious and
easy-to-prepare-and-tote suggestions. Lunch boxes have never
been so chic!

BROWN BAG 1   Start with a pita pocket—but don't open it. Instead, place it flat on your counter. Add two slices of turkey breast, 1 tablespoon reduced-calorie mayonnaise, a few raw onion rings, and two slices of tomato, and spice it up with some Italian seasonings. Roll it up and wrap well in plastic wrap. Eat it as you would a hot dog when the lunch bell rings!

BROWN BAG 2   Pack 1 to 2 tablespoons of peanut butter (remember: 1 tablespoon is equivalent to 1 high-fat meat exchange) wrapped in foil along with your apple. Spread it on your apple with every bite. A great—and healthy—taste sensation!

BROWN BAG 3   Tired of plain old tuna salad? Be creative. Try your very own "Salad Niçoise" by adding cold blanched string beans, sun-dried tomatoes, fresh dill, a few chopped walnuts, and a splash of oil and vinegar. Scoop your salad into a plastic container lined with lettuce. By the time you're ready for lunch, your salad will be deliciously marinated and ready to eat.

BROWN BAG 4   Pineapple and cottage cheese is an old standby lunch. But most of the "fruit-and-cheese" combos on your grocery shelf contain more fat than you need. Instead of buying ready-made concoctions, try making your own. Start with 1-percent cottage cheese and add whatever fruit you want. Be creative! Try strawberries and bananas. Pineapple packed in its own juice. Drained mandarin oranges. Kiwi fruit. Honeydew and cantaloupe. Mix well and fold into a plastic container. Add a touch of artificial sweetener to taste right before you eat. Enjoy!

BROWN BAG 5   Cold chicken can be delicious—especially when you get inventive. Cut up white meat into chunks. Add blanched cold broccoli, a sprinkle of sesame seeds, a splash of sesame oil, and salt and pepper to taste. Put into a pita pocket for a chicken sandwich that's delightfully different.

III

FOR THE
REST OF
YOUR LIFE

5

THE LIFETIME
EXCHANGE SYSTEM

Congratulations! You have changed your life. You have discovered how eating the low-fat way doesn't mean deprivation. You have proven how easily you can lose weight by combining exercise with a healthy diet. You have joined the successful ranks of our Rockport Walking Program subjects who have learned how wonderful change can be—to every aspect of their lives.

Your Rockport Walking Program is more than a 30-Day (20-Week) Program. To lose one to two pounds a week, you must keep to your Meal Plan—and use our exchange system.

These exchanges are designed to make low-calorie eating easy to live with—and to enjoy. You can substitute one food serving in a specific exchange-list category for another in the same category—without sacrificing your nutritional needs for the day. For example, if you are on our 1,500-Calorie-a-Day Meal Plan, you will be eating four fruit exchanges—which you are free to choose from your fruit-exchange list. You might decide to use one of your exchanges for a small apple, or ¾ cup blueberries, or two medium plums. Another example: If you are on the 1,200-Calorie-a-Day Meal Plan, you'll need to eat four starch/breads. You might decide to spread your starch exchanges throughout the day, eating one exchange for breakfast, one for lunch, and two for dinner. Or you might decide to use up all your starch exchanges at dinner—and treat yourself to that bowl of pasta. The choice is yours!

The Rockport Walking Program incorporates the American Heart Association (AHA) guidelines with the American Diabetes Association/

The American Dietetic Association Exchange Lists for Meal Planning.*
The 1,200-, 1,500-, and 1,800-calorie Meal Plans in the 30-Day Program Calendar are designed to provide no more than 30 percent fat.
The ADA/ADA Exchange Lists include guidelines for sodium and fiber.
Foods high in sodium and fiber have been highlighted throughout the
exchange lists. The Rockport Walking Program's major focus is on fat
and calories. We make no specific guidelines for sodium as do the
ADA/ADA Exchange Lists, but this information has been included for
those of you who would like to decrease the sodium in your diet.

Increasing fiber in your diet is beneficial for the prevention of
gastrointestinal difficulties and disease. Use the footnotes regarding
fiber to help guide you in choosing foods with a higher fiber content.

At the end of the ADA/ADA Exchange Lists you will find an
additional list that the nutritionists from The Rockport Walking Program
have developed. For more variety, you may include any of the foods on
this list in your diet.

The Six Exchange Lists

The foods listed within each category have approximately the same
amount of protein, fat, carbohydrate, and calories per serving. *Every
food is listed with a serving size that equals one exchange.*

1. Starch/Bread List

Each item in this list contains approximately 15 grams of carbohydrate,
3 grams of protein, a trace of fat, and 80 calories. Whole-grain products average about 2 grams of fiber per exchange. Some foods are
higher in fiber. Those foods that contain 3 or more grams of fiber per
exchange are footnoted.

You can choose your starch exchanges from any of the items on
this list. If you want to eat a starch food that is not on this list, the
general rule is that:

- ½ cup of cereal, grain, or pasta is one exchange
- 1 ounce of a bread product is one exchange

*The exchange lists are the basis of a meal-planning system designed by a committee of the
American Diabetes Association and The American Dietetic Association. While designed
primarily for people with diabetes and others who must follow special diets, the exchange lists
are based on principles of good nutrition that apply to everyone. Copyright © 1986 American
Diabetes Association, The American Dietetic Association.

CEREALS/GRAINS/PASTA

Bran cereals*, concentrated	⅓ cup
(such as Bran Buds®, All Bran®)	
Bran cereals*, flaked	½ cup
Bulgur (cooked)	½ cup
Cooked cereals	½ cup
Cornmeal (dry)	2½ Tbsp.
Grape-Nuts®	3 Tbsp.
Grits (cooked)	½ cup
Other ready-to-eat unsweetened cereals	¾ cup
Pasta (cooked)	½ cup
Puffed cereal	1½ cups
Rice, white or brown (cooked)	⅓ cup
Shredded wheat	½ cup
Wheat germ*	3 Tbsp.

*3 grams or more of fiber per exchange.

DRIED BEANS/PEAS/LENTILS

Beans* and peas* (cooked),	⅓ cup
such as kidney, white, split, black-eyed	
Lentils* (cooked)	⅓ cup
Baked beans*	¼ cup

*3 grams or more of fiber per exchange.

STARCHY VEGETABLES

Corn*	½ cup
Corn on cob*, 6 in. long	1
Lima beans*	½ cup
Peas, green* (canned or frozen)	½ cup
Plantain*	½ cup
Potato, baked	1 small (3 oz.)
Potato, mashed	½ cup
Squash, winter* (acorn, butternut)	1 cup
Yam, sweet potato, plain	⅓ cup

*3 grams or more of fiber per exchange.

BREAD

Bagel	½ (1 oz.)
Breadsticks, crisp, 4 in. long × ½ in.	2 (⅔ oz.)
Croutons, low-fat	1 cup

BREAD *(cont.)*

English muffin	½
Frankfurter or hamburger bun	½ (1 oz.)
Pita, 6 in. across	½
Plain roll, small	1 (1 oz.)
Raisin, unfrosted	1 slice (1 oz.)
Rye, pumpernickel	1 slice (1 oz.)
Tortilla, 6 in. across	1
White (including French, Italian)	1 slice (1 oz.)
Whole-wheat	1 slice (1 oz.)

CRACKERS/SNACKS

Animal crackers	8
Graham crackers, 2½ in. square	3
Matzoh	¾ oz.
Melba toast	5 slices
Oyster crackers	24
Popcorn (popped, no fat added)	3 cups
Pretzels	¾ oz.
Rye crisp*, 2 in. × 3½ in.	4
Saltine-type crackers	6
Whole-wheat crackers*, no fat added (crisp breads, such as Finn®, Kavli®, Wasa®)	2–4 slices (¾ oz.)

*3 grams or more of fiber per exchange.

STARCH FOODS PREPARED WITH FAT

(Count as 1 starch/bread exchange, plus 1 fat exchange.)

Biscuit, 2½ in. across	1
Chow mein noodles	½ cup
Corn bread, 2 in. cube	1 (2 oz.)
Cracker, round butter type	6
French-fried potatoes, 2 in. to 3½ in. long	10 (1½ oz.)
Muffin, plain, small	1
Pancake, 4 in. across	2
Stuffing, bread (prepared)	¼ cup
Taco shell, 6 in. across	2
Waffle, 4½ in. square	1
Whole-wheat crackers*, fat added (such as Triscuit®)	4–6 (1 oz.)

*3 grams or more of fiber per exchange.

2. Meat List

Each serving of meat and substitutes on this list contains about 7 grams of protein. The amount of fat and number of calories varies, depending on what kind of meat or substitute you choose. The list is divided into three parts based on the amount of fat and calories: lean meat, medium-fat meat, and high-fat meat. One ounce (one meat exchange) of each of these includes:

	CARBOHYDRATE (GRAMS)	PROTEIN (GRAMS)	FAT (GRAMS)	CALORIES
Lean	0	7	3	55
Medium-Fat	0	7	5	75
High-Fat	0	7	8	100

You are encouraged to use lean meat, poultry, and fish in your meal plan. This will help decrease your fat intake, which may help decrease your risk for heart disease. The items from the high-fat group are high in saturated fat, cholesterol, and calories. Meat and substitutes do not contribute any fiber to your meal plan.

Meats and meat substitutes that have 400 milligrams or more of sodium per exchange are footnoted.

Meats and meat substitutes that have 400 mg or more of sodium if two or more exchanges are eaten are footnoted.

TIPS

- Bake, roast, broil, grill, or boil these foods rather than frying them with added fat.
- Use a nonstick pan spray or a nonstick pan to brown or fry these foods.
- Trim off visible fat before and after cooking.
- Do not add flour, bread crumbs, coating mixes, or fat to these foods when preparing them.
- Weigh meat after removing bones and fat, and after cooking. Three ounces of cooked meat is about equal to 4 ounces of raw meat. Some examples of meat portions are:

2 ounces meat (2 meat exchanges) =
    1 small chicken leg or thigh
    ½ cup cottage cheese or tuna

3 ounces meat (3 meat exchanges) =
    1 medium pork chop
    1 small hamburger
    ½ of a whole chicken breast
    1 unbreaded fish fillet
    cooked meat, about the size of a deck of cards
- Restaurants usually serve prime cuts of meat, which are high in fat and calories.

LEAN MEAT AND SUBSTITUTES

(One exchange is equal to any one of the following items.)

Beef:	USDA Select or Choice grades of lean beef, such as round, sirloin, and flank steak; tenderloin; and chipped beef*	1 oz.
Pork:	Lean pork, such as fresh ham; canned, cured, or boiled ham*; Canadian bacon*, tenderloin	1 oz.
Veal:	All cuts are lean except for veal cutlets (ground or cubed). Examples of lean veal are chops and roasts.	1 oz.
Poultry:	Chicken, turkey, Cornish hen (without skin)	1 oz.
Fish:	All fresh and frozen fish	1 oz.
	Crab, lobster, scallops, shrimp, clams (fresh or canned in water)	2 oz.
	Oysters	6 medium
	Tuna** (canned in water)	¼ cup
	Herring** (uncreamed or smoked)	1 oz.
	Sardines (canned)	2 medium
Wild Game:	Venison, rabbit, squirrel	1 oz.
	Pheasant, duck, goose (without skin)	1 oz.
Cheese:	Any cottage cheese**	¼ cup
	Grated Parmesan	2 Tbsp.
	Diet cheeses* (with less than 55 calories per ounce)	1 oz.
Other:	95% fat-free luncheon meat*	1½ oz.
	Egg whites	3 whites
	Egg substitutes with less than 55 calories per ½ cup	½ cup

*400 mg or more of sodium per exchange.
**400 mg or more of sodium if two or more exchanges are eaten.

MEDIUM-FAT MEAT AND SUBSTITUTES

(One exchange is equal to any one of the following items.)

Beef:	Most beef products fall into this category. Examples are: all ground beef, roast (rib, chuck, rump), steak (cubed, Porterhouse, T-bone), and meatloaf.	1 oz.
Pork:	Most pork products fall into this category. Examples are: chops, loin roast, Boston butt, cutlets.	1 oz.

MEDIUM-FAT MEAT AND SUBSTITUTES *(cont.)*

Lamb:	Most lamb products fall into this category. Examples are: chops, leg, and roast.	1 oz.
Veal:	Cutlet (ground or cubed, unbreaded)	1 oz.
Poultry:	Chicken (with skin), domestic duck or goose (well drained of fat), ground turkey	1 oz.
Fish:	Tuna* (canned in oil and drained)	¼ cup
	Salmon* (canned)	¼ cup
Cheese:	Skim or part-skim milk cheeses, such as:	
	Ricotta	¼ cup
	Mozzarella	1 oz.
	Diet cheeses** (with 56–80 calories per ounce)	1 oz.
Other:	86% fat-free luncheon meat*	1 oz.
	Egg (high in cholesterol, limit to 3 per week)	1
	Egg substitutes with 56–80 calories per ¼ cup	¼ cup
	Tofu (2½ in. × 2¾ in. × 1 in.)	4 oz.
	Liver, heart, kidney, sweetbreads (high in cholesterol)	1 oz.

*400 mg or more of sodium if two or more exchanges are eaten.
**400 mg or more of sodium per exchange.

HIGH-FAT MEAT AND SUBSTITUTES

Remember, these items are high in saturated fat, cholesterol, and calories.
(One exchange is equal to any one of the following items.)

Beef:	Most USDA Prime cuts of beef, such as ribs, corned beef*	1 oz.
Pork:	Spareribs, ground pork, pork sausage** (patty or link)	1 oz.
Lamb:	Patties (ground lamb)	1 oz.
Fish:	Any fried fish product	1 oz.
Cheese:	All regular cheeses, such as American**, Blue**, Cheddar*, Monterey Jack*, Swiss	1 oz.
Other:	Luncheon meat**, such as bologna, salami, pimento loaf	1 oz.
	Sausage**, such as Polish, Italian smoked	1 oz.
	Knockwurst**	1 oz.
	Bratwurst*	1 oz.
	Frankfurter** (turkey or chicken)	1 frank (10/lb.)
	Peanut butter (contains unsaturated fat)	1 Tbsp.

Count as one high-fat meat plus one fat exchange

Frankfurter** (beef, pork, or combination)		1 frank (10/lb.)

*400 mg or more of sodium if two or more exchanges are eaten.
**400 mg or more of sodium per exchange.

3. Vegetable List

Each vegetable serving on this list contains about 5 grams of carbohydrate, 2 grams of protein, and 25 calories. Vegetables contain 2 to 3 grams of dietary fiber. Vegetables that contain 400 milligrams or more of sodium per exchange are footnoted.

Vegetables are a good source of vitamins and minerals. Fresh and frozen vegetables have more vitamins and less added salt. Rinsing canned vegetables will remove much of the salt.

Unless otherwise noted, the serving size for vegetables (one vegetable exchange) is:

- ½ cup of cooked vegetables or vegetable juice
- 1 cup of raw vegetables.

Starchy vegetables such as corn, peas, and potatoes are found on the Starch/Bread List.

Artichoke (½ medium)
Asparagus
Beans (green, wax, Italian)
Bean sprouts
Beets
Broccoli
Brussels sprouts
Cabbage, cooked
Carrots
Cauliflower
Eggplant
Greens (collard, mustard, turnip)
Kohlrabi
Leeks
Mushrooms, cooked
Okra
Onions
Pea pods
Peppers (green)
Rutabaga
Sauerkraut*
Spinach, cooked
Summer squash (crookneck)
Tomato (one large)
Tomato/vegetable juice*
Turnips
Water chestnuts
Zucchini, cooked

*400 mg or more of sodium per exchange.

4. Fruit List

Each item on this list contains about 15 grams of carbohydrate and 60 calories. Fresh, frozen, and dried fruits have about 2 grams of fiber per exchange. Fruits that have 3 or more grams of fiber per exchange are footnoted.

The carbohydrate and calorie content for a fruit exchange are based on the usual serving of the most commonly eaten fruits. Use fresh fruits or fruits frozen or canned without sugar added. Whole fruit is more filling than fruit juice and may be a better choice for those who are trying to lose weight. Unless otherwise noted, the serving size for one fruit exchange is:

- ½ cup of fresh fruit or fruit juice
- ¼ cup of dried fruit

FRESH, FROZEN, AND UNSWEETENED CANNED FRUIT

Apple (raw, 2 in. across)	1 apple
Applesauce (unsweetened)	½ cup
Apricots (medium, raw)	4 apricots
Apricots (canned)	½ cup, or 4 halves
Banana (9 in. long)	½ banana
Blackberries* (raw)	¾ cup
Blueberries* (raw)	¾ cup
Cantaloupe (5 in. across)	⅓ melon
(cubes)	1 cup
Cherries (large, raw)	12 cherries
Cherries (canned)	½ cup
Figs (raw, 2 in. across)	2 figs
Fruit cocktail (canned)	½ cup
Grapefruit (medium)	½ grapefruit
Grapefruit (segments)	¾ cup
Grapes (small)	15 grapes
Honeydew melon (medium)	⅛ melon
(cubes)	
Kiwi (large)	1 kiwi
Mandarin oranges	¾ cup
Mango (small)	½ mango
Nectarine* (2½ in. across)	1 nectarine
Orange (2½ in. across)	1 orange
Papaya	1 cup
Peach (2¾ in. across)	1 peach, or ¾ cup
Peaches (canned)	½ cup, or 2 halves
Pear	½ large, or 1 small
Pears (canned)	½ cup, or 2 halves
Persimmon (medium, native)	2 persimmons
Pineapple (raw)	¾ cup
Pineapple (canned)	⅓ cup
Plum (raw, 2 in. across)	2 plums
Pomegranate*	½ pomegranate
Raspberries* (raw)	1 cup
Strawberries* (raw, whole)	1¼ cup
Tangerine* (2½ in. across)	2 tangerines
Watermelon (cubes)	1¼ cup

*3 grams or more of fiber per exchange.

DRIED FRUIT

Apples*	4 rings
Apricots*	7 halves
Dates	2½ medium
Figs*	1½
Prunes*	3 medium
Raisins	2 Tbsp.

*3 grams or more of fiber per exchange.

FRUIT JUICE

Apple juice/cider	½ cup
Cranberry juice cocktail	⅓ cup
Grapefruit juice	½ cup
Grape juice	⅓ cup
Orange juice	½ cup
Pineapple juice	½ cup
Prune juice	⅓ cup

5. Milk List

Each serving of milk or milk products on this list contains about 12 grams of carbohydrate and 8 grams of protein. The amount of fat in milk is measured in percent (%) of butterfat. The calories vary, depending on what kind of milk you choose. The list is divided into three parts based on the amount of fat and calories: skim/very low-fat milk, low-fat milk, and whole milk. One serving (one milk exchange) of each of these includes:

	CARBOHYDRATE (GRAMS)	PROTEIN (GRAMS)	FAT (GRAMS)	CALORIES
Skim/Very Low-fat	12	8	trace	90
Low-fat	12	8	5	120
Whole	12	8	8	150

Milk is the body's main source of calcium, the mineral needed for growth and repair of bones. Yogurt is also a good source of calcium. Yogurt and many dry or powdered milk products have different amounts of fat. If you have questions about a particular item, read the label to find out the fat and calorie content.

Milk is good to drink, but it can also be added to cereal, and to other foods.

SKIM AND VERY LOW-FAT MILK

Skim milk	1 cup
½% milk	1 cup
1% milk	1 cup
Low-fat buttermilk	1 cup
Evaporated skim milk	½ cup
Dry nonfat milk	⅓ cup
Plain nonfat yogurt	8 oz.

LOW-FAT MILK

2% milk	1 cup fluid
Plain low-fat yogurt (with added nonfat milk solids)	8 oz.

WHOLE MILK

The whole milk group has much more fat per serving than the skim and lowfat groups. Whole milk has more than 3¼ percent butterfat. Try to limit your choices from the whole milk group as much as possible.

Whole milk	1 cup
Evaporated whole milk	½ cup
Whole plain yogurt	8 oz.

6. Fat List

Each serving on the fat list contains about 5 grams of fat and 45 calories.

The foods on the fat list contain mostly fat, although some items may also contain a small amount of protein. All fats are high in calories and should be carefully measured. Everyone should modify fat intake by eating unsaturated fats instead of saturated fats.

UNSATURATED FATS

Avocado	⅛ medium
Margarine	1 tsp.
Margarine*, diet	1 Tbsp.
Mayonnaise	1 tsp.
Mayonnaise*, reduced-calorie	1 Tbsp.
Nuts and Seeds:	
Almonds, dry roasted	6 whole
Cashews, dry roasted	1 Tbsp.
Pecans	2 whole
Peanuts	20 small, or 10 large
Walnuts	2 whole
Other nuts	1 Tbsp.
Seeds, pine nuts, sunflower (without shells)	1 Tbsp.
Pumpkin seeds	2 tsp.
Oil (corn, cottonseed, safflower, soybean, sunflower, olive, peanut)	1 tsp.
Olives*	10 small, or 5 large
Salad dressing, mayonnaise-type	2 tsp.

UNSATURATED FATS *(cont.)*

Salad dressing, mayonnaise-type, reduced-calorie	1 Tbsp.
Salad dressing* (oil varieties)	1 Tbsp.
Salad dressing**, reduced-calorie	2 Tbsp.

*400 mg or more of sodium if two or more exchanges are eaten.
**400 mg or more of sodium per exchange.

SATURATED FATS

Butter	1 tsp.
Bacon*	1 slice
Chitterlings	½ ounce
Coconut, shredded	2 Tbsp.
Coffee whitener, liquid	2 Tbsp.
Coffee whitener, powder	4 tsp.
Cream (light, coffee, table)	2 Tbsp.
Cream, sour	2 Tbsp.
Cream (heavy, whipping)	1 Tbsp.
Cream cheese	1 Tbsp.
Salt pork*	¼ ounce

*400 mg or more of sodium if two or more exchanges are eaten.

Free Foods

A free food is any food or drink that contains less than 20 calories per serving. You can eat as much as you want of those items that have no serving size specified. You may eat two or three servings per days of those items that have a specific serving size. Be sure to spread them out through the day.

DRINKS

Bouillon, or broth without fat*
Bouillon, low-sodium
Carbonated drinks, sugar-free
Carbonated water
Club soda

Cocoa powder, unsweetened (1 Tbsp.)
Coffee/Tea
Drink mixes, sugar-free
Tonic water, sugar-free

*400 mg or more of sodium per exchange.

NONSTICK PAN SPRAY

FRUIT

Cranberries, unsweetened (½ cup)   Rhubarb, unsweetened (½ cup)

VEGETABLES *(raw, 1 cup)*

Cabbage   Hot peppers
Celery   Mushrooms
Chinese cabbage*   Radishes
Cucumber   Zucchini*
Green onion

*3 grams or more of fiber per exchange.

SALAD GREENS

Endive   Romaine
Escarole   Spinach
Lettuce

SWEET SUBSTITUTES

Candy, hard, sugar-free   Pancake syrup, sugar-free (1–2 Tbsp.)
Gelatin, sugar-free   Sugar substitutes (saccharin, aspartame)
Gum, sugar-free   Whipped topping (2 Tbsp.)
Jam/Jelly, sugar-free
   (less than 20 cal./2 tsp.)

CONDIMENTS

Ketchup (1 Tbsp.)   Salad dressing**, low-calorie (2 Tbsp.)
Horseradish   Taco sauce (3 Tbsp.)
Mustard   Vinegar
Pickles*, dill, unsweetened

*400 mg or more of sodium per exchange.
**The nutritionists who developed the diet for The Rockport Walking Program suggest that only those salad dressings with 10 calories or less per tablespoon be considered "free foods."

Seasonings (next page) can be very helpful in making food taste better. Be careful of how much sodium you use. Read the label, and choose those seasonings that do not contain sodium or salt.

Basil (fresh)
Celery seeds
Chili powder
Chives
Cinnamon
Curry
Dill
Flavoring extracts (vanilla, almond, wal-
    nut, peppermint, butter, lemon, etc.)
Garlic
Garlic powder
Herbs
Hot pepper sauce
Lemon
Lemon juice

Lemon pepper
Lime
Lime juice
Mint
Onion powder
Oregano
Paprika
Pepper
Pimento
Spices
Soy sauce*
Soy sauce*, low-sodium ("lite")
Wine, used in cooking (¼ cup)
Worcestershire sauce

*400 mg or more of sodium per exchange.

Combination Foods

Much of the food we eat is mixed together in various combinations. These combination foods do not fit into only one exchange list. It can be quite hard to tell what is in a certain casserole dish or baked food item. This is a list of average values for some typical combination foods. This list will help you fit these foods into your meal plan.

FOOD	AMOUNT	EXCHANGES
Casseroles, homemade	1 cup (8 oz.)	2 starch, 2 medium-fat meat, 1 fat
Cheese pizza*, thin crust	¼ of 15 oz., or ¼ of 10″	2 starch, 1 medium-fat meat, 1 fat
Chili with beans* **, (commercial)	1 cup (8 oz.)	2 starch, 2 medium-fat meat, 2 fat
Chow mein* (without noodles or rice)	2 cups (16 oz.)	1 starch, 2 vegetable, 2 lean meat
Macaroni and cheese*	1 cup (8 oz.)	2 starch, 1 medium-fat meat, 2 fat
Soup		
Bean* **	1 cup (8 oz.)	1 starch, 1 vegetable, 1 lean meat
Chunky, all varieties*	10¾ oz. can	1 starch, 1 vegetable, 1 medium-fat meat
Cream* (made with water)	1 cup (8 oz.)	1 starch, 1 fat
Vegetable* or broth-type*	1 cup (8 oz.)	1 starch
Spaghetti and meatballs* (canned)	1 cup (8 oz.)	2 starch, 1 medium-fat meat, 1 fat
If beans are used as a meat substitute		
Dried beans**, peas**, lentils	1 cup (cooked)	2 starch, 1 lean meat

*400 mg or more of sodium per exchange.
**3 grams or more of fiber per exchange.

The Rockport Walking Program
Additional Exchange List

STARCH/BREAD LIST

Bread, low-calorie (40 calories or less per slice)	2 slices
Bread crumbs, dried	3 Tbsp.
Popcorn (popped in oil), plain	1 to 1½ cups
Rice cakes	2
Zwieback cookies	2
Arrowroot cookies	4
Fig bars	1
Vanilla wafers	5
Gingersnaps	3
Mixed vegetables (peas, corn, etc.)	½ cup
Flour	3 Tbsp.
Cornstarch	3 Tbsp.

FRUIT LIST

Fruit/juice bars	1 bar
Ice pop	1
Sherbet	¼ cup
Sorbet	¼ cup
Honey	1 Tbsp.
Sugar	1 Tsp.
Jelly	1 Tbsp.

MILK LIST

Sugar-free hot cocoa (40 calories)	2 packets
Sugar-free pudding, made with skim milk	½ cup
Sugar-free shake mix (70 calories)	1 packet
Frozen yogurt (any flavor), low-fat	½ cup
Frozen yogurt bar, low-fat	1 bar
Fudge bar, Fudgesicle, etc.*	1 bar
Ice milk (no more than 110 calories per serving)	½ cup

*There are many low-calorie frozen desserts on the market today. Many of them are made with low-fat milk and have less than 100 calories. These may be included in the diet and counted as one milk exchange.

ADDITIONAL FREE FOODS

Butter-flavored crystals (Butter Buds, Molly McButter, etc.)
Crystal Light bars (14 calories/bar)
Tabasco
Salsa
Teriyaki
Salt
Celery salt
Garlic salt
Onion salt
All spices and herbs
Ginger, fresh or powder
Tenderizers
No-oil salad dressing

Alcohol

Drinking can be a pleasant social activity. Because The Rockport Walking Program is a lifelong plan, not something you go on or off, we've included alcoholic beverages in reasonable amounts. Alcohol provides "empty calories"—that is, it provides calories and almost nothing else. We've used it as part of our fat exchanges—though in reality, of course, alcohol is not a fat. Alcohol is a concentrated source of calories, and provides 7 calories per gram, similar to fat which provides 9 calories per gram.

ALCOHOLIC BEVERAGE LIST

TYPE	AMOUNT	EXCHANGE
Table wine	4 oz.	2 fats
Beer	12 oz.	1 starch, 2 fats
Beer, light	12 oz.	2 fats
Whiskey, Vodka, Gin, Scotch, etc.	1.5 oz. (1 shot)	2 fats

Making Your 1,200, 1,500, or 1,800-Calorie Meal Plan Work for You

The Rockport Walking Program provides a flexible diet. In addition to the wide variety of foods found in your exchange lists, you can also modify your basic Meal Plan to make it work with your particular life-style. For example, if you're a late-night snacker, save some of your exchanges for the "yawning hungries" after dinner. If you like to nibble all day long, you can divide your exchanges into six light meals.

But do try to eat something in the morning—even if you're not hungry until 10:30 or so. You don't have to eat a huge breakfast, but even a small glass of juice or a slice of dry toast will do. It's important to "break your fast" to get your metabolism going and begin your day. Your body needs to be refueled. "We've seen a pattern in people," says registered dietitian Merry Yamartino. "One of the reasons they don't eat breakfast is because they are snacking so much at night, and they are full in the morning. If you eat throughout the day you won't be as hungry at night—and you'll be less likely to snack." What's more, going to bed on a full stomach can be detrimental to your "weight-loss health." Sleep doesn't burn off those late-night calories.

If you do decide to modify your basic plan, follow these guidelines:

• Women should always keep two milk exchanges to meet their calcium requirements. Men should have at least one milk exchange every day.
• Do not go below four proteins a day.
• Always use at least two fat exchanges daily.
• Don't go below 1,200 calories.
• Keep your vegetable and fruit exchanges high for maximum health benefits.

Behavior That Brings Success

It's a fact of life. There will be times when our motivation will nose-dive, when our maintenance takes a steel will, when our measurement of success looks bleak. But discouragement can be broken, and negative attitudes can be turned around. Here are some ways our Rockport Walking Program subjects kept their "3 Ms" high. These motivational tools worked for them—and they can work for you.

Keep a Food Diary

Registered dietitian Paula Cuneo found that when people started writing down everything they ate, they became more aware—and cut down on their calories considerably. Writing out a food diary will also help you keep your focus on your exchanges—and show you how well you're eating since you started The Rockport Walking Program.

Rethink "Only" One or Two Pounds a Week

Four pounds a month might seem slow—but not if you multiply them by 12. Look back at the "One-Year Weight-Loss Chart" in chapter 2. In 12 months, you will have lost close to 50 pounds—and you'll be keeping them off for good.

Don't underestimate the value of 4 pounds. Those 4 extra pounds you're carrying around are the equivalent of 4 pounds of potatoes. A 4-pound chicken. Four pounds of paper. Four pounds is heavy weight—and it feels great to shed them.

Make a "Vat of Fat"

Fill a jelly glass or an old juice glass with vegetable shortening. Whenever you get the desire for French fries or a bagel spread with cream cheese, take a look at your fat-filled glass. Chances are, you'll lose that urge fast!

Psychological Triggers—And How to Stop Them in Their Tracks

The world would be a sleek place indeed if we all ate only when we were hungry. Real physical hunger is the result of a physiological process that involves metabolic factors, physical arousal, and a stimulus/reaction response from the brain to the body that you need fuel.

But, as we all know, there are many "triggers" that set off our appetites that have nothing at all to do with physical hunger:

• *Sometimes your surroundings can set you off.* A delicious smell coming from the restaurant's kitchen, a cocktail party, the coffee wagon outside your office door—all of these situations can be circumvented.

Here are some things you can do to keep your surroundings safe:

1. Ask the waiter or waitress to remove the bread and butter.
2. Order salad dressing on the side.
3. Have a small snack before going to a highly tempting cocktail party.
4. Wait until everyone else has been to the buffet table before you line up. The food won't look as appetizing.
5. Eat lightly during the day in preparation for the party or holiday event.
6. Don't even bother looking at the dessert menu in the restaurant. If others order, ask if there is any fresh fruit.

• *Sometimes you eat out of just plain habit.* Watching television, reading a book, or just because the food is there—all of these are cues to start eating. Before you can break habits like these, you must first become aware of them. The problem with habit eating is that it is almost an unconscious act, a behavior that's intertwined with the habit itself. Think about the times and places you eat. Write them down. If the television gets you going, get moving! Fold the laundry, pick up some knitting, polish your nails, or do some stretches. If you eat because the clock says it's time to eat, ask yourself if you are *really* hungry. If not, ignore the signal. If you're eating because the food is in the house—throw it out! Studies have shown that avoidance techniques are the most successful ways to break bad eating habits. "Out of sight, out of mind" is the best way to go. If your family loves their chocolate-chip cookies, ask them to munch in another room. Leave leftovers in the restaurant—or really feed them to your dog. Throw away the remains of your dinner party. As an added plus, your refrigerator will be free of those strange, moldy, long-forgotten leftovers.

Here are some other ways to break bad eating habits:

1. Put your proper portions on your plate—and don't go back for seconds.
2. Don't eat standing at the kitchen counter. Sit at the table and savor your food.
3. Eat slowly. Concentrate on the conversation around you, on the taste of the food, or on the background music.
4. Use one room in the house to eat in—and don't eat anywhere else. (This also includes the couch in front of the television set.)
5. Substitute lower-calorie snack foods for high-calorie, fat-laden ones. If you really love to eat and watch television, try air-popped popcorn or a piece of fruit instead of chips.
6. Enlist the support of your family. As many participants in our

study found out, families not only help individuals stick to the diet plan, but they themselves learn to eat the low-fat way—and love it!

7. Tell your co-workers and friends that you are watching your weight. By proclaiming your dieting plans, you won't be as quick to backslide. And you just might receive some needed understanding and support.

• *Emotions can set off "triggers" to eat.* We are all too familiar with the depression or the anger that makes us reach for a chocolate bar or a pint of ice cream. Or the feelings of camaraderie that make us reach for a drink. Or the delights of a delicious high-fat feast. But your emotions can be controlled. Whether you're feeling happy, sad, frustrated, anxious, or exhilarated—you don't have to turn to food. If you're filled with good feelings, relish them—and just go easy on the food and drink. If you are angry, try going for a walk to let off steam. If you're anxious, try meditation or a deep-breathing exercise. Remind yourself that if you binge, you will have *two* problems—the original problem *and* the eating problem.

Here are some more ways to stop emotions from weighing you down:

1. A hot, relaxing bath will make you feel good without the calories.
2. If you are feeling vulnerable, avoid people or situations that make you anxious.
3. Try not to take things so seriously.
4. Turn on the shower and scream—or punch a pillow.
5. Talk to a close friend.
6. Go to a movie.
7. Get enough sleep. Fatigue can make you feel sorry for yourself.
8. Make sure you eat three meals a day so you don't feel even more deprived.
9. Stop thinking! Tell yourself not to be so critical of others—and of yourself. Everyone makes mistakes.
10. Distract yourself with another thought if you can't get that ice cream out of your mind. Pick up the latest magazine. Look out the window and watch the people go by. Anything. In a few moments the desire for food will pass. This technique has been used successfully for people who have quit smoking—and it can work for food as well.

The Maintenance Program

How do you maintain what you've so proudly accomplished?

The best way to maintain your weight loss is by adding more calories. But how many? Too many calories and you'll start putting the weight back on. Too few and you'll lose weight you might not want to lose. Our studies have found that an additional 300 calories is a good standard to use to maintain your weight loss—especially if this is combined with at least three days of walking a week.

If you were on the *1,200-Calorie Plan*, you can maintain your weight by going on the *1,500-Calorie Plan*.

If you were on the *1,500-Calorie Plan*, you can maintain your weight by going on the *1,800-Calorie Plan*.

If you were on the *1,800-Calorie Plan*, you can maintain your weight by *adding 300 calories* to your daily diet.

Weigh yourself every week. If you see the numbers creeping up, cut back on your food intake or do more exercise. And remember: It's easier to lose 3 or 5 pounds than another 30!

A lifetime of good, healthy eating also means continuing your low-fat diet. It means adding more bread, protein, or fruit—rather than fat. It means keeping up your exercise to help maintain your weight loss, your motivation, and your improved good health. The two work together, keep your internal setpoint at its new low level and your metabolism "revved up."

As we have seen, this does not imply struggle or deprivation. Many of our subjects found that the less fat they ate, the less they craved it. At one time, Moire Johnson found a take-out fried-chicken dinner a meal made in heaven. Today, the grease is unappealing, and she'll actually opt for broiled chicken and a baked potato topped with yogurt and chives. Others, too, have found that the rich foods they once loved no longer tempt them. Katie Allen prefers skim milk in her coffee instead of cream. Ceile Burgess chooses fresh fruit instead of ice cream when she orders dessert—not out of "will power" but because she really wants fresh fruit.

And all of these people have found that exercise is key. You can counteract a few nights—or even a few weeks—of overindulgence with more exercise. We all know people who maintain their trim weight throughout their lives. Whenever they *choose* to eat more, they simply remember to exercise the next day—and eat a little less.

After six months, your new behavior will have boosted your self-esteem. Our Rockport Walking Program subjects, armed with confidence and real pleasure at their results, would never want to go back to their old ways.

The same can happen to you.

6

YOUR PERSONAL
20-WEEK WALKING
PROGRAM—AND BEYOND

*"I've lost weight before, and I have looked different before,
but there's something different about this exercise for me.
My energy is different. My stress is different. What I can
control by walking 4.5 miles per day amazes me."*
—Kathy Madden, 50, wife, mother of four,
secretary, and Rockport Walking Program
subject

We already gave you the first four weeks of the 20-Week Program in
chapter 4 (see pages 60–194 for the 30-Day Program). Though you're
on your own now, you're not forgotten. We still have specific goals for
you—but calculated by weeks instead of days. Since you have already
completed the first four weeks of the program, you should go to week
5 in the program that follows. You should warm up by walking slowly
for 5 minutes and then stretch for 5 minutes before each walk. The
cool down after the walk should include 5 minutes of slower walking
and 5 minutes of stretching.

BLUE PROGRAM

WEEK	1–2	3–4	5–6	7–8	9–10	11–12	13–14	15–16	17–18	19–20
Mileage	1.5	2.0	2.5	2.5	2.75	2.75	3.0	3.0	3.0	3.25
Pace (mph)	2.5	2.5	2.5	2.6	2.6	2.7	2.7	2.9	3.0	3.0
(min/mi)	24	24	24	23	23	22	22	21	20	20
Heart Rate (% max)	50	50	50	50–60	50–60	60	60	60–70	70	70
Frequency (days per week)	5–7	5–7	5–7	5–7	5–7	5–7	5–7	5–7	5–7	5–7

WHITE PROGRAM

WEEK	1–2	3–4	5–6	7–8	9–10	11–12	13–14	15–16	17–18	19–20	Maintenance
Mileage	2.0	2.5	3.0	3.0	3.25	3.25	3.5	3.5	3.75	4.0	3.5–4.0
Pace (mph)	3.0	3.0	3.0	3.2	3.2	3.3	3.3	3.5	3.5	3.5	3.5
(min/mi)	20	20	20	19	19	18	18	17	17	17	17
Heart Rate (% max)	60	60	60	60–70	60–70	70	70	70–80	70–80	70–80	70–80
Frequency (days per week)	5–7	5–7	5–7	5–7	5–7	5–7	5–7	5–7	5–7	5–7	4–5

RED PROGRAM

WEEK	1–2	3–4	5–6	7–8	9–10	11–12	13–14	15–16	17–18	19–20	Maintenance
Mileage	3.0	3.5	4.0	4.0	4.0	4.5	4.5	4.5	5.0	5.0	4–5
Pace (mph)	3.5	3.5	3.5	3.75	4.0	4.0	4.3	4.6	4.6	5.0	4.5–5.0
(min/mi)	17	17	17	16	15	15	14	13	13	12	13–12
Heart Rate (% max)	60	60	60	60–70	70	70	70–80	70–80	70–80	80	70–80
Frequency (days per week)	5–7	5–7	5–7	5–7	5–7	5–7	5–7	5–7	5–7	5–7	4–7

Each of the programs above contains five categories that make up your new personal walking prescription. Use the same program that you used for your 30-Day Plan. To understand exactly how your new program works, let's go over each one of the categories now.

- *Week.* Here you'll find each week's program—with a total of 20 weeks.

- *Mileage.* Here you'll find your walking goal for the week.
- *Pace.* How fast you walk is determined by the speed that keeps your heart rate at the appropriate range. The pace is listed in miles per hour and minutes per mile. Aim for the pace listed. Check your heart rate every 10 to 15 minutes and adjust your pace so that you're at your target heart-rate zone.
- *Heart Rate.* Here you'll find the percentage of maximum heart rate you should aim for during the week. This category is linked to pace. If you are below your target heart rate, increase your pace slightly and if you're above your target heart rate, decrease your pace.
- *Frequency.* This category tells you how many times during the week you should walk.

Making Your 20-Week Personal Walking Program Work for You

Like your daily meal plans, these exercise programs are meant to be adjusted to your life-style. They are not etched in stone. It's important not to get too bogged down in your target heart-rate zone percentages—or in taking your pulse. Enjoy your walk. Relish the exercise. Chances are if you are walking at a brisk pace, you're reaching your target heart-rate zone. The fact is, you're walking—and that means moving, toning, shaping up, and feeling great! But do try to meet your walking goal—and don't overdo it. If you start to feel breathless, you're walking too fast. Just keep to your specified program as best you can.

If your life-style seems too hectic to fit in your daily walk, here's a tip: Twice a day can be better than once—as many people in The Rockport Walking Program study discovered. If putting in your miles in one fell swoop takes more time than you have available, take two walks a day! Simply divide your day's mileage by half; every other category stays the same. And, as an added plus, you'll probably get more of a workout because your energy level will remain high. With two shorter walks, your pace will start out faster and stay faster throughout your workout.

Remember: A brisk 45-minute walk every day burns about 300 calories—and you can lose 18 pounds in a year without even trying by following your 20-Week Walking Program!

CALORIC COST OF WALKING (CALORIES/MILE)*

WALKING PACE (MPH)	CALORIES BURNED					
	100 lbs.	125 lbs.	150 lbs.	175 lbs.	200 lbs.	225 lbs.
3.0	52	66	79	92	105	118
3.5	54	67	80	94	107	120
4.0	58	72	87	101	116	131
4.5	65	81	97	113	129	145

Source: Anne Kashiwa and James Rippe, M.D. *Fitness Walking for Women.* New York: Perigee Books, 1987, 77.
*Based on Bubb, et al. *Journal of Cardiac Rehabilitation* 5:462–65, 1985.

Staying With It

- Katie Allen was embarrassed to go outside that first day. She felt dumpy and self-conscious. So she bought a brand-new sweatsuit that fit so well she could walk with confidence.

- Kathy Madden had trouble sticking to her diet in the late afternoon. But instead of sitting on her sofa thinking about food, she turned her "temptation hour" into her walking hour.

- Joyce Danielson was afraid that work would get in the way of her walk. So she organized a "walkathon" at her office—getting her colleagues to join her for a two-mile walk during lunch.

- Nick Rioux knew that the coming New England winter would discourage him from walking. Before the first snow fell, he had already called a local mall and discovered he could walk in climate-controlled temperature all winter long.

- Moire Johnson writes her walking goals and her walking hour right in her appointment book—and keeps to it just like she would any business meeting.

These Rockport Walking Program subjects have learned to adapt walking into their life-styles and make exercise a part of their daily routine.

Seduce Yourself Into Shape

Based on the work we did for the President's Council on Physical Fitness, here are ten ways to make walking a lifetime commitment to good health and steady weight loss—starting right now:

1. *Develop a Specific Plan.* A specific walking agenda will point you in the right direction.

    For added reinforcement, try writing a "contract" to yourself that you will commit to your walking program for another week or month.
2. *Set Realistic Goals.* Accept the fact that things take time—and work toward goals that you can meet. Walking 1 block further each day. Going past 12 more telephone poles. Doing your walk 5 times a week. Walking 2 days in a row.

    If you go out and do something for yourself each day—one day at a time and one step at a time—all these small daily steps will add up to a long journey.
3. *Use Equipment That Motivates.* There's nothing worse than walking shoes that don't provide adequate support. At the first ache, you'll be ready to put your shoes in the closet—permanently. Spending the time to purchase a pair of shoes that fit right and do the job will translate into more enjoyable walking—and a program you'll stick with for the "long run."

    Similarly, spending money on, say, a new sweatsuit or shorts, a comfortable pair of socks, or a walking gadget or two will help motivate you to stay with it, making walking fun as you "protect your investment."

    Here are some gadgets and equipment that can make your walk easier and more fun:
    - A *pedometer* will help you keep track of your mileage. You can find one in any sporting goods store for approximately $15. Check the accuracy by walking a couple of miles on a track. Adjust the stride length until the pedometer reads accurately.
    - A light *backpack* or fanny pack will keep your essentials handy when you're out for longer distances. Water, a stopwatch, a piece of fruit—all will be in easy reach.
    - A *walking stick* is useful for keeping a consistent stride, and it can also help you get up hills with less strain.

- A *heart-rate monitor* will calculate your pulse rate for you as you walk. It's a gadget consisting of two pieces: a small electrode strip you place on your chest, and a wristwatch. One glance at the watch and you can immediately see if you are in your target heart-rate zone—without stopping in midstride to take your pulse. It will also give you your walking time to the second. A heart-rate monitor is expensive; it costs approximately $300. But if you have difficulty finding your pulse, if you hate the inconvenience of taking it every five or ten minutes, or if you just love gadgets, it can be well worth the investment.
- A *compass* is a good tool to have if you like to explore new areas when you walk.
- *Hand weights* used correctly can increase energy cost—but they can also increase shoulder and back problems. They are only recommended for people who can't achieve their target heart-rate zone through walking alone. Hold a one- to three-pound weight in each hand. When you walk, move your arms from the shoulder in a smooth, controlled swing. Don't jerk! If you have arthritic or orthopedic problems, check with your physician before using weights.

4. *Know Your Time and Place.* Studies show that people who commit themselves to exercise at a specific time and place will be more likely to stay with it than those who leave their exercise plans to chance. Decide on your route beforehand, and develop a walking routine. Gee Mahassel always walks first thing in the morning. Nick Rioux likes to go to the track at Lake Quinsigamond in Worcester. Katie Allen likes to take a break around 4:30 in the afternoon. She finds walking through her neighborhood at dusk soothing. Whatever your best walking time and place is, write it in your appointment book as Moire Johnson does—and stick to it.

5. *Involve Your Family and Friends.* Nothing helps you succeed more than support. A family member, a significant other, or a good friend who cheers you along will help you keep your motivation strong. Explain what you are doing and why. Go shopping with your spouse. Have your children help prepare your low-fat meals. Walk with a friend. One woman in our study said, "I can't keep my husband away from me. He says I look sexy!" Another woman said that her family "applauded it. My kids say, 'Hey, Mom, you look great! You're happier. We love seeing you like this.' "

  If you establish a "buddy system," there's always someone there to get you walking on days you'd rather stay in, a friendly voice of encouragement when you feel down. Sometimes knowing that your friends are counting on you to meet them for your scheduled walk is all you need to "stay with it."

6. *Make Room for Variation.* Variety is the spice of life—and it can overcome the boredom that occurs from time to time in even the most enthusiastic walker. Use a portable cassette player when you walk, changing the tapes to fit your mood. (But do make sure you keep the volume low enough to hear the passing traffic.) Change your route on occasion. Walk with a buddy. Vary your routine, walking at dusk instead of early morning. Try walking in a mall on rainy or wintery days. Join a walking group and participate in local walkathons. Train for a walking event. Even something as simple as purchasing a new pair of shorts in a different color can keep boredom at bay.

7. *Avoid Injury.* If you injure yourself, you'll most likely quit. By following your Rockport Walking Program, you will avoid injury—and discouragement. Don't overexert yourself. Choose level routes that are fairly smooth your first few times out. Make sure your shoes fit properly. Include your warm-up and cool-down whenever you exercise.

8. *Build Up Gradually.* Just as our Rockport Walking Program subjects gradually worked themselves up to 4.5 miles a day, you can too—but you must do it slowly. Overexerting yourself will only lead to discouragement—which will make you quit. A lifelong, consistent program depends on a slow and steady pace—with progress that shows over the long haul. Remember the 2-percent rule. Gradually build up the intensity of your workout, the length of time you exercise, and the amount of days you walk. By following your Rockport Walking Program, you'll be assured of a steady, safe progression—with enough challenge to keep boredom away. As you progress, you might try walking up hills or adding a light backpack for weight. Meeting new challenges is exciting—and they'll help burn more calories. But be realistic and don't try too much too soon.

9. *Keep a Record.* There it is in black and white: your ability to reach realistic goals and your inspiring progress. All our subjects kept exercise logs, detailing the time they took to walk their miles, their heart rates, and the number of miles they actually walked. Serious athletes always keep exercise logs of their progress, detailing their perceptions of their performance. See the sample exercise logs in appendix C. We included a blank log that you can use at home.

Another great motivator is retaking the tests you took before you started walking. They are visual proof of how far you've come—especially on days when you feel discouraged. Retake the "Be a Fat Detective" quiz and you will see the results of your walking and dieting in less body fat—and more muscle tone.

10. *Reward Yourself.* After one month on The Rockport Walking Program, we gave our subjects free hats. One month later, we gave them T-shirts. And, after three months, they each received a sweatshirt for a job well done. Rewards don't have to be big to make you feel good. A small reward when you've accomplished a goal can keep motivation strong. The next time you walk an extra half mile, reward yourself with a pedicure or a movie or tickets to a ball game. When you've reached your 20-week goal, why not reward yourself with a heart-rate monitor—or a weekend away for two?

We all need to stop and give ourselves a pat on the back from time to time. Just as rewards will help keep you to your diet plan, they will also help you stay with your walking.

No Pain, No Gain

It's time this old cliché was laid to rest. The fact is that consistency is much more important than intensity. If you feel pain when you exercise, you're overexerting yourself—and setting yourself up to quit. A more moderate workout like walking will directly translate into more enjoyment—which will help you stay with it. Studies show that regular moderate exercise will not only increase your sense of well-being but make pain a thing of the past.

We know that in virtually every field of behavior modification—whether it be starting an exercise program, getting your weight under control, or stopping smoking—six months is the key. At the six-month point, you can see significant improvements in your self-esteem—and that will keep you going. Think of it: If you can carry out your new behavior for six months, the chances of adapting it for the rest of your life are high. Even if you eventually drop out, you will make that new behavior stick in a future attempt.

But six months is still some steps away. For now, we urge you to keep going without making any judgments. Just go out there and walk and say, "I'm just going to do this because I think it's important to me." As members of Alcoholics Anonymous, Smokers Anonymous, and Overeaters Anonymous do, give yourself up to a "higher power" and simply follow your diet and walking plan. Within six months, any initial muscle soreness will be a dim memory. In six months, you may very well feel the exhilarating euphoria we call "walker's high." In six months, you will have turned a new behavior into a habit—one you'll never want to give up.

The Walking Maintenance Program

As your strength, your endurance, and your VO$_2$max increase, you'll need to readjust your walking program to meet your new requirements—and to continue to reap the rewards of walking.

To maintain your new improved physical fitness—and your weight-loss goal—simply change your Walking Program:

- If you have completed the *Blue Program*, retake The Rockport Fitness Walking Test. You'll not only see that your relative fitness level has improved but you will find that you're ready to start a new, more advanced program. You should start the White Program at approximately week 9.
- If you have completed the *White Program*, retake The Rockport Fitness Walking Test to determine your new relative fitness level. You can then go to the White Maintenance Program or start the Red Program at week 7.
- If you have completed the *Red Program*, retake The Rockport Fitness Walking Test to determine your new relative fitness level and then follow the Red Maintenance Program.

WHITE MAINTENANCE PROGRAM

WARM-UP: 5–7 minutes before-walk stretches
AEROBIC WORKOUT: mileage: 3.5–4.0 miles at 3.5 mph
HEART RATE: 70–80 percent of maximum
COOL-DOWN: 5–7 minutes after-walk stretches
FREQUENCY: 4–7 times per week
WEEKLY MILEAGE: 14–28 miles

RED MAINTENANCE PROGRAM

WARM-UP: 5–7 minutes before-walk stretches
AEROBIC WORKOUT: mileage: 4–5 miles at 4.5 to 5.0 mph
HEART RATE: 70–80 percent of maximum
COOL-DOWN: 5–7 minutes after-walk stretches
FREQUENCY: 4–7 times per week
WEEKLY MILEAGE: 16–35 miles

The more you walk, the more energy you'll have and the more you'll want to use it. Walking up the stairs will be easier. Walking to work will seem like a great idea on a beautiful day. Perhaps you'll investigate health-club facilities when you take a vacation or go away on business. And, as you get fit, you might want to incorporate other forms of exercise into your walking program. You might want to try a calisthenics class, yoga, bicycling, swimming, even water aerobics— and a whole new world of exercise will open up!

TO YOUR HEALTH

Self-confidence. It's one of the most exciting things we saw in our Rockport Walking Program study subjects. The confidence they felt projected out into the room: in the way they sat, in the way they talked about themselves. These were people who for most of their adult lives had had no control over their lives. They were ordinary people who proved, some for the very first time, that they *could* assert control over themselves and their future.

But our excitement goes beyond the very real pleasure of seeing such confident, hopeful, and healthy people. Their self-confidence was visible proof of what we have been preaching for years: that if individuals *believe* they can make a difference in their own lives, they will heed our words of advice. When we suggest they lose weight, they know they can do it. When we advise them to stop smoking or drinking, our words will have an impact. When we discuss an exercise program, they are ready and willing to start. And when we ask them to take pre-scribed medications we know they will follow through.

Best of all, if our patients and research subjects can see that they can change their lives, they won't stop with just diet and exercise.

To us this is the greatest achievement of The Rockport Walking Program.

Jesse Jackson touched us with his words about the working men and women in our country: "They go back to work every day." Being an adult means responsibility. It means that there are going to be days when you don't want to go to work. But you have responsibilities. Bills to pay. Children to raise. You go to work every day because you care about the kind of life you want to live.

The Rockport Walking Program understands this. It is the first diet and exercise book to address the realities of life as an adult—who goes out to work every day. As an adult, you understand that you have to earn a living. You understand and accept responsibility for your family and for yourself. You care about your quality of life. The Rockport Walking Program has been proven to work—*if you do it on a consistent, daily basis.* Remember:

- You can do something about your present situation.
- You can change for the better in only one month.
- You can have more energy and more vitality.
- You can have good health and a longer life.
- You can be self-confident and happier.

It all comes down to taking a walk and cutting back on your fat.

Simple? Yes. But sometimes it's the shortest distance between two points that takes the longest to cross. You have the knowledge and the latest scientific findings on the benefits of a low-fat diet and a regular walking routine. You have your basic walking and exercise plans. You have a one-month, day-by-day diary to put your plans into action. You have (in the section that follows) delicious recipes to use and enjoy. And you have a maintenance program to create a lifetime of total fitness.

It's our great hope that you succeed as our 80 subjects did.

One of our subjects told us, "Thank you for all that you have allowed me to do."

Our reply? "*You* did it."

You can do it, too.

We wish you all the success and happiness in the world.

The Rockport Recipes

Variety and good taste. They make all the difference between a diet that makes you feel deprived and a diet plan that becomes a part of your life. To add spice to The Rockport Walking Program, we're pleased to present 109 recipes prepared especially for this program by California food expert Judy Fredal Pang and her testers Melinda Morris, R.D., Susan Greene, Francis Fredal, and Beverly Dedonatis.

All of these recipes are low-fat and low-calorie—and the results will delight the most discriminating palates. Just ask our Rockport Walking Program subjects. They tried them out at home—and loved them!

Each recipe is simple to prepare and follow. For each one, you'll find a per-serving calorie, fat, and cholesterol analysis. And best of all, each recipe contains an exchange breakdown per serving so you can easily fit it into your daily meal planning.

Browse through them. Use them. Adapt them. And most of all, enjoy them.

Hors D'Oeuvres

CLAM-STUFFED ARTICHOKES

Yield: 8 servings

4 artichokes
1 cut lemon
1 tablespoon margarine
1 tablespoon olive oil
1 cup finely chopped onion (2 medium onions)
1 cup finely chopped celery (3 stalks celery)
3 cloves garlic, minced
⅓ cup chopped fresh parsley
2 tablespoons chopped fresh basil leaves
2 cups soft bread crumbs
1 cup oat bran
½ teaspoon salt
⅛ teaspoon pepper
½ cup nonfat evaporated milk
1 16½-ounce can chopped clams, drained and cleaned of shell bits
Lemon wedges

Cut the stems from the artichokes and remove any loose bottom leaves. Cut 1 inch off the top of each artichoke; trim the thorny tips of the leaves with kitchen shears. Wash the artichokes well. Rub the cut surfaces with lemon. Stand the artichokes in a 4-quart pot in 1 inch of boiling water. Return the water to a boil, reduce heat to low, cover, and simmer for 30 minutes. Drain the artichokes upside-down on paper towels; cool them slightly. Gently pull out the prickly leaves in the center of each artichoke. Using a small spoon, carefully scrape away the fuzzy choke; discard it. In a nonstick skillet, heat the margarine and oil. Add the onion, celery, garlic, parsley, and basil; cook until tender. Remove from heat. Stir in the bread crumbs, oat bran, salt, pepper, and evaporated milk; fold in the clams. Gently spoon the dressing between the leaves and into the center of each artichoke. Pour 1 cup of boiling water into an 8-inch square glass baking dish. Stand the artichokes in the dish, and cover them tightly with foil. Bake at 400 degrees until a leaf can be easily plucked from the artichoke (about 45 minutes). Let the artichokes sit for 10 minutes. Cut them in half lengthwise before serving. Set out bowls to hold the discarded leaves. Pass lemon wedges at the table.

Exchanges per serving: 1 bread, 2 vegetable, ½ meat, 1 fat

Calories per serving: 189
Fat per serving (gm): 5.0
Cholesterol per serving (mg): 19.0

CRUDITÉS IN A BASKET

Yield: Approximately twelve 1-cup servings

1 red bell pepper
Green leaf lettuce (enough to cover serving dish)
2 cups low-fat dip
1 cup mushrooms
1 cup cauliflower flowerets
1 cup jicama root, peeled and sliced in long strips
1 cup fennel, sliced
1 cup palm hearts, sliced
1 cup celeriac, sliced, blanched, and cooled
Other white vegetables, as desired

Slice off the stem end of the bell pepper, and level off the bottom so the pepper will stand upright. Remove the seeds and membranes from the inside. Cut the top edge in a zigzag pattern. Line a large oblong straw or wire basket with well-shaped lettuce leaves. (If a straw basket is used, line it first with foil or paper towel.) Fill the pepper with dip,* and place it at one end of the basket. Arrange the vegetables in the basket, with the cauliflower flowerets and mushrooms at the dip end and the longer strips arranged lengthwise in the basket.

Exchanges per serving: 1 vegetable (does not include exchanges for dips)

Calories per serving: 18
Fat per serving (gm): less than 1.0
Cholesterol per serving (mg): 0

*Use one of the dip recipes in the "Dressings, Dips, Sauces, and Spreads" section.

STUFFED ENDIVE STARS

Belgian endive is often confused with curly endive (chicory). Belgian endive has a small, smooth compact head with white, tapering leaves.

Yield: 2 dozen appetizer servings (4 stars/serving)

4 ounces Neufchâtel cheese, at room temperature
3 ounces Danish Blue cheese (or other soft-textured blue cheese), at
    room temperature
¼ to ⅓ cup nonfat evaporated milk
2 large bunches Belgian endive, leaves separated, washed, and drained
Green leaf lettuce, washed and drained
Paprika for garnish

Combine the cheeses in a blender or food processor and mix until creamy, adding the milk a little at a time until the desired consistency is reached. Spoon the mixture into a pastry bag fitted with a star tip; squeeze it onto the endive leaves. Spread the lettuce on a platter. Arrange the endive leaves in a spoke pattern on top of the lettuce and sprinkle them with paprika. Cover them lightly with plastic wrap or waxed paper—insert toothpicks upright at four points to prevent the wrap from sticking to the cheese—and refrigerate until ready to serve.

Exchanges per serving: 1 high-fat meat, free vegetable

Calories per serving: 120.5
Fat per serving (gm): 8.7
Cholesterol per serving (mg): 25.5

GOLDEN TREES

The appearance of these baked appetizers inspired their fanciful name.

Yield: about 4 dozen appetizers (5 per serving)

½ bunch broccoli
½ head cauliflower
¼ cup plain nonfat yogurt
½ cup egg whites (from about 4 eggs)
½ teaspoon Worcestershire sauce
½ teaspoon garlic salt
¾ cup crushed cornflakes, divided into thirds

Wash and pat dry the broccoli and cauliflower; cut them into flowerets with 1-inch stems and set them aside. In a mixing bowl, whip the yogurt with a fork until it is smooth. Add the egg whites, Worcestershire sauce, and garlic salt, and blend well. Dip a floweret top (not a stem) in the yogurt mixture; shake off any excess. Roll the floweret in crushed cornflakes to coat, then place it on a greased baking sheet. Repeat this procedure with all the flowerets, replacing the crushed cornflakes with fresh ones when they get too wet. Bake at 400 degrees until the vegetables are tender and the coating is crisp (17 to 20 minutes). Serve hot.

Exchanges per serving: 1 vegetable

Calories per serving: 30
Fat per serving (gm): .2
Cholesterol per serving (mg): .1

PARTY MEATBALLS

Yield: about 18 servings

1 pound extra-lean ground beef
1½ tablespoons seasoned bread crumbs
1 small onion, minced
½ tablespoon horseradish
2 small cloves garlic, minced
½ cup tomato juice
½ teaspoon salt
Pepper to taste
½ tablespoon margarine
½ tablespoon olive oil
1 small onion, finely chopped
1 cup beef broth, defatted
1½ tablespoons all-purpose flour
⅓ cup red wine
1½ tablespoons brown sugar
1½ tablespoons ketchup
2 teaspoons lemon juice
½ teaspoon salt
Pepper to taste

Combine the ground beef, bread crumbs, onion, horseradish, garlic, tomato juice, salt, and pepper in mixing bowl, and mix well. Shape the mixture into 1-inch balls. Place the meatballs in a shallow pan and bake at 350 degrees until they are browned (about 10 minutes), turning once. Remove them from the pan and drain them; set them aside. Heat the margarine and oil in a small saucepan; add the onion, and cook over medium heat until it is tender. Add the beef broth. Combine the flour and red wine in a small cup and blend until smooth. Slowly add this mixture to the saucepan, stirring constantly. Add the brown sugar, ketchup, lemon juice, salt, and pepper, and stir until smooth. Bring the mixture to a boil; then reduce the heat to low and simmer for 15 minutes. Add the meatballs and simmer 5 more minutes; serve hot.

Exchanges per serving: 1 meat

Calories per serving: 70
Fat per serving (gm): 3.9
Cholesterol per serving (mg): 15.8

BAKED WONTON CHIPS

These chips are a tasty, low-fat alternative to regular chips and crackers. Serve them alone or with Ginger Dip (p. 306).

Yield: about 8 dozen chips

1 12-ounce package fresh wonton skins

SEASONING SUGGESTIONS Parmesan cheese, grated
Garlic powder
Herb seasoning
Minced onion

Cut the wonton skins diagonally. Arrange them on cookie sheets in a single layer. Spray them lightly with water, and sprinkle them with your choice of seasoning(s). Bake them in a preheated 325-degree oven until they are puffy and crispy (about 7 minutes). Remove the wontons from the cookie sheets; serve them warm or cooled.

Exchanges per serving: 1½ bread (about 1 dozen chips)

Calories per serving: 109
Fat per serving (gm): 2.2
Cholesterol per serving (mg): 1.5 (analysis includes Parmesan cheese)

Soups

BOSTON CLAM CHOWDER

Yield: six ¾-cup servings

1½ cups fish stock (or fish bouillon)
2 cups diced cauliflower
1½ cups peeled and cubed potato
1 cup chopped onion
1 cup sliced mushrooms
⅛ teaspoon dried tarragon
⅛ teaspoon dried marjoram
½ teaspoon salt (omit if salted stock is used)
Dash white pepper
1 cup nonfat evaporated milk
1 10-ounce can clams, drained
1 tablespoon fresh chopped dill

Heat the stock to boiling and add the cauliflower. Cover and heat to boiling; simmer for 10 to 12 minutes. With a strainer, remove the cauliflower and let it cool. To the stock, add the potato, onion, mushrooms, tarragon, marjoram, salt, and pepper, and return to a boil. Cover and simmer for 15 minutes, stirring occasionally. While the soup is cooking, blend the cauliflower and milk in a blender until smooth. After the soup has cooked, gradually stir in the pureed cauliflower and cook over low heat until thickened. Add the clams. Turn up the heat to medium and bring the soup to a boil. Boil for 1 minute. Pour into soup bowls and garnish with chopped dill.

Exchanges per serving: 1 meat, 1 vegetable, ½ milk

Calories per serving: 109
Fat per serving (gm): .7
Cholesterol per serving (mg): 16.7

LENTIL SOUP WITH HAM

This is a hearty main-dish soup. Serve it with rye bread and coleslaw or salad for a complete and satisfying meal.

Yield: twelve 1-cup servings

2 teaspoons peanut oil
1 cup diced onion
1 cup sliced carrot
1 cup sliced celery with leaves
1 ham bone (for flavor)
2 cups chopped lean ham
1 cup chopped cabbage
1 pound dry lentils, rinsed and drained
8 cups water
1 bay leaf
½ teaspoon thyme leaves
½ teaspoon salt
½ teaspoon pepper
2 tablespoons cider vinegar

In a 5-quart Dutch oven over medium flame, heat peanut oil. Add the onion, carrot, and celery, and cook until tender. Add the ham bone, ham, cabbage, lentils, water, bay leaf, thyme, salt, and pepper. Heat the mixture to boiling over high heat; reduce the heat to low. Cover and simmer for 1 hour or until the lentils are tender. Remove the ham bone. Stir in the vinegar; simmer for 1 to 2 minutes. Remove the bay leaf before serving.

Exchanges per serving: 1 bread, 1 meat, 1 vegetable

Calories per serving: 185
Fat per serving (gm): 2.7
Cholesterol per serving (mg): 13.3

CREAMY SPINACH SOUP

Yield: six ¾-cup servings

2 tablespoons margarine
1 medium onion, chopped
4 cups packed torn spinach leaves (about 1 large bunch spinach)
½ cup packed coarsely chopped arugula leaves
2 cups chicken broth, defatted
2 tablespoons cornstarch
1 cup nonfat evaporated milk
1 teaspoon salt (omit if salted broth is used)
⅛ teaspoon white pepper
1 tablespoon dry sherry

Melt the margarine in a large saucepan over medium heat. Add the onion and cook until it is tender. Add the spinach and arugula; cook, stirring for 1 minute. Add 1 cup chicken broth to the spinach mixture; stir. Blend mixture in blender at low speed until smooth. Return to saucepan; stir in remaining chicken broth and heat over medium flame. Blend cornstarch into evaporated milk until smooth. Gradually stir milk into soup; add salt, pepper, and sherry. Cook and stir soup until it is thickened and begins to boil; serve.

Exchanges per serving: ½ milk, 1 vegetable, 1 fat

Calories per serving: 98.7
Fat per serving (gm): 4.3
Cholesterol per serving (mg): 1.7

SWEET DUMPLING SQUASH BISQUE

Sweet dumpling squash is shaped like a miniature pumpkin and has a yellow-orange color.

Yield: 4 servings

2 pounds sweet dumpling squash
2 cups nonfat evaporated milk
1 teaspoon salt
⅛ teaspoon white pepper
1 cube chicken bouillon
2 to 4 tablespoons nonfat milk
Paprika
4 thin lemon slices

Cut each squash in half through the stem; remove and discard the seeds. Cut the squash halves crosswise into 1-inch slices; remove the peel. Steam or microwave the squash slices until they are very tender. Place the squash in a blender or food processor, and blend at low speed until very smooth. (Pour in a little of the evaporated milk, if necessary.) In a medium-size saucepan over low to medium heat, combine the squash, evaporated milk, salt, pepper, and bouillon cube, and cook until hot, stirring frequently. Add a little milk to thin soup to desired consistency. Spoon the soup into soup bowls. Sprinkle on paprika; top with lemon slices.

Exchanges per serving: 1 vegetable

Calories per serving: 190
Fat per serving (gm): .9
Cholesterol per serving (mg): 4.5

VICHYSSOISE

Here is a refreshing soup for a hot summer evening.

Yield: six ⅔-cup servings

2 small leeks (about 10 ounces total)
1 tablespoon margarine
1 small stalk celery, chopped
2 small potatoes (about 8 ounces total), peeled and thinly sliced
1 14-ounce can chicken broth, defatted
1 cup nonfat evaporated milk
¼ teaspoon salt
⅛ teaspoon white pepper
Fresh snipped chives

Remove the roots and tough leaves from the leeks. Cut the leeks in half lengthwise; rinse them thoroughly under running water to wash away any sand. Cut the white part crosswise and as much of the green top as needed to make 1 cup; refrigerate the remaining portion for use in another recipe.

Melt the margarine in a small saucepan over medium heat. Add the leeks and celery; cook for 5 minutes. Add the potatoes and broth, and heat to boiling. Reduce the heat to low; cover and simmer for 30 minutes.

Spoon half of the leek mixture into a blender, and blend at low speed until smooth. Pour the resulting puree into a 2-quart saucepan and repeat the procedure with the remaining leek mixture. Stir the milk, salt, and pepper into the puree; cook and stir over low heat just to heat through. Pour the soup into a large bowl; cover and refrigerate for at least 4 hours. When ready to serve, pour the soup into bowls; sprinkle snipped chives on top.

Exchanges per serving: ½ milk, ½ bread, ½ fat

Calories per serving: 102
Fat per serving (gm): 2.5
Cholesterol per serving (mg): 1.5

Salads

BELGIAN SALAD WITH RASPBERRY DRESSING

Yield: 4 servings

3 tablespoons pine nuts
1 large head escarole (about 6 cups)
1 5-ounce head radicchio, leaves rinsed and separated
2 medium-size heads Belgian endive, leaves rinsed and separated
4 thin leaves of chicory
4 tablespoons raspberry vinegar
2 teaspoons salad oil
1 tablespoon walnut oil
¼ teaspoon granulated sugar
¼ teaspoon grated lemon peel
Salt to taste
Fresh pepper to taste

Bake the pine nuts in an 8-inch square pan at 350 degrees until they are golden brown in the center (about 3 to 5 minutes). Set them aside to cool. Rinse the escarole, then shake it and gently pat it dry. Remove the core and arrange the leaves on a large platter, pulling them out slightly to make serving easier. Tuck the radicchio and Belgian endive between the lettuce leaves. Place chicory leaves over all. Sprinkle with pine nuts.

In a small jar, combine the vinegar, salad oil, walnut oil, sugar, lemon peel, and salt; shake vigorously. Spoon or pour the dressing evenly over the arranged salad; season to taste with fresh-ground pepper.

Exchanges per serving: 2 fat, free vegetable

Calories per serving: 102
Fat per serving (gm): 8.2
Cholesterol per serving (mg): 0

CUCUMBER SALAD

This is a delicious, light, summertime salad.

Yield: 6 servings

1 large cucumber, peeled and thinly sliced
1 small onion, chopped
Salt to taste
Black pepper to taste
1 teaspoon light olive oil
2 to 3 tablespoons nonfat evaporated milk
1 tablespoon white vinegar

Combine the cucumber slices, onion, salt, pepper, and oil thoroughly. Stir in the milk and then the vinegar.

Exchanges per serving: free vegetable

Calories per serving: 20
Fat per serving (gm): .8
Cholesterol per serving (mg): .2

TWO-BEAN SALAD

High in cholesterol-reducing fiber, this bean salad is also delicious!

Yield: eight ½-cup servings

1½ cups cooked chick-peas, drained
1½ cups cooked kidney beans, drained
1 cup diced celery
1½ tablespoons minced fresh cilantro (leaves of coriander used as a flavoring or garnish)
1½ tablespoons minced fresh parsley
⅔ cup plain low-fat yogurt
4 teaspoons lemon juice
2 teaspoons granulated sugar
⅓ cup nonfat dry milk
¼ teaspoon salt
⅛ teaspoon ground cumin
Dash black pepper
Dash cayenne pepper

Combine the chick-peas, kidney beans, celery, cilantro, and parsley in a salad bowl. Pour the yogurt into a small mixing bowl. Beat it with a fork until it is smooth and creamy. Stir in the lemon juice, sugar, and dry milk until smooth. Blend in the salt, cumin, black pepper, and cayenne pepper. Combine the dressing with the bean mixture.

Exchanges per serving: 1 bread, ½ milk

Calories per serving: 118
Fat per serving (gm): 1.0
Cholesterol per serving (mg): 1.7

DELICIOUS GOLD AND RED COLESLAW

Here is a delicious slaw with a different taste—and color!

Yield: twelve ½-cup servings

7 cups finely shredded red cabbage
1 large Golden Delicious apple (with skin), cored and diced
2 tablespoons light olive oil
5 tablespoons cider vinegar
1 teaspoon Dijon mustard
1 teaspoon caraway seeds
½ teaspoon salt
⅛ teaspoon pepper
1 teaspoon granulated sugar

In a large bowl, combine the cabbage and apple. In a small jar, combine the oil, vinegar, mustard, caraway seeds, salt, pepper, and sugar. Pour the dressing onto the cabbage-apple mixture and toss well. Cover and refrigerate for several hours before serving.

Exchanges per serving: ½ fat, free vegetable

Calories per serving: 45
Fat per serving (gm): 2.5
Cholesterol per serving (mg): 0

HEARTY CAESAR SALAD

This egg-free version of a classic salad, along with French or Italian bread, can be served as a satisfying meal in itself!

Yield: 6 side-dish servings

1 medium clove garlic, crushed
¼ teaspoon dry mustard
¼ teaspoon salt
¼ teaspoon ground pepper
1½ tablespoons olive oil
1½ tablespoons water
1½ teaspoons Worcestershire sauce
8 anchovy fillets, drained and chopped (1 ounce)
1 large bunch romaine lettuce, torn (8 cups)
¼ cup grated Parmesan cheese
¼ cup crumbled blue cheese (1.2 ounces)
1½ tablespoons lemon juice
1 cup seasoned croutons

Combine the crushed garlic, mustard, salt, pepper, oil, water, Worcestershire sauce, and anchovies in a jar; cover and shake vigorously. Pour this dressing over the lettuce in a salad bowl. Add the cheeses and toss the salad until it is well coated. Add the lemon juice and toss. Add the croutons, toss gently, and serve immediately.

Exchanges per serving: ½ bread, ½ meat, 1 fat

Calories per serving: 124
Fat per serving (gm): 8.2
Cholesterol per serving (mg): 9.5

RAINBOW ROTELLE SALAD

This salad is perfect for a tailgate party, barbeque, or other informal gathering.

Yield: twelve 1-cup servings

12 ounces dry rainbow rotelle pasta (5 cups cooked)
2 cups fresh broccoli flowerets
2 medium carrots, diagonally sliced
1 medium onion, sliced
2 cups sliced tomatoes
1 2-ounce can black olives, drained and sliced
¼ cup fresh grated Parmesan cheese
1 cup reduced-calorie Italian dressing
½ teaspoon garlic powder
Salt and pepper to taste

Cook the pasta according to the package directions; drain it and rinse it under cold water. Place the pasta in a large serving bowl. Add the vegetables, olives, cheese, dressing, garlic powder, and salt and pepper. Toss gently. Refrigerate for several hours before serving.

Exchanges per serving: 1 bread, 1 vegetable, ½ fat

Calories per serving: 115
Fat per serving (gm): 3.4
Cholesterol per serving (mg): 2.7

RED-AND-WHITE SALAD

Here's a change-of-pace salad with a striking presentation.

Yield: 6 servings

4 medium-size beets (2 pounds, or 4 cups, total)
½ cup cider vinegar
2 tablespoons honey
2 teaspoons prepared horseradish
1 small European-style cucumber, thinly sliced
1½ cups peeled, julienned jicama
6 radishes, cut into flower shapes (optional)

Cut all but 1 inch of the tops off the beets; scrub the beets. In a 5-quart pot, combine the beets and 3 quarts of water. Bring to a boil; cover and simmer until the beets are tender (about 35 minutes). Drain and cool them. Trim the beet ends and rub the skins off under running water. Quarter and thinly slice the beets.

In a small jar or bowl, combine the vinegar, honey, and horseradish. In a container, mix the cucumber and jicama; add half of the marinade and toss. In a separate container, combine the beets and the remaining marinade. Cover and refrigerate both for several hours. Pour the beets into a wide serving bowl. Spoon the jicama-cucumber mixture over the center of the beets. Garnish each plate with radish flowers.

Exchanges per serving: 2 vegetable

Calories per serving: 81
Fat per serving (gm): .3
Cholesterol per serving (mg): 0

SPINACH SALAD WITH SLIVERED ALMONDS

This salad is tangy and ready in minutes—a perfect accompaniment to broiled or steamed fish!

Yield: 2 servings

---

3 cups fresh spinach, washed and patted dry
1 cup fresh sliced mushrooms
3 tablespoons rice vinegar
½ tablespoon brown sugar
½ tablespoon soy sauce
1 thin slice fresh ginger, minced
1 tablespoon slivered blanched almonds

Place the spinach leaves in a salad bowl; top them with the sliced mushrooms. Combine the vinegar, sugar, soy sauce, and ginger in a small jar; cover, and shake vigorously to blend. Pour the dressing over the salad; toss gently. Divide the salad onto salad plates; top with slivered almonds.

Exchanges per serving: ½ fat, free vegetable

Calories per serving: 73
Fat per serving (gm): 2.9
Cholesterol per serving (mg): 0

TABBOULEH

A refreshing Middle Eastern salad, tabbouleh is traditionally served on lettuce leaves or stuffed in pita bread.

Yield: eight 1-cup servings

¾ cup bulgur
2 large or 3 small bunches parsley
1 cup chopped onion
1 cup chopped tomato
2 tablespoons finely chopped fresh mint
1½ teaspoons salt
½ teaspoon pepper
Dash each of cinnamon, allspice, nutmeg
6 tablespoons lemon juice
4 tablespoons salad oil

Mix the bulgur with just enough water to wet it; set it aside. Remove the stems from the parsley and chop the leaves in a food processor or with a knife. Place the parsley and onion in a large salad bowl. Add the bulgur to the middle of the bowl and top with the tomato. Add the remaining ingredients and toss well. Cover and refrigerate for at least several hours before serving.

Exchanges per serving: ½ bread, 1 vegetable, 1½ fat

Calories per serving: 127
Fat per serving (gm): 7.2
Cholesterol per serving (mg): 0

TUNA SALAD

Yield: 2 servings

1 6½-ounce can water-packed tuna, drained
2 dill pickles, finely chopped
2 tablespoons reduced-calorie mayonnaise
1½ to 2 tablespoons plain low-fat yogurt
½ teaspoon granulated sugar
Pepper to taste

Flake the tuna with a fork; add the remaining ingredients and mix well.

Exchanges per serving: 2 meat, 1 fat

Calories per serving: 189
Fat per serving (gm): 5.5
Cholesterol per serving (mg): 63.4

SALAD D'AMOUR

Yield: 2 servings

3 cups torn fresh spinach
1 4-ounce jar quartered marinated artichoke hearts, drained (reserve marinade)
1 4-ounce jar hearts of palm, drained and sliced (reserve liquid)
2 teaspoons snipped sun-dried tomato
3 tablespoons rosemary vinegar

Place the spinach on two salad plates. Arrange the artichoke and hearts of palm slices decoratively on top of the spinach. Sprinkle tomato bits over the salads. Combine the vinegar and 1 tablespoon reserved marinade; pour over the salads.

Exchanges per serving: 1 vegetable, 1 fat

Calories per serving: 77
Fat per serving (gm): 4.1
Cholesterol per serving (mg): 0

Entrées

BEEF TENDERLOIN WITH CAPERS

If you can't find small tenderloin steaks, have your butcher cut whole filet mignon into 1- to 1½-inch steaks.

Yield: 6 servings

2 tablespoons margarine
6 beef tenderloin steaks, 1½ to 2 pounds total weight
⅔ cup water
4 teaspoons prepared mustard
⅔ cup dry vermouth
1 green onion, chopped
2 tablespoons capers, drained
¼ teaspoon salt
1 beef bouillon cube
1 tablespoon cornstarch
2 tablespoons cold water
Watercress for garnish

In a 12-inch nonstick pan over medium heat, heat the margarine and brown the steaks 3 to 4 minutes per side (for 1-inch steaks) or to desired doneness. Meanwhile, combine the water and mustard and stir until smooth; set aside. Remove the steaks to a heated platter when done, and keep them warm. Add the vermouth and green onion to the pan. Cook for 2 minutes, stirring to loosen any brown bits on the bottom. Stir in the mustard mixture, capers, salt, and bouillon cube. Blend the cornstarch into the cold water until smooth; slowly add this mixture to the pan liquid and heat to boiling, stirring constantly. Pour the sauce over the meat or into a gravy boat to pass at the table. Garnish the platter with sprigs of watercress.

Exchanges per serving: 4 meat, 1 fat

Calories per serving: 260
Fat per serving (gm): 11.0
Cholesterol per serving (mg): 95.0

PRISCILLA'S TERIYAKI STEAK

This dish is guaranteed to get rave reviews!

Yield: 4 servings

1 pound thinly sliced lean steak (such as top round) (12 ounces cooked)
⅓ cup soy sauce (to reduce sodium content, use low-sodium soy sauce)
5 tablespoons brown sugar
1¼-inch slice fresh ginger, crushed
1 green onion, chopped
¼ cup white wine
1 teaspoon sesame oil

Trim the steak of all visible fat; wash it and pat it dry. Combine the soy sauce, sugar, ginger, green onion, wine, and oil. Pour this mixture over the steak in a glass dish or marinade container. Cover the dish and marinate in the refrigerator overnight. Broil or barbeque the steak to desired doneness. This marinade can also be used to make teriyaki chicken.

Exchanges per serving: 3 meat

Calories per serving: 185
Fat per serving (gm): 5.6
Cholesterol per serving (mg): 71.4

STEAK JARDINIÈRE

The liquid used to cook this steak helps keep it moist and tender. The slicing method also affects the tenderness of the meat.

Yield: 6 servings

1 tablespoon olive oil
1 1½-pound top round steak, ½-inch thick
1 medium onion, chopped
3 cloves garlic, minced
¾ teaspoon salt
½ teaspoon freshly ground black pepper
2 small green peppers, seeded and cut into strips
3 medium tomatoes, cut in small wedges
2 medium carrots, sliced (¼-inch slices)
1½ cups beef broth
1 tablespoon Worcestershire sauce
2 tablespoons water
1½ tablespoons cornstarch

Heat the oil in a large nonstick skillet over high heat. Add the steak and brown well on one side; turn the steak and add the onion and garlic. When the steak is browned and the onion is limp, add the salt, pepper, green pepper, tomatoes, carrots, and beef broth. Cover—leaving the lid slightly open—and simmer for 15 minutes. Remove the steak to a warm platter and keep it warm.

Combine the Worcestershire sauce and water in a small cup; blend in the cornstarch until the mixture is smooth. Slowly add this mixture to the skillet, stirring constantly, until the sauce thickens and begins to boil. Remove the skillet from the heat. Slice the steak into thin strips across the grain, cutting on a diagonal (almost parallel to the platter). Pour the sauce over the steak; serve.

Exchanges per serving: 3 meat, 1 vegetable

Calories per serving: 230
Fat per serving (gm): 8.0
Cholesterol per serving (mg): 71.4

GRILLED ALBACORE WITH HERBS

Pacific albacore, a member of the tuna family, is a firm fish with a mild flavor and light color. It is an excellent source of omega-3 fatty acids—a heart-healthy nutrient. Swordfish can be used also.

Yield: 4 servings

1½ tablespoons olive oil
2 tablespoons white wine
2 tablespoons white vinegar
1 teaspoon chopped fresh rosemary
2 tablespoons finely chopped fresh parsley
1 tablespoon finely chopped fresh dillweed
¼ teaspoon salt
⅛ teaspoon pepper
1 pound fresh albacore steak, ¼-inch thick
Vegetable oil

Combine all of the ingredients except the albacore and vegetable oil. Rub the mixture onto both sides of the albacore; let it sit for 30 minutes. Brush the grill grates with vegetable oil to prevent sticking. Grill for 1 to 2 minutes per side or until medium-rare. (It should be slightly pink in the center.)

Exchanges per serving: 3 meat, 1 fat

Calories per serving: 246
Fat per serving (gm): 13.0
Cholesterol per serving (mg): 62.4

GILBERT'S CALAMARI

Yield: 4 servings

1 pound small cleaned squid, tentacles included (12 ounces cooked)
1 tablespoon olive oil
1 teaspoon fresh diced garlic
½ tablespoon fresh dillweed, minced
4 cups cooked linguine, hot
1 tablespoon olive oil

Cleaned squid should be ready to cook, but sometimes it still contains a long, transparent, sword-shaped shell inside the body (tail). Check for this, and remove and discard it before cooking. Wash the squid inside and out; slice into ½-inch strips.

Heat the olive oil over a medium flame in a black iron skillet. Add the garlic and stir until golden. Add the squid and the dillweed, stirring constantly. Cook until the tentacles curl and meat is cooked, approximately 2 to 4 minutes total. Do not overcook. Toss the linguine with olive oil and serve onto individual plates. Top each serving with calamari.

Exchanges per serving: 3 meat, 2 bread, 1 fat

Calories per serving: 367
Fat per serving (gm): 8.5
Cholesterol per serving (mg): 62.3

CIOPPINO

This hearty seafood soup is extremely low in fat and calories.

Yield: 8 servings

1½ dozen cherrystone or littleneck clams
Nonstick cooking spray
1 tablespoon olive oil
1 large onion, coarsely chopped
1 medium green pepper, coarsely chopped
2 cloves garlic, minced
1 28-ounce can tomatoes
1 8-ounce can tomato sauce
½ cup dry white wine
¼ cup chopped parsley
1 teaspoon salt
1 teaspoon dry leaves of each: basil, thyme, marjoram, oregano
1 12-ounce package frozen Alaska King crab legs (split), thawed
1 pound red snapper fillets, cut into 2-inch pieces
1 pound large shrimp, shelled and deveined
½ pound medium-size sea scallops

With a stiff brush, scrub the clams under running cold water to remove any sand and dirt. In an 8-quart Dutch oven over high heat, boil ½ inch of water and cook the clams just until the shells open (about 5 minutes). Remove and discard the top shells; rinse the clams in the pan liquid to remove any remaining sand and set them aside. After the sand has settled in the pan, spoon out ¾ cup of clear broth and reserve. Clean and dry the Dutch oven. Spray it with nonstick cooking spray. Add the oil, and heat over a medium flame. Add the onion, green pepper, and garlic, and cook until tender. Add the tomatoes with their liquid, the tomato sauce, wine, parsley, salt, basil, thyme, marjoram, oregano, and reserved clam broth; heat to boiling. Reduce the heat to low; simmer, covered, for 15 minutes. Meanwhile, cut the crab legs into chunks. Turn the heat to high and add the crab-leg chunks, fillet pieces, shrimp, and scallops; heat to boiling. Cook for 1 minute or until the fish flakes easily when tested with a fork, and the shrimp turns pink. Add the clams and heat through. Serve in large bowls, with side bowls to hold the empty shells.

Exchanges per serving: 2 meat, 2 vegetable

Calories per serving: 198
Fat per serving (gm): 4.7
Cholesterol per serving (mg): 122.7

PARSLEYED FISH FILLETS WITH PINE NUTS

Yield: 4 servings

3 tablespoons chopped pine nuts
¼ cup all-purpose flour
¾ teaspoon salt
¼ teaspoon paprika
4 4-ounce fish fillets (½-inch thick or less)
½ tablespoon olive oil
½ tablespoon margarine
3 tablespoons lime juice
5 tablespoons white wine
⅓ cup minced parsley
1 pickled jalapeño, seeded and minced

Brown the pine nuts in a nonstick pan until they are golden, stirring frequently; set them aside. Combine the flour, salt, and paprika; spread onto a large plate. Rinse the fillets under running water; pat them dry with paper towels. Coat the fillets with the flour mixture. Heat the oil and margarine in a nonstick pan. Sauté the fillets over high heat, browning them on both sides, until the fish flakes easily with a fork (about 5 minutes total time per ½-inch thickness). Remove from heat; place fish on a heated platter. Over low heat, add the lime juice, wine, parsley, and jalapeño to the skillet, stirring to dissolve any bits on the bottom. Cook, stirring, 1 minute. Pour the sauce over the fish; top with the pine nuts. Serve immediately.

Exchanges per serving: 3 meat, 1 fat

Calories per serving: 153
Fat per serving (gm): 6.3
Cholesterol per serving (mg): 51.0

POACHED SALMON

This elegant dish, quick and easy to prepare, is an excellent source of the beneficial omega-3 fatty acids.

Yield: 2 servings

2 cups boiling water
2 chicken bouillon cubes
1 tablespoon white vinegar
1 small onion, sliced
1 lemon, sliced
¼ teaspoon pepper
2 salmon fillets (5 ounces each, raw)

Combine all of the ingredients, except the salmon, in a wok or wok-shaped skillet. Heat them to boiling; then cover and simmer for 5 minutes. Add the salmon skin-side down. Cover and simmer until the fish flakes easily (about 10 minutes per inch at the thickest point). Remove and drain the fillets; arrange them on dinner plates with the onion and lemon slices. Serve with Cucumber Sauce (p. 305).

Exchanges per serving (Poached Salmon): 4 meat
Exchanges per serving (Cucumber Sauce): free exchange

Calories per serving: 296; with sauce, 308
Fat per serving (gm): 16.0; with sauce, 16.3
Cholesterol per serving (mg): 46.7; with sauce, 47.6

STEAMED SEA BASS, CHINESE STYLE

Yield: four 3½-ounce servings

1 2-pound whole sea bass, dressed
2 tablespoons dry sherry
½ teaspoon salt
¼ teaspoon pepper
3 tablespoons soy sauce
1 tablespoon peanut oil
1 teaspoon sesame oil
1 teaspoon cornstarch
1 teaspoon granulated sugar
2 green onions, greens cut in 1-inch pieces, whites finely chopped
2 tablespoons chopped Chinese parsley
1 1½-inch piece peeled fresh ginger, slivered
Water

Rinse the sea bass under cold water; pat it dry with paper towels. To improve the speed and evenness of cooking, cut several crosswise slashes about ½-inch deep at intervals of ¾ inch on each side of the fish. Place the fish on a heatproof platter or a baking dish large enough to hold the fish but small enough to fit inside an oval roasting pan or steamer. Rub the inside and outside of the fish with sherry, salt, and pepper. Marinate in the refrigerator for 1 hour.

Combine the soy sauce, peanut and sesame oils, cornstarch, and sugar until smooth. Combine the green onion, parsley, and ginger; place half of this mixture in the fish cavity. Pour the soy sauce mixture over the fish; top with the remaining green-onion mixture.

Pour 1 to 2 inches of water into a roasting pan or steamer. Place three small custard cups upside-down in the roasting pan, or place a wire rack in the steamer. (The top of the cups or rack should be above water level.) Boil the water, then set the platter with the fish on the cups or rack. Reduce the heat to medium-high, cover, and steam the fish until it flakes easily with a fork (about 10 minutes per each inch of thickness at the thickest point). Serve with the liquid on the platter.

Exchanges per serving: 3 meat, 1 fat

Calories per serving: 192
Fat per serving (gm): 7.7
Cholesterol per serving (mg): 74.0

SUMMERTIME SEAFOOD KABOBS

Quick, light, and delicious, these kabobs should be served with steamed rice.

Yield: 4 servings

¼ cup Worcestershire sauce
¼ cup oyster sauce (available in oriental markets/sections)
¼ cup dry white wine
1 tablespoon olive oil
½ pound boned and skinned sea bass or other firm fish
½ pound sea scallops
16 small button mushrooms
1 medium green bell pepper, stemmed, seeded, and cut into 1-inch pieces
8 baby yellow summer squash
16 cherry tomatoes

In a bowl, combine the Worcestershire sauce, oyster sauce, wine, and oil. Rinse and cut the sea bass and scallops into 1-inch cubes and add to the bowl; mix well. Cover and refrigerate for several hours, mixing occasionally.

When you are ready to broil the kabobs, rinse the mushrooms, pepper, squash, and tomatoes. Remove the seafood from the bowl, and reserve the marinade. Thread seafood cubes and vegetables onto eight skewers, alternating the ingredients in an attractive arrangement. Place the skewers slightly apart on a broiler rack or barbeque, 3 inches from the heat source. Brush them with marinade and cook until the seafood just turns opaque in the center (about 8 minutes total). Turn the skewers once and brush them with marinade.

Exchanges per serving: 2 meat, 2 vegetable

Calories per serving: 139
Fat per serving (gm): 3.0
Cholesterol per serving (mg): 50.8

SHRIMP CURRY

Yield: 8 servings

2 pounds fresh medium shrimp
½ tablespoon each ground cumin and coriander
½ teaspoon each chili powder and ground red pepper (cayenne)
¼ teaspoon each ground cinnamon and cardamom
1 small onion, minced
1 tablespoon margarine
1 cup chicken broth, cooled
1½ teaspoons granulated sugar
1 teaspoon salt
¼ teaspoon ground ginger
2 tablespoons plus 2 teaspoons cornstarch
12 ounces nonfat evaporated milk
4 ounces water
1 teaspoon lemon juice
5 cups cooked rice, hot
Chutney (optional)
Golden raisins (optional)
Salted peanuts (optional)

Shell and devein the shrimp; rinse them under cold water. Add the shrimp to 3 inches of boiling water in a large saucepan. Reheat the water to boiling, reduce the heat to low, and cook the shrimp until they turn pink and opaque (45 to 60 seconds). Drain and set aside.

Combine the cumin, coriander, chili powder, red pepper, cinnamon, and cardamom; set aside. In a 3-quart saucepan, cook the onion in melted margarine until it is tender. Slowly stir in ½ cup of the chicken broth, the sugar, salt, ginger, and spice mixture; cook for 1 minute. Add the cornstarch to the remaining ½ cup of chicken broth; stir until smooth. Gradually combine the milk, water, and cornstarch mixture in a saucepan. Cook, stirring until the mixture thickens. Add the shrimp and lemon juice; heat through. Serve over rice; sprinkle with chutney, raisins, and/or peanuts.

Exchanges per serving: 2 meat, 2 bread, ½ milk

Calories per serving: 327
Fat per serving (gm): 4.2
Cholesterol per serving (mg): 155.0

COMPANY LEG OF LAMB

Yield: 12 servings

1 5-pound boneless leg of lamb with shank bone left in* (approximately
    42 ounces meat, cooked)
6 cloves garlic, finely chopped
⅓ cup each chopped fresh mint and parsley
1 teaspoon salt
½ tablespoon freshly ground pepper
2 teaspoons brown sugar
1 tablespoon lemon juice
1 beef bouillon cube
1 cup hot water
About ⅔ cup red wine

Trim the lamb of excess fat. With a sharp knife, make several 2-inch-long
by ¼-inch-deep slices on the inside of the meat, so that the seasonings
can penetrate more fully. Combine the garlic, mint, parsley, salt, pepper,
sugar, and lemon juice; spread this mixture over the inner surface of
the meat. Roll the meat and tie it with string at 1- to 2-inch intervals.
Insert a meat thermometer at the thickest part, without touching bone.
Place the lamb fat-side up on a rack in an open roasting pan. Roast at
325 degrees until the thermometer reaches 160 degrees for medium
(about 25 to 30 minutes per pound), or 170 degrees for well-done.

Combine the bouillon cube and the water. Mix ½ cup each of the
broth and wine. Baste the lamb with the wine mixture every 15 to 20
minutes. When the lamb is done, remove it from the pan and let it
stand for 15 minutes. Meanwhile, pour the meat drippings into a cup;
freeze for 5 to 10 minutes to separate the fat. Skim and discard the fat;
add 2 tablespoons of wine and the remaining ½ cup of beef broth.
Return the juices to the roasting pan. Over medium-high heat, bringing
the mixture to a boil, stirring to loosen any bits on the bottom of the
pan; pour the gravy into a gravy boat. Remove the strings from the
lamb; cut the meat into thin slices. Serve with gravy.

Exchanges per serving: 4 meat

Calories per serving: 322
Fat per serving (gm): 23.8
Cholesterol per serving (mg): 97.2

*Ask your butcher to butterfly the lamb for rolling, leaving the shank bone intact.

CAPELLINI WITH CLAM SAUCE

A very thin pasta, capellini is also known as vermicelli or angel hair pasta.

Yield: 4 servings

2 10-ounce jars whole baby clams
1 cup clam juice (reserved from clams)
2 teaspoons cornstarch
6 ounces capellini (3½ cups cooked)
1 tablespoon olive oil
1 tablespoon margarine
2 shallots, sliced
3 small or 2 large cloves garlic, minced
Salt to taste
White pepper to taste
½ teaspoon dry oregano
3 tablespoons chopped Italian parsley

Drain the clams, reserving 1 cup of juice. Add the cornstarch to the juice and blend well. Cook the capellini according to the package directions. Meanwhile, heat the oil and margarine in a pan; add the shallots, garlic, salt, and pepper, and cook until golden. Add the oregano, clams, and clam juice–cornstarch mixture. Stir over low heat until the mixture is thickened. Add the parsley, turn up the heat, and bring the sauce to a boil. Boil for 1 minute. Serve over drained pasta.

Exchanges per serving: 2 meat, 2 bread, 1 fat

Calories per serving: 337
Fat per serving (gm): 8.0
Cholesterol per serving (mg): 45.3

FETTUCCINE WITH TOMATOES AND BASIL

This would be excellent with Hearty Caesar Salad (p. 245) and warm Italian bread.

Yield: 4 servings

6 medium tomatoes
6 ounces dry fettuccine (3½ cups cooked)
1 medium onion, chopped
1 large clove garlic, minced
1 tablespoon olive oil
1 bunch fresh basil, minced
1 teaspoon dry oregano
½ teaspoon salt
¼ teaspoon pepper
2 tablespoons grated Parmesan cheese
Basil leaves, for garnish

To remove the tomato skins, place the tomatoes in boiling water for 30 seconds; then transfer them to cold water. They can then be easily peeled. Dice and seed the tomatoes, drain well, and set aside. Prepare the fettuccine according to the package instructions.

Meanwhile, sauté the onion and garlic in the olive oil in a nonstick pan until the onion is tender. Add the tomatoes, minced basil, oregano, salt, and pepper. Cook for 5 to 7 minutes, stirring frequently. Mix the sauce with the drained pasta; transfer to a serving dish. Sprinkle with Parmesan cheese, and garnish with basil leaves.

Exchanges per serving: 2 bread, 1 vegetable, 1 fat

Calories per serving: 246
Fat per serving (gm): 5.4
Cholesterol per serving (mg): 2.0

PASTA AND BEAN SOUP

This nutrient-rich soup is high in complex carbohydrates and soluble fiber.

Yield: 10 main-dish servings

1½ cups (8 ounces) dry Great Northern beans, sorted and rinsed
5 cups water (for beans)
½ pound ground turkey
1 large onion, chopped
3 cloves garlic, minced
1 large carrot, chopped
2 tablespoons dried currants
6 cups chicken broth, defatted
1 cup water
1 teaspoon dry basil
½ teaspoon cumin
6 drops Tabasco sauce
1 14-ounce can plum tomatoes
1 cup dry small shell pasta

To prepare the beans, bring them to a boil in hot water; let them boil for 3 minutes. Cover, remove them from the heat, and let them sit for 1 hour. Drain and rinse the beans; set them aside. Cook the ground turkey in a 5-quart nonstick pot until it is lightly browned, breaking it into large chunks as it cooks. Drain any excess fat. Add the onion, garlic, and carrot; stir until the onion is tender. Add the currants, broth, water, beans, basil, cumin, and Tabasco sauce. Cover and bring to a boil; then simmer until the beans are soft (1½ to 2 hours).

Coarsely chop the tomatoes; add them (with their liquid) and the pasta to the soup. Cover and simmer until the pasta is barely tender (about 10 minutes).

Exchanges per serving: 1 bread, 1 vegetable, 1 meat

Calories per serving: 179
Fat per serving (gm): 2.9
Cholesterol per serving (mg): 16.2

GRILLED PORK WITH RASPBERRY SAUCE

This pork dish is very low in fat, yet tender and flavorful.

Yield: 4 servings

1 pound boneless pork tenderloin (12 ounces cooked)
1 medium clove garlic, minced
1 teaspoon fresh ginger, peeled and minced
½ cup sliced onion
¼ teaspoon ground cinnamon
½ teaspoon curry powder
⅓ cup orange juice
¼ cup lemon juice
Coarse salt
Freshly ground pepper
Orange slices
Fresh parsley

SAUCE   1 pearl onion, minced
            1 teaspoon olive oil
            ½ cup chicken broth
            Reserved marinade
            ¼ cup raspberry jam
            1 tablespoon lemon juice
            1 teaspoon cornstarch

Slice the pork in half lengthwise if it is more than 1 or 2 inches thick. In a bowl, mix the garlic, ginger, onion, cinnamon, curry powder, and orange and lemon juices. Place the pork in a glass dish or airtight plastic bag and add the marinade. Marinate it in the refrigerator for at least 8 hours, turning it frequently. Remove the pork and pat it dry; sprinkle it with salt and pepper. Strain and reserve the marinade, discarding the solids.

Broil or barbeque the pork until it is done (about 30 minutes per inch of thickness), turning it once. (The meat should have an internal temperature of 150 degrees.) Meanwhile, prepare the sauce: Sauté the onion in the oil, but do not brown. Add the chicken broth (except 2 tablespoons) and marinade, and cook until the liquid is reduced to ⅓ cup. Add the jam and lemon juice. Remove from the heat. Mix the cornstarch with the reserved broth until smooth. Add this mixture to the sauce, stirring constantly. Return the sauce to the heat and bring it to a boil. Slice the pork thinly and serve with sauce. Garnish with orange slices and parsley.

Exchanges per serving: 3 meat, 1 fruit

Calories per serving: 247
Fat per serving (gm): 5.5
Cholesterol per serving (mg): 79.0

DIJON CHICKEN

Serve this with pasta or steamed rice.

Yield: 3 servings

Nonstick cooking spray
3 chicken-breast halves, boneless and skinless (3 ounces each, cooked)
Salt and pepper to taste
⅔ cup white wine
3 tablespoons Dijon mustard
4 ounces marinated artichoke hearts, drained and quartered
Fresh parsley

Spray a pan with nonstick cooking spray. Sprinkle the chicken pieces with salt and pepper; place them in the pan in one layer. Brown the chicken on both sides over medium heat. Meanwhile, blend the wine and mustard together thoroughly. Pour the wine-mustard mixture over the chicken; top with the artichoke hearts. Simmer uncovered until the meat is tender and white (about 20 minutes). Cover the pan when the sauce thickens to the desired consistency. Serve, garnished with parsley.

Exchanges per serving: 3 meat

Calories per serving: 175
Fat per serving (gm): 5.0
Cholesterol per serving (mg): 72.2

PEPPERED PORK WITH BLACK BEANS

Pork tenderloin is an excellent source of thiamine and is similar to lean beef in fat and cholesterol content. Serve it with white rice.

Yield: 4 servings

1 pound boneless pork tenderloin
1 tablespoon light olive oil
1 each red and yellow bell peppers, cut into strips
2 medium-size carrots, julienned
1 beef or pork bouillon cube
1 cup water
¼ teaspoon pepper
1 16-ounce can black beans, drained

Trim the pork of all visible fat; cut it into ¾-inch cubes. In a large nonstick skillet over medium heat, brown the pork cubes in hot oil. Add the bell pepper strips, carrot, bouillon, water, and pepper, and heat to boiling over high heat. Reduce the heat to low; cover and simmer until the pork is done and the vegetables are fork-tender (approximately 10 to 15 minutes). Add the black beans; heat through.

Exchanges per serving: 3 meat, 2 vegetable, 1 bread

Calories per serving: 294
Fat per serving (gm): 8.2
Cholesterol per serving (mg): 79.0

CHICKEN FAJITAS

These are a favorite among Mexican-food lovers. Serve them with Spanish-Style Rice (p. 295).

Yield: 4 servings

4 chicken-breast halves, boned and skinned (4 ounces each, raw)
Salt and pepper to taste
1 cup lemon juice
4 tablespoons red-wine vinegar
2 teaspoons granulated sugar
4 large cloves garlic, crushed
1 tablespoon light olive oil
1 green bell pepper, cut into strips
1 onion, sliced into wedges
1 large tomato, sliced into wedges
6 sprigs cilantro, chopped
8 6-inch flour tortillas, warmed
Salsa Cruda (optional) (p. 311)

Cut the chicken into 3-by-½-inch strips; sprinkle it with salt and pepper to taste. Place the strips in an enamel or glass dish or marinade container. Combine the lemon juice, vinegar, sugar, and garlic; pour this mixture over the chicken strips to coat them thoroughly. Marinate the chicken for 1 hour or more.

Heat the olive oil in a 12-inch nonstick skillet. Brown the chicken quickly on both sides over medium-high heat; remove it to a warm plate. Cook the pepper and onion over medium heat for 3 minutes, stirring frequently. Add a little marinade if the vegetables begin to burn and stick. Return the chicken to the pan and cook over medium-high heat until done (2 to 3 minutes), stirring occasionally. Add the tomato and cilantro and cook to heat through (about 1 minute). Serve immediately.

To eat, place the chicken strips, vegetables, and salsa in a warm tortilla and fold over the sides.

Exchanges per serving: 3 meat, 2 bread, 1 vegetable, 1 fat

Calories per serving: 417
Fat per serving (gm): 11.3
Cholesterol per serving (mg): 72.3

CHICKEN PASTA PRIMAVERA

This is a very colorful and very tasty dish!

Yield: 4 servings

6 ounces dry fettuccine
1 tablespoon margarine
1 teaspoon olive oil
½ large onion, chopped
2 cloves garlic, finely chopped
1 cup sliced mushrooms
1 cup broccoli flowerets
2 medium carrots, thinly sliced
⅓ cup chicken broth
¾ cup nonfat evaporated milk
2 tablespoons dry sherry
⅓ cup fresh chopped, packed basil leaves
½ teaspoon salt
⅛ teaspoon pepper
1 tablespoon cornstarch
2 tablespoons water
8 ounces (1¾ cups) boneless, skinless, cooked, coarsely chopped
    chicken

Prepare the pasta according to the package directions, until it is tender but firm inside (al dente). Rinse it under hot water, drain, and transfer to a heated platter.

In a 3-quart saucepan, heat the margarine and oil over medium heat. Add the onion and garlic; cook for 1 to 2 minutes. Add the mushrooms, broccoli, and carrots, and cook just until tender. Stir in the chicken broth, evaporated milk, sherry, basil, salt, and pepper. Blend the cornstarch into the water until smooth; slowly stir the mixture into the sauce. Add the chicken; heat until the sauce just begins to boil, stirring constantly. Pour the sauce over hot pasta; serve immediately.

Exchanges per serving: 2 meat, ½ milk, 1½ bread, 1 vegetable, 1 fat

Calories per serving: 399
Fat per serving (gm): 9.3
Cholesterol per serving (mg): 89.8

JANE'S CHICKEN PICCATA

Yield: 4 servings

4 chicken-breast halves, skinned and boned (3 ounces each, cooked)
¼ cup all-purpose flour
¾ teaspoon salt
¼ teaspoon paprika
1½ tablespoons extra virgin olive oil
1 tablespoon margarine
2 tablespoons Madeira wine or cream sherry
2 tablespoons lemon juice
½ lemon, thinly sliced
2 tablespoons capers
2 tablespoons chopped fresh parsley

Pound the chicken breasts with a mallet to ¼-inch thickness. Mix the flour, salt, and paprika in a plastic bag; add the chicken and shake to coat thoroughly. Heat the oil and margarine in a large nonstick skillet over medium heat. Sauté the chicken on each side until it is golden and cooked through. Remove it to a warm platter. Add the Madeira to the skillet; cover over medium heat, stirring to dissolve any bits that have adhered to the skillet bottom. Add the lemon juice and heat briefly.

Return the chicken, with the lemon slices, to the skillet to reheat. Top them with capers and parsley; serve immediately.

Exchanges per serving: 3 meat, 1 fat

Calories per serving: 217
Fat per serving (gm): 10.3
Cholesterol per serving (mg): 72.3

CORNISH GAME HENS

Here's a dish that is very simple yet extra special.

Yield: 6 servings

3 Cornish game hens (22–24 ounces each)
Lemon-herb seasoning (or other seasonings) to taste
Pepper
1 tablespoon lemon juice
4 cups Savory Almond Rice (p. 296)
Parsley

Remove the giblets from the hens' cavities and rinse the hens well. Cut them in half along their spines. Cut away any loose, excess fat and discard. Turn the wing tips onto the back sides. Sprinkle both sides liberally with seasoning and pepper to taste. Place the halves skin-side down on a foil-lined broiler rack 7 to 9 inches from the flame in a 450-degree oven. Drizzle the hens with lemon juice. Broil them for about 15 minutes. Turn the halves and broil them until the skins are browned and the meat is fork-tender (12 to 15 minutes). Place the hen halves on a serving platter on top of the rice; garnish with fresh parsley.

Exchanges per serving (Cornish Game Hens): 3 meat
Exchanges per serving (Savory Almond Rice): ½ bread, ½ vegetable, ½ fat

Calories per serving: 190; with rice, 349
Fat per serving (gm): 10.0; with rice, 12.1
Cholesterol per serving (mg): 72.2; with rice, 72.2

TURKEY-ASPARAGUS ROLL-UPS

Yield: 1 serving

2 ounces thinly sliced low-fat turkey-ham
½ tablespoon Dijon mustard
5–6 asparagus spears, lightly cooked and chilled

If the turkey-ham slices are large, cut them in half crosswise. Spread the mustard evenly over one side of each turkey slice. Place one spear of asparagus along the edge of each turkey slice, exposing its tip and end; roll up. Arrange the rolls on a platter.

Exchanges per serving: 2 meat, 1 vegetable

Calories per serving: 105
Fat per serving (gm): 3.7
Cholesterol per serving (mg): 31.7

CHEESY TURKEY-HAM BAKE

This would be perfect for a weekend lunch. Or, bake it a day ahead and microwave it briefly to reheat.

Yield: 4 servings

Nonstick cooking spray
4 slices whole-wheat bread, toasted and cut into cubes
4 ounces turkey-ham, cut into thin strips
3 ounces low-fat sharp Cheddar cheese, shredded
1 cup evaporated skim milk
4 egg whites
2 eggs
2 tablespoons finely chopped parsley
¼ cup finely chopped onion

Preheat the oven to 350 degrees. Spray a 9-inch pie pan with nonstick cooking spray. Arrange the bread cubes evenly over the bottom and sides of the pan. Spread the meat and then the cheese over the bread cubes. Beat the milk, egg whites, and eggs lightly until blended; stir in the parsley and onion. Pour this mixture into the pie pan. Bake it for 40 to 45 minutes, until it is lightly browned and puffy. (A knife inserted in the center should come out clean.) Let it cool for 10 minutes before cutting.

Exchanges per serving: 2 bread, 2 meat, ½ milk

Calories per serving: 270
Fat per serving (gm): 8.5
Cholesterol per serving (mg): 157.0

TURKEY WITH BLACK BEAN SAUCE

If you like spicy food, this dish is for you!

Yield: 4 servings

1 pound skinless turkey breast (12 ounces cooked)
1 tablespoon soy sauce
2 tablespoons cooking sherry
4 teaspoons fermented black beans (available in oriental markets)
2 cloves garlic, finely chopped
1 tablespoon cornstarch
2 tablespoons chicken broth
2 teaspoons sesame oil
1 teaspoon granulated sugar
⅓ cup chicken broth
2 green onions, chopped

Cut the turkey in thin strips; marinate it in a mixture of the soy sauce and cooking sherry for ½ hour. Rinse the black beans; add the garlic and crush. Blend the cornstarch and the 2 tablespoons of chicken broth until smooth; set aside.

Heat the oil in a nonstick pan, and sauté the beans and garlic over a medium flame. Add the turkey; cook and stir until the meat is just white. Sprinkle it with sugar and cook for 1 minute. Add the ¼ cup of broth and the green onions, and cook for 2 minutes. Add the cornstarch mixture and cook until thickened.

Exchanges per serving: 3 meat, ½ fat

Calories per serving: 195
Fat per serving (gm): 5.3
Cholesterol per serving (mg): 58.6

VEAL MARSALA

Tender veal slices are served with a Marsala wine sauce.

Yield: 4 servings

1 pound veal cutlets, each ¼-inch thick
¼ cup all-purpose flour
¾ teaspoon salt
¼ teaspoon pepper
Nonstick cooking spray
2 teaspoons margarine
1 tablespoon olive oil
1 cup thinly sliced mushrooms
2 tablespoons lemon juice
½ cup dry Marsala
1 teaspoon cornstarch
1 tablespoon water
Chopped parsley

With a meat mallet, pound each cutlet to ⅛-inch thickness. Cut the veal into 3-by-3-inch pieces. Combine the flour, salt, and pepper. Spread the flour mixture on a plate or a sheet of waxed paper; coat the veal lightly with the mixture.

In a skillet sprayed with nonstick cooking spray, heat 1 teaspoon each of the margarine and oil over medium-high heat. Cook half of the cutlets until they are lightly browned on both sides. Remove the cutlets to a warm platter, add the remaining margarine and oil, and repeat the procedure with the remaining pieces. Add the mushrooms to the skillet, and sauté until tender. Reduce the heat to medium-low, add the lemon juice and Marsala, and cook for 1 minute, stirring to loosen any brown bits. Stir the cornstarch into the water until smooth; slowly pour this into the mushroom mixture and stir until thickened. Pour the sauce over the veal; sprinkle with parsley; serve.

Exchanges per serving: 3 meat, ½ bread, 1 fat

Calories per serving: 282
Fat per serving (gm): 16.8
Cholesterol per serving (mg): 85.8

BLACK BEAN CHILI

Yield: six 1¼-cup servings

1 cup dry black beans, sorted and washed
4 cups water
1 16-ounce can whole tomatoes, drained (reserve liquid)
1½ cups coarsely chopped Spanish onion
3 cloves garlic, minced
1½ cups chopped green pepper
12 ounces ground turkey or extra-lean ground beef
3 tablespoons minced fresh cilantro (Chinese parsley)
1 can tomato soup
1 tablespoon chili powder
¾ teaspoon ground cumin
¾ teaspoon oregano leaves
⅛–¼ teaspoon red-pepper sauce
¼ teaspoon salt

Soak the beans in the 4 cups of water overnight; *or* bring them to a boil in water, boil for 3 minutes, cover, remove from heat, and let them sit for 1 hour. Drain and rinse the beans.

Add just enough fresh water to cover the beans. Bring the water to a boil, then cover and simmer over a low flame for 1½ hours. Add the reserved tomato liquid to cover the beans, if needed. Sauté the onion, garlic, green pepper, and ground turkey until the vegetables are tender and the turkey is cooked. Add this mixture to the beans, along with the tomatoes, cilantro, tomato soup, chili powder, cumin, oregano, red-pepper sauce, and salt. Simmer uncovered until hot and thickened (about 15 minutes or longer).

Exchanges per serving: 2 meat, 1½ bread, 2 vegetable

Calories per serving: 309
Fat per serving (gm): 9.4
Cholesterol per serving (mg): 39.4

CRUSTLESS GARDEN QUICHE

Patty-pan squash are shaped like pie crusts, with large scalloped edges. They are light yellow, pale green, or white in color and about four inches in diameter.

Yield: 6 servings

⅓ cup sun-dried tomatoes
Nonstick cooking spray
3 cups (about 1 pound) coarsely shredded, ripe patty-pan (scallop) squash
4 ounces (1 cup) shredded low-fat Swiss cheese
2 eggs
3 egg whites
1 cup buttermilk baking mix (Bisquick)
3 tablespoons chopped fresh cilantro
½ tablespoon olive oil
¼ cup nonfat evaporated milk
½ teaspoon salt
½ teaspoon Italian seasoning

Place the tomatoes in boiling water and boil them for 2 minutes; drain and chop. Preheat the oven to 375 degrees. Spray a 9-inch pie pan with nonstick cooking spray. In a large bowl, combine the squash, cheese, eggs, egg whites, baking mix, cilantro, oil, evaporated milk, tomatoes, salt, and Italian seasoning; mix thoroughly. Pour the mixture into the pie pan. Bake until the surface is golden brown and a toothpick inserted in the center comes out clean (about 40 minutes).

Exchanges per serving: 1 bread, 1 vegetable, 1 meat, ½ fat

Calories per serving: 182
Fat per serving (gm): 7.2
Cholesterol per serving (mg): 96.7

EASTERN OMELETTE

The use of only one egg yolk makes this omelette relatively low in cholesterol.

Yield: 2 servings

8 ounces firm tofu, drained
3 egg whites
1 egg
1 tablespoon soy sauce
½ teaspoon honey
2 teaspoons sesame oil
1 thin slice fresh ginger, minced
3 large fresh mushrooms, sliced
3 green onions, chopped
Fresh coriander

Press the tofu carefully between layers of paper towel to extract any excess liquid. Finely dice the tofu; set it aside. Beat the egg whites and egg lightly in a medium-size bowl. Add the tofu, soy sauce, and honey. Heat the oil in a 12-inch nonstick skillet. Add the ginger, mushrooms, and green onions, and sauté for 2 minutes or until slightly cooked. Gently blend the ginger, mushrooms, and green onions into the egg-tofu mixture. Pour the mixture back into the skillet and cook over low heat, periodically lifting the edges gently to allow the uncooked egg to flow underneath. When the omelette is cooked, fold it and cut it in half. Garnish each half with fresh coriander.

Exchanges per serving: 2 meat, 1 fat

Calories per serving: 218
Fat per serving (gm): 13.0
Cholesterol per serving (mg): 136.5

EGGPLANT PARMESAN

This version is lighter than restaurant-style eggplant parmesan because the eggplant is steamed, not fried.

Yield: 6 servings

1 28-ounce can tomato puree
2 tablespoons minced fresh basil
1 large clove garlic, minced
½ teaspoon crumbled dry thyme
1 large eggplant
2 tablespoons finely chopped parsley
¼ teaspoon salt
⅛ teaspoon pepper
1 cup part-skim ricotta cheese
4 ounces (1 cup) part-skim Mozzarella cheese
9 ounces tofu, regular, drained and cut into cubes
¼ cup grated Parmesan cheese, divided
1 tablespoon all-purpose flour

Heat the tomato puree, basil, garlic, and thyme, and simmer the mixture uncovered to cook it down. Meanwhile, slice the eggplant crosswise into ½-inch wheels. Steam them for 10 minutes. Mix together the parsley, salt, pepper, ricotta cheese, Mozzarella cheese, tofu, half of the Parmesan cheese, and the flour. Into a 2-quart casserole, pour a thin layer of tomato puree. On top of that, put a layer of eggplant, then cheese mixture, then tomato puree. Repeat the layers twice. (There may be extra tomato puree that can be saved for later use.) Top with the remaining Parmesan cheese. Bake uncovered at 350 degrees for 30 minutes.

Exchanges per serving: 2 vegetable, 2 meat

Calories per serving: 237
Fat per serving (gm): 9.6
Cholesterol per serving (mg): 26.4

NOUVELLE PIZZA

This recipe was inspired by the light, West-Coast style of eating.

Yield: two 6-slice pizzas

MARINARA SAUCE 1 small clove garlic, minced
1 teaspoon olive oil
1 8-ounce can tomato sauce
1 teaspoon oregano leaves
½ tablespoon chopped Italian parsley

1 package active dry yeast
1 cup warm water (105 to 115 degrees)
1 teaspoon salt
2 tablespoons olive oil
2½ cups whole-wheat flour
1 ounce sun-dried tomatoes
½ pound medium shrimp, shelled and deveined
½ cup chopped Maui onion
2 ounces feta cheese
2 tablespoons finely chopped fresh basil
4 ounces part-skim Mozzarella cheese

For the marinara sauce, sauté the garlic in oil until it is golden. Stir in the tomato sauce, oregano, and parsley; cover and simmer for 20 minutes.

Dissolve the yeast in the warm water. Stir in the salt, oil, and flour; beat vigorously for 20 strokes. Let the dough sit for 5 minutes. Meanwhile, place the sun-dried tomatoes in boiling water for 2 minutes. Drain them, then slice. Pat the pizza dough into the bottoms and halfway up the sides of two greased 9-inch round cake pans. Spread the sauce evenly over both pizzas. Top them with the shrimp, onion, tomatoes, feta cheese, basil, and Mozzarella cheese. Bake at 425 degrees until the crusts are lightly browned (20 to 25 minutes).

Exchanges per serving (2 slices): 2 bread, 2 meat, 1 fat, 1 vegetable

Calories per serving: 341
Fat per serving (gm): 12.2
Cholesterol per serving (mg): 62.3

SPAGHETTI SQUASH MARINARA

Spaghetti squash is a large, oblong, yellow summer squash. When cooked, it is removed from the skin in spaghettilike strands.

Yield: 5 servings

1 pound lean ground turkey (12 ounces cooked)
1 large onion, chopped
1 clove garlic, crushed
1 teaspoon salt
1 teaspoon granulated sugar
1 teaspoon chili powder
¾ cup chopped green pepper
⅔ cup water
1 8-ounce can tomato sauce
1 6-ounce can tomato paste
1 spaghetti squash, cut in half lengthwise, seeded and cleaned (8 cups)
2 ounces (½ cup) shredded low-fat cheese (Mozzarella or Cheddar)
¼ cup grated Parmesan cheese

Cook and stir the ground turkey with the onion and garlic in a large nonstick skillet until the turkey is lightly browned and the onion and garlic are limp. Drain. Stir in the salt, sugar, chili powder, green pepper, water, tomato sauce, and tomato paste. Heat to boiling; reduce the heat. Cover and simmer for about 15 minutes.

Meanwhile, fill two saucepans large enough to hold the squash halves with 2 inches of water each; heat to boiling. Place the squash halves in the pans cut-sides down; cover, and simmer until tender (about 20 to 25 minutes). Remove the squash from the pans; allow it to drain thoroughly in a colander. Holding the squash upright, scrape the insides with a fork to release the spaghettilike strands. Pour the squash into a greased 2-quart casserole, top with sauce, and toss. Sprinkle the top with the low-fat and Parmesan cheeses. Bake uncovered in a 375-degree preheated oven until the cheese melts and the sauce is bubbly (about 10 minutes).

Exchanges per serving: 3 meat, 4 vegetable

Calories per serving: 319
Fat per serving (gm): 13.0
Cholesterol per serving (mg): 72.8

SPINACH QUESADILLAS WITH BLACK BEAN SAUCE

These are spicy quesadillas with a cheesy spinach filling. The pasilla chile called for is large, green, resembles a bell pepper, but is cone-shaped. It is mild to medium-hot in flavor. One 4-ounce can of chopped chilies can be substituted, if necessary.

Yield: 4 servings

8 medium cloves garlic, unpeeled
1 medium pasilla chile
½ large bunch spinach
1 tablespoon water
¼ teaspoon salt
4 ounces (1 cup) shredded low-fat Jack cheese
4 6-inch flour tortillas
Olive oil
1 cup Black Bean Sauce (p. 302)
Fresh chopped cilantro for garnish (if desired)

Bake the garlic at 350 degrees for 5 to 10 minutes or until it is soft. Peel and finely chop the garlic; set it aside. Roast the chile over a gas flame until the skin turns black and bubbles. Place it in a plastic bag and seal for 2 to 3 minutes. Take it out and remove the skin under running water. Remove the seeds and stem and finely dice the chile; set it aside. Clean and coarsely chop the spinach leaves. Cook them with the water over medium heat in a large nonstick skillet for 30 seconds. Add the salt, garlic, and chile, and cook until the spinach is fully wilted. Cool slightly; fold in the cheese.

Spread one-quarter of the spinach mixture onto each tortilla. Fold the tortillas in half and place them on a baking sheet. Brush the tops lightly with olive oil; bake for 5 minutes. Heat the Black Bean Sauce until it is hot.

To serve the quesadillas, pour ¼ cup of Black Bean Sauce onto each plate. Place the quesadillas on the prepared plates; sprinkle them with cilantro.

Exchanges per serving (analysis includes Black Bean Sauce): 1 meat,
    2 bread, 1 vegetable, 1 fat

Calories per serving: 292
Fat per serving (gm): 11.1
Cholesterol per serving (mg): 2.3

GARDEN TOSTADA

This makes a perfect luncheon diversion from the sandwich routine.

Yield: 1 serving

⅓ cup cooked or canned pinto beans, drained
1 6-inch flour tortilla, warmed
1 ounce shredded Cheddar cheese
Shredded lettuce
Chopped tomato
Chopped green onion
Salsa
2 tablespoons sour cream

VARIATION Tostada Grande
To above ingredients add:
1 ounce extra-lean ground beef or shredded chicken
⅛ avocado, sliced

Lightly mash the pinto beans with a fork or potato masher; heat them in a microwave oven or a small saucepan until hot. Spread the beans over the tortilla. Top the tortilla with cheese, lettuce, tomato, green onion, salsa, and sour cream.

For the Tostada Grande, spread the meat or chicken over the beans, then add the cheese, lettuce, tomato, green onion, salsa, avocado slices, and sour cream.

Exchanges per serving: 1 high-fat meat, 2 bread, 1 vegetable, 1 fat

Calories per serving: 389
Fat per serving (gm): 18.0
Cholesterol per serving (mg): 42.7

Exchanges per serving (variation): 1 high-fat meat, 1 meat, 2 bread, 1 vegetable, 2 fat

Calories per serving: 502
Fat per serving (gm): 26.3
Cholesterol per serving (mg): 66.3

BLACK 'N RED BEANS

These Cajun-style beans can be served over cooked rice, warmed tortillas, or hearty corn bread.

Yield: 4 servings

½ cup chopped onion
½ cup diced green pepper
1 large clove garlic, minced
1 tablespoon light olive oil
1 15-ounce can red beans, drained and rinsed
1 15-ounce can black beans, drained and rinsed
1 cup beef broth, defatted
¼ teaspoon black pepper
¼ bunch cilantro, chopped
¼ cup chopped celery leaves
2 tablespoons imitation bacon bits
⅛ to ¼ teaspoon red pepper sauce

In a 3-quart saucepan, sauté the onion, green pepper, and garlic in hot oil until tender. Add the red and black beans, beef broth, pepper, cilantro, celery leaves, bacon bits, and red pepper sauce to taste. Bring the mixture to a boil, stirring occasionally. Reduce the heat to low, cover, and simmer until thickened (about 30 minutes).

Exchanges per serving: 1 meat, 2 bread, 1 fat

Calories per serving: 305
Fat per serving (gm): 5.3
Cholesterol per serving (mg): 0

Side Dishes

STIR-FRIED ASPARAGUS WITH OYSTER MUSHROOMS

Yield: four ¾-cup servings

1 pound asparagus, trimmed
2 tablespoons soy sauce
2 teaspoons cornstarch
1 teaspoon granulated sugar
1 tablespoon peanut oil
1 teaspoon grated fresh ginger
1 clove garlic, minced
½ pound oyster mushrooms, sliced (or regular mushrooms)
½ cup chicken broth
1 tablespoon toasted sesame seeds (optional)

To prepare the asparagus, make a diagonal cut through one end of an asparagus spear. Roll the asparagus spear one-quarter turn. Make another diagonal cut ½-inch from the first one. Continue rolling and slicing, leaving the tip whole. Cut all of the asparagus this way. In a small bowl, combine the soy sauce, cornstarch, and sugar until smooth; set aside.

In a 12-inch nonstick skillet, heat the oil over medium-high heat until it is bubbling. Stir-fry the ginger and garlic over high heat for 30 seconds. Add the asparagus and mushrooms and stir-fry for 1 minute, stirring constantly. Reduce the heat to medium, add the chicken broth, and simmer until the vegetables are crisp-tender (3 to 4 minutes). Slowly stir in the soy sauce mixture and cook until the mixture boils and thickens. Spoon the mixture onto a serving dish; top it with sesame seeds.

Exchanges per serving: 2 vegetable, 1 fat

Calories per serving: 103
Fat per serving (gm): 3.6
Cholesterol per serving (mg): 0

BROCCOLI WITH MUSTARD SAUCE

Serve with Grilled Albacore with Herbs (p. 254).

Yield: 4 servings

1½ pounds fresh broccoli
¼ cup nonfat evaporated milk
1 teaspoon dry mustard
½ teaspoon granulated sugar
⅛ teaspoon pepper
2 teaspoons margarine

Remove the large leaves and tough stem ends of the broccoli; wash the broccoli. Make lengthwise ¼-inch gashes in each broccoli stem to allow for even cooking. Steam the broccoli until it is tender (about 12 minutes). Meanwhile, blend the milk, mustard, sugar, and pepper thoroughly. Heat the mixture in a small saucepan over low heat, but do not boil. Transfer the broccoli to a serving dish. Stir in the margarine; top with mustard sauce.

Exchanges per serving: 2 vegetable, ½ fat

Calories per serving: 79
Fat per serving (gm): 2.6
Cholesterol per serving (mg): .6

SLICED CARROTS WITH SNOW PEAS

Yield: eight ½-cup servings

½ pound snow peas (Chinese peas)
4 pieces (about 2 tablespoons) sun-dried tomatoes
1 large clove garlic, halved
1 thin slice fresh ginger
1 tablespoon olive oil
½ teaspoon sesame oil
4 medium-size raw carrots, sliced diagonally

Remove the stems and strings from the snow peas. Place the tomatoes in boiling water for 2 minutes (or follow the package instructions); drain. Slice the tomatoes into thin strips. Sauté the garlic and ginger in the hot olive and sesame oils in a nonstick pan over medium heat for 1 minute. Add the carrots; heat and stir until they are barely tender. Add the snow peas and sliced tomatoes; heat and stir until the vegetables are tender. Add water to the pan if it becomes too dry and the vegetables begin to stick. Remove the garlic and ginger before serving.

Exchanges per serving: 1 vegetable, ½ fat

Calories per serving: 49
Fat per serving (gm): 2.2
Cholesterol per serving (mg): 0

STIR-FRIED BROCCOLI AMANDINE

This dish is an excellent source of calcium, vitamins A and C, and fiber.

Yield: 4 servings

1 tablespoon slivered almonds
1 pound fresh broccoli
1 tablespoon peanut oil
1 clove garlic, crushed
¼ teaspoon salt
1 teaspoon rice wine or dry sherry
¼ teaspoon granulated sugar
3 tablespoons chicken broth
¼ cup water

Brown the almonds in a nonstick skillet over low heat; set them aside. Remove the large leaves and trim the tough stalk ends of the broccoli. Discard the leaves and ends, and rinse the broccoli. Cut it into 2-inch flowerets and 2-inch-long by ¼-inch-thick pieces of stalk. Heat the oil in a nonstick skillet over high heat; cook the garlic stirring, until it is golden (about 30 seconds). Add the broccoli-stalk pieces and salt; cook and stir for 30 seconds. Add the flowerets; cook and stir for 1 minute. Add the wine, sugar, broth, and water. Reduce the heat to medium-low and cook until the water is almost gone and the broccoli is tender-crisp, stirring frequently (3 to 5 minutes). Transfer the broccoli to a serving dish; top with the slivered almonds.

Exchanges per serving: 1 vegetable, 1 fat

Calories per serving: 79
Fat per serving (gm): 5.0
Cholesterol per serving (mg): 0

SWEET-AND-SOUR LEEKS

Known in Europe as the "asparagus of the poor," the leek is actually a giant scallion that is sweet and mild in taste. Select specimens with bright green tops, white bulbs, and pliable stalks.

Yield: four ½-cup servings

2 pounds leeks (about 4)
1 thin slice fresh ginger
1 clove garlic, halved
2 teaspoons margarine
1 teaspoon sesame oil
2 tablespoons brown sugar
¼ cup cider vinegar
1 teaspoon soy sauce
½ cup water
1 tablespoon toasted sesame seeds

Remove the outer leaves from the leeks. Slice off the roots and all but 2 inches of the leek greens. Cut the leeks in half lengthwise and then in half again. Rinse them well to remove grit.

In a large nonstick skillet, cook the leeks, ginger, and garlic in margarine and oil over low to medium heat, stirring occasionally and adding a little water if the leeks begin to stick. Cook until soft (about 15 to 20 minutes). Stir in the sugar, vinegar, soy sauce, and ½ cup water. Bring the liquid to a boil, then cover—but with lid cracked—and simmer, stirring occasionally, until most of the liquid is gone (about 10 minutes). Remove the garlic and ginger; top with sesame seeds.

Exchanges per serving: 1 vegetable, 1 fat

Calories per serving: 76
Fat per serving (gm): 3.1
Cholesterol per serving (mg): 0

COUSCOUS

Couscous is a North African staple made from hard durum wheat (semolina) that has been processed into tiny nuggets. It is yellow in color, varies in grain size, and can be purchased precooked.

Yield: six ½-cup servings

1 cup couscous
1 teaspoon olive oil
¼ cup golden raisins
2 tablespoons finely chopped cilantro
½ teaspoon salt
½ teaspoon ground cumin

Place the couscous in a couscousière or steamer over boiling water. If a steamer is used it should be lined with cheesecloth to keep the couscous grains from falling through the perforations. Cook the couscous until it is fluffy and just tender, according to the package instructions, but do not add additional ingredients. Place the couscous in a saucepan; stir in the oil, raisins, cilantro, salt, and cumin. Cover and heat through over a low flame, stirring occasionally.

Exchanges per serving: 1 bread, ½ fruit

Calories per serving: 117
Fat per serving (gm): .1
Cholesterol per serving (mg): 0

DELICATE ANGEL PASTA

This would be perfect with veal or sautéed chicken or fish.

Yield: six ½-cup servings

9 ounces fresh angel hair pasta (or 6 ounces dry pasta) (about 3 cups cooked)
4 teaspoons olive oil
2 small shallots, minced
3 tablespoons chopped parsley
¼ teaspoon salt
Dash pepper
1 tablespoon margarine
1 ounce sliced olives (½ of a 2¼-ounce can, drained)

Prepare the pasta in a large saucepan according to the package instructions; drain. Loosen and place on heated dish. Meanwhile, in a nonstick pan, heat the olive oil; add the shallots and parsley and cook over medium heat until the shallots are tender. Pour over pasta; add the salt, pepper, margarine, and olives. Heat through, gently tossing with two forks. Serve immediately.

Exchanges per serving: 1 bread, 1 fat

Calories per serving: 157
Fat per serving (gm): 5.9
Cholesterol per serving (mg): 0

POTATOES MEDITERRANEAN

These potatoes are very appealing when served right from the skillet.

Yield: 4 servings

3 medium potatoes with skins
2 teaspoons margarine
2 teaspoons olive oil
1 shallot, chopped
Salt and pepper to taste
4 tablespoons sherry
2 tablespoons lemon juice
2 tablespoons finely chopped fresh parsley
2 tablespoons capers

Slice the potatoes in half lengthwise; then cut them into ¼-inch slices. Heat the margarine and oil in a large nonstick pan; add the potatoes and the shallot. Cook until the shallot is tender, stirring frequently. Add the salt and pepper. Cook until the potatoes are browned, stirring frequently. Add the sherry and lemon juice, cover, and cook over low to medium heat until tender (7 to 10 minutes), stirring once. Stir in the parsley; top with the capers. Cook for 1 minute; serve.

Exchanges per serving: 1 bread, 1 fat

Calories per serving: 106
Fat per serving (gm): 4.3
Cholesterol per serving (mg): 0

CHEDDAR POTATOES

Tender, baked strips of potato are baked in a cheesy sauce.

Yield: 6 servings

1 pound, 5 ounces (about 4 medium) potatoes
Pepper
¾ teaspoon garlic salt
2 tablespoons chopped parsley
1 small onion, minced
3 ounces thinly sliced low-fat Cheddar cheese
¾ cup evaporated whole milk, at room temperature

Wash and pare the potatoes, removing any eyes. Cut them into lengthwise strips, ¼- to ⅜-inch wide. Arrange half of the potato strips in a greased 2-quart casserole, topping them with a dash of pepper and half each of the garlic salt, parsley, onion, and cheese. Repeat layers of potato, pepper, garlic salt, parsley, and onion, but not cheese. Pour the milk over all. Lay the remaining cheese slices on top. Cover and cook at 350 degrees until the potatoes are tender (about 60 minutes). If a crusty top is desired, remove the cover for the last 15 minutes.

Exchanges per serving: 1 bread, ¼ milk, ½ meat

Calories per serving: 142
Fat per serving (gm): 4.7
Cholesterol per serving (mg): 10.5

SWEET RUTABAGAS

Often called yellow or Swedish turnips, rutabagas are actually unrelated to the smaller, more perishable root. Choose ones that are heavy for their size and free of cracked or bruised skins.

Yield: eight ½-cup servings

2 pounds rutabagas (about 2)
¼ cup packed light brown sugar
¼ cup nonfat evaporated milk, at room temperature
1 tablespoon plus 1 teaspoon margarine, softened
1½ teaspoons ground ginger
1 teaspoon salt
¼ teaspoon pepper
Snipped chives for garnish

Quarter and peel the rutabagas, then cut them into ½-inch cubes. In a large saucepan, boil 1 inch of water; add the rutabagas and return to a boil. Cover and simmer over low heat until the rutabagas are fork-tender (10 to 15 minutes); drain. Place the rutabagas in a large mixing bowl. Add the sugar, milk, margarine, ginger, salt, and pepper, and beat with a mixer at low speed until smooth and fluffy. Return the mixture to the saucepan and reheat, if necessary. Garnish with snipped chives.

Exchanges per serving: 1 vegetable, ½ fruit, ½ fat

Calories per serving: 91
Fat per serving (gm): 2.2
Cholesterol per serving (mg): .3

SPANISH-STYLE RICE

Try this for a zesty change of pace from white rice.

Yield: nine ½-cup servings

Nonstick cooking spray
1 teaspoon light olive oil
1 clove garlic, finely chopped
1 small onion, chopped (about ⅔ cup)
⅔ cup finely chopped green pepper
2 cups water
1 cup uncooked rice
1 teaspoon salt
¼ teaspoon pepper
1 16-ounce can stewed tomatoes, broken up
1 teaspoon chili powder
¾ teaspoon dried oregano leaves

Heat the olive oil in a 3-quart saucepan sprayed with nonstick cooking spray. Add the garlic, onion, and green pepper, and cook over low to medium heat until tender, stirring occasionally. Do not brown. Stir in the remaining ingredients. Heat to boiling; reduce the heat. Cover and simmer, stirring occasionally, until the rice is tender (about 30 minutes).

Exchanges per serving: 1 bread, 1 vegetable

Calories per serving: 117
Fat per serving (gm): 1.8
Cholesterol per serving (mg): 0

SAVORY ALMOND RICE

This would be a tasty accompaniment to a simple entrée, such as Cornish Game Hens (p. 272).

Yield: twelve ⅔-cup servings

1 cup brown rice
1 package Rice A Roni (Fried Rice with Almonds flavor)
4 cups hot water
1 clove garlic, minced
¼ cup slivered, blanched almonds
½ cup raisins
2 tomatoes, chopped
2 green onions, sliced

Brown the brown rice in a 2-quart nonstick skillet over a medium flame. Add the contents of the Rice A Roni package (except seasoning packet) and brown lightly. Pour in the hot water and garlic and bring to a boil. Reduce to a simmer and add the almonds, raisins, tomato, green onion, and seasoning packet. Stir lightly, then cover and simmer for 15 to 20 minutes.

Exchanges per serving: 2 bread

Calories per serving: 159
Fat per serving (gm): 2.1
Cholesterol per serving (mg): 0

WILD RICE WITH FENNEL

Wild rice is actually the seed of a water grass, not a grain at all. It is long, grayish-brown in color, and has a strong, nutty flavor.

Yield: nine ½-cup servings

Nonstick cooking spray
1 tablespoon olive oil
2 cups sliced mushrooms
1 cup chopped fennel bulb
1 cup wild rice
2 cups water
1 chicken bouillon cube
2 tablespoons chopped parsley

Heat the oil in a 2-quart saucepan sprayed with nonstick cooking spray. Add the mushrooms and fennel and cook them over medium heat for 7 minutes, stirring frequently. Rinse the wild rice thoroughly under running water. Add the wild rice, 2 cups of water, bouillon cube, and chopped parsley to the vegetables. Heat to boiling over high heat. Reduce the heat to low, cover, and simmer 30 to 45 minutes or just until kernels pull open. Uncover; fluff with fork. Simmer 5 additional minutes. Drain excess liquid (it should be moist, not dry).

Exchanges per serving: 1 bread

Calories per serving: 84
Fat per serving (gm): 1.8
Cholesterol per serving (mg): 0

STUFFED TABLE QUEEN SQUASH

Table queen squash looks like small acorn squash.

Yield: 4 servings

2 table queen squash
1 cup peeled, diced apple
¼ cup raisins
1 tablespoon brown sugar
1 teaspoon ground cinnamon

Remove the bottoms of the squash so that they will stand upright, taking care not to cut through to the insides. Bake the squash on a sheet at 375 degrees until they are soft when pressed (about 40 minutes). Let them cool slightly.

Mix the diced apple, raisins, brown sugar, and cinnamon. Cook this mixture uncovered in a saucepan over a medium flame, stirring occasionally, until the apple is tender and most of the juice is gone (about 10 minutes).

Remove the tops of the squash, again being careful not to cut through to the insides. Cut the squash in half crosswise. Remove the seeds, and fill the squash halves with the apple mixture. Place the squash on a foil-lined baking sheet or in a greased casserole dish, cover, and bake until heated through (5 to 10 minutes).

Exchanges per serving: 1 bread, ½ fruit

Calories per serving: 115
Fat per serving (gm): .3
Cholesterol per serving (mg): 0

PETITE VEGETABLES IN LEMON SAUCE

Yield: 4 servings

⅔ cup baby carrots
½ cup baby corn
½ cup petite onions, peeled
½ tablespoon margarine
1 teaspoon cornstarch
¼ cup lemon juice
1 4-ounce jar petite marinated asparagus, drained
½ teaspoon lemon zest
¼ teaspoon salt
¼ cup water

Steam the carrots and corn until they are just tender; set them aside. In a nonstick pan over a medium flame, sauté the onions in margarine until they are tender, but do not brown. Add the cornstarch to the lemon juice, and blend until smooth; set the mixture aside. Add the asparagus to the onions and stir; then stir in the lemon zest, salt, and steamed vegetables. Remove the pan from the heat; stir in the lemon-cornstarch mixture and water. Heat over a medium flame until the sauce is thick and the vegetables are heated through.

Exchanges per serving: 1 vegetable, ½ fat

Calories per serving: 55
Fat per serving (gm): 2.0
Cholesterol per serving (mg): 0

SKILLET TURNIPS

Yield: six ½-cup servings

½ pound (1⅔ cups) peeled and cubed turnips
½ pound (1⅔ cups) peeled and sliced parsnips
1 tablespoon olive oil
1 medium onion, chopped
½ teaspoon salt
⅛ teaspoon pepper
3 tablespoons fresh chopped parsley

In a 3-quart saucepan, boil 1 inch of water. Add the turnips, cover, and cook over medium-low heat for 5 minutes. Add the parsnips and cook until the vegetables are just tender (about 8 minutes); drain. In a 12-inch nonstick skillet, heat the oil. Add the onion and cook over medium heat until tender. Stir in the turnips, parsnips, salt, and pepper. Cook, stirring frequently, 3 minutes. Add parsley and turnip, heat slightly, and continue cooking and stirring until lightly browned, 3 to 4 minutes.

Exchanges per serving: 1 vegetable, ½ fat

Calories per serving: 64
Fat per serving (gm): 2.5
Cholesterol per serving (mg): 0

Dressings, Dips, Sauces, and Spreads

CHEDDAR CHEESE SPREAD

This spread livens up celery sticks, apple slices, or low-fat crackers (rye crisp bread, Melba toast, bagel chips, etc).

Yield: about sixteen 2-tablespoon servings

1¼ cups low-fat cottage cheese
3 ounces (¾ cup) grated sharp Cheddar cheese
1 teaspoon Worcestershire sauce
⅛ teaspoon garlic salt
1 teaspoon prepared mustard
Pinch black pepper
Pinch cayenne pepper

In a blender or food processor, blend all of the ingredients together until smooth. Refrigerate for several hours in a covered container before serving.

Exchanges per serving: ½ meat

Calories per serving: 35
Fat per serving (gm): 2.0
Cholesterol per serving (mg): 6.4

BLACK BEAN SAUCE

Serve this sauce with Spinach Quesadillas (p. 282), or with other Mexican or Caribbean dishes. Alter the heat of the sauce by adjusting the amount of chile used.

Yield: about twelve ¼-cup servings

1 cup dry black beans
2 tablespoons chopped onion
3 medium cloves garlic, chopped
½ teaspoon salt (omit if salted broth is used)
2 to 2½ cups chicken broth, defatted
½ to 1 teaspoon pureed canned chiles
½ bunch cilantro, chopped

Soak the black beans in water all day or overnight. Drain and rinse the beans; set them aside. Cook the onion and garlic over medium heat in a nonstick saucepan until they are tender, stirring frequently. Add the beans and salt; cook for 1 minute. Add enough chicken broth to just cover the beans, and bring to a boil. Reduce the heat, cover, and simmer until the beans are tender (1 to 1½ hours). Add more broth, if necessary, to keep the beans covered while cooking. Cool slightly.

Spoon beans with a slotted spoon into a blender or food processor and blend them until smooth. Thin sauce to desired consistency with a little lemon juice or chicken broth. Add the pureed chiles to taste and the cilantro. Reheat sauce to serve, or refrigerate in covered container for later use (sauce can also be frozen).

Exchanges per serving: 1 bread

Calories per serving: 62
Fat per serving (gm): .3
Cholesterol per serving (mg): 0

MUSHROOM SAUCE

Use this creamy sauce as a topping for beef, poultry, or fresh pasta.

Yield: seven ¼-cup servings

1½ tablespoons margarine
2 small shallots, minced
1½ tablespoons cornstarch
½ cup chicken broth
¾ cup nonfat milk
1 4-ounce can sliced mushrooms, drained
¼ cup dry sherry
2 tablespoons chopped fresh parsley
½ tablespoon Worcestershire sauce
¼ teaspoon salt
Dash pepper
Parsley for garnish

In a small nonstick saucepan, heat the margarine. Add the shallots and sauté them until tender. Stir in the cornstarch; blend until smooth. Remove the pan from the heat. Stir in the broth, milk, mushrooms, sherry, parsley, Worcestershire sauce, salt, and pepper. Cook over medium-low heat, stirring constantly, until the mixture thickens and begins to boil gently. Remove the pan from the heat. Pour the sauce over meat, poultry, or pasta; garnish with fresh parsley.

Exchanges per serving: 1 vegetable, ½ fat

Calories per serving: 47
Fat per serving (gm): 2.7
Cholesterol per serving (mg): 3.3

CRAZY GARLIC SPREAD

Garlic has a very mild flavor when cooked. In this form, it's also a treat to eat!

Yield: about 10 servings (1 clove/serving)

1 large head garlic, unpeeled
½ tablespoon margarine
1 tablespoon water

Trim the roots from the garlic head to flatten the bottom. Stand the garlic on a sheet of aluminum foil. Top it with margarine. Bring up the sides of the foil; pour the water onto foil. Fold up the foil around the garlic, and close the top and side edges tightly. Bake the garlic at 350 degrees until the cloves are very soft and mushy (60 to 70 minutes). To serve, take a clove between your fingers and squeeze garlic paste through its skin onto a slice of bread; discard the skin. Spread the paste as you would butter.

Exchanges per serving: free exchange

Calories per serving: 6
Fat per serving (gm): .6
Cholesterol per serving (mg): 0

CUCUMBER SAUCE

Here's a delicious low-fat accompaniment to fish.

Yield: about three ¼-cup servings

3 tablespoons plain low-fat yogurt
¼ teaspoon celery salt
¼ teaspoon pepper
Dash salt
½ teaspoon lemon juice
½ cup finely diced cucumber, well drained

Blend the yogurt with the celery salt, pepper, and salt until smooth. Add the lemon juice and cucumber, one at a time, until mixed.

Exchanges per serving: free exchange

Calories per serving: 12
Fat per serving (gm): .3
Cholesterol per serving (mg): .9

GINGER DIP

This tangy dip has an oriental flavor.

Yield: twelve 2-tablespoon servings

¾ cup plain low-fat yogurt
¼ cup reduced-calorie mayonnaise
2 ounces water chestnuts, chopped
1 tablespoon chopped green onion
1 tablespoon minced shallot
1 tablespoon grated fresh ginger
2 teaspoons soy sauce

Stir the yogurt in a small bowl until it is smooth. Stir in the mayonnaise; then add the remaining ingredients and mix well. Chill for several hours before serving.

Exchanges per serving: ½ fat

Calories per serving: 28
Fat per serving (gm): 1.7
Cholesterol per serving (mg): 2.4

GINGER SAUCE

An elegant dessert sauce, this can be ready to serve in minutes. Use it over Kiwi Cups (p. 326) or over yogurt or angel food cake.

Yield: about ⅔ cup (ten 1-tablespoon servings)

½ cup plus 1 tablespoon granulated sugar
1 tablespoon cornstarch
⅔ cup water
1 tablespoon lemon juice
¼ teaspoon ground ginger

Mix the sugar and cornstarch in a small saucepan. Stir in the remaining ingredients. Heat to boiling over low-medium heat, stirring constantly. Boil and stir for 1 minute.

Exchanges per serving: 1 fruit

Calories per serving: 59
Fat per serving (gm): 0
Cholesterol per serving (mg): 0

MARINARA SAUCE

This is a tangy, meatless, low-fat sauce for pasta and other Italian dishes.

Yield: about six ½-cup servings

1 tablespoon olive oil
1 small onion, chopped
1 clove garlic, minced
1 16-ounce can tomatoes, including liquid
1 6-ounce can tomato paste
1 teaspoon granulated sugar
2 tablespoons fresh chopped basil leaves
1 tablespoon fresh chopped parsley
½ teaspoon salt

In a 2-quart nonstick saucepan, heat the olive oil. Add the onion and garlic, and cook over medium-low heat until tender. Stir in the tomatoes with their liquid, the tomato paste, sugar, basil, parsley, and salt. Heat to boiling, then reduce the heat, cover, and simmer for 20 to 30 minutes. Stir occasionally and break up the tomatoes.

Exchanges per serving: 1 vegetable, ½ fat

Calories per serving: 69
Fat per serving (gm): 2.8
Cholesterol per serving (mg): 0

MEDIUM WHITE SAUCE

Also known as béchamel, *this sauce is lower in fat than the traditional version. It is delicious over hot cooked vegetables, pasta, or seafood.*

Yield: about four ¼-cup servings

1 tablespoon cornstarch
½ cup nonfat milk
½ cup nonfat evaporated milk
1 tablespoon plus 1 teaspoon margarine
¼ teaspoon salt
⅛ teaspoon white pepper
Dash paprika

In a small saucepan, blend the cornstarch into the nonfat milk until smooth. Stir in the evaporated milk. Add the margarine, salt, pepper, and paprika. Bring to a boil over medium heat, stirring constantly; boil for 1 minute.

Exchanges per serving: ½ milk, 1 fat

Calories per serving: 77
Fat per serving (gm): 3.9
Cholesterol per serving (mg): 1.7

ORANGE SAUCE

Serve this sauce with Holiday Gingerbread (p. 319), or as a topping for fresh fruit.

Yield: about 1 cup (eight 2-tablespoon servings)

¼ cup granulated sugar
1 tablespoon cornstarch
½ teaspoon ground cinnamon
⅛ teaspoon ground ginger
⅛ teaspoon ground cloves
1 cup orange juice
1 teaspoon grated lemon zest

Blend the sugar, cornstarch, cinnamon, ginger, and cloves in a small saucepan. Slowly stir in the orange juice and lemon zest over medium heat. Cook and stir until the sauce is thickened and begins to boil; remove from heat. Serve warm.

Exchanges per serving: ½ fruit

Calories per serving: 40
Fat per serving (gm): .1
Cholesterol per serving (mg): 0

SALSA CRUDA

The tomatillo (toe-mah-TEE-yo) looks like a small green tomato and is covered with a dry, papery skin or husk that is easily removed. Choose fruits that are firm and have close-fitting skins.

Yield: about 1½ cups (twelve 2-tablespoon servings)

5 medium tomatillos
1 small onion, chopped
1 chile pepper (serrano or jalapeño), seeded and finely chopped
2 medium cloves garlic, minced
½ teaspoon salt
5 cilantro sprigs, chopped
Juice of ½ medium lemon (or 1 small lime)

Peel off the husks from the tomatillos; wash the fruit thoroughly to remove the sticky substance near the stems. Remove the stems. Place the tomatillos in a small pan and barely cover them with cold water. Poach them gently—do not boil—until they are tender (12 to 15 minutes). Chop the tomatillos; combine them in a serving bowl with the remaining ingredients and mix well. Cover them and refrigerate until served. (To prevent burning, wear rubber gloves while handling jalapeño, wash hands immediately after touching it, and do not touch face with hands.)

Exchanges per serving: free exchange

Calories per serving: 18
Fat per serving (gm): .1
Cholesterol per serving (mg): 0

SHRIMP 'N CHEESE SPREAD

Slightly sweet, with a mild shrimp flavor.

Yield: eight 2-tablespoon servings

2 tablespoons nonfat milk
3 ounces reduced-calorie Laughing Cow Pasteurized Process Cheese Spread,
    softened
¼ cup reduced-calorie mayonnaise
6–7 drops red pepper sauce
Dash of Worcestershire Sauce
1 green onion, chopped
1 4½-ounce can tiny peeled shrimp, drained
Paprika

With mixer, blend milk, a little at a time, into cheese spread in a small
mixing bowl. Add mayonnaise, red pepper sauce, and Worcestershire
Sauce and beat until smooth. Stir in green onion; then shrimp. Sprinkle
with paprika lightly. Cover and refrigerate at least one hour.

Exchanges per serving: ½ meat, ½ fat

Calories per serving: 56
Fat per serving (gm): 3.0
Cholesterol per serving (mg): 27.1

YOGURT CHEESE

Here's a great low-fat, high-calcium substitute for cream cheese! Spread it on bagels or muffins, or mix it with a little honey and serve it with fresh fruit. It is the "cheese" in Kiwi Cheesecake (p. 332).

Yield: about 1 cup (eight 2-tablespoon servings)

2 cups plain nonfat yogurt

Place the yogurt in the middle of a triple-thickness square of cheese-cloth, large enough to be hung. Bring the four corners of the cheese-cloth together and tie them. Suspend the bundle where it can drip, or place it inside a funnel suspended in a 1-quart measuring cup or other large container. Refrigerate the yogurt and let it drip for 8 to 12 hours, periodically squeezing the bundle to drain excess fluid. When the yogurt is ready, it should be the consistency of cream cheese. Transfer it from the cheesecloth to a covered container and refrigerate until used.

Exchanges per serving: ½ milk

Calories per serving: 32
Fat per serving (gm): .1
Cholesterol per serving (mg): 1.0

Breads

HAWAIIAN TOAST

French toast for the connoisseur. Serve it plain or with powdered sugar, warm applesauce, maple syrup, or flavored yogurt.

Yield: 4 servings

¼ cup nonfat dry milk
½ cup water
6 large egg whites, slightly beaten
3 tablespoons granulated sugar
½ teaspoon vanilla
⅛ teaspoon ground cinnamon
⅛ teaspoon ground nutmeg
Nonstick cooking spray
4 ¾-inch slices King's Hawaiian bread (or other sweet, soft bread), halved and allowed to dry slightly

Add the nonfat dry milk to the water and blend until smooth. Pour the milk into a mixing bowl. Add the egg whites, sugar, vanilla, cinnamon, and nutmeg, and mix well. Heat a skillet sprayed with nonstick cooking spray. Dip the bread slices, one at a time, into the egg mixture, turning them to coat both sides well; do not soak. Place the slices immediately in the skillet, and cook them over medium heat until they are browned on both sides, turning once.

Exchanges per serving: 2 bread, ½ meat

Calories per serving: 224
Fat per serving (gm): 2.6
Cholesterol per serving (mg): 51.8

OAT BRAN MUFFINS

These are a good source of cholesterol-lowering fiber.

Yield: 12 muffins (1 muffin/serving)

1 cup whole-wheat flour
1½ cups oat bran
2½ teaspoons baking powder
1 teaspoon salt
¼ teaspoon baking soda
⅓ cup brown sugar, packed
½ cup nonfat dry milk
1 teaspoon ground cinnamon
½ teaspoon ground nutmeg
3 tablespoons olive oil
1 cup plain nonfat yogurt
2 egg whites
1 cup unsweetened applesauce

Preheat the oven to 400 degrees.

In a large bowl, mix the dry ingredients together thoroughly. In a separate bowl, beat the oil, yogurt, and egg whites together. Blend in the applesauce. Add the wet ingredients to the dry ingredients, and blend just until moistened; do not overmix. Grease the bottoms of 12 muffin tins; pour the batter into the tins. Bake for 20 minutes.

Exchanges per serving: 1½ bread, 1 fat

Calories per serving: 169
Fat per serving (gm): 4.3
Cholesterol per serving (mg): .9

TROPICAL PUFF PANCAKE

Try these as a special dish for Sunday brunch.

Yield: 3 servings

½ cup egg white (about 4 egg whites)
1 egg
⅔ cup all-purpose flour
½ cup nonfat evaporated milk
1 teaspoon baking powder
1 teaspoon powdered ginger
4 teaspoons margarine, melted
Nonstick cooking spray
1½ cups sliced feijoa (or kiwi, or other sliced tropical fruit)
2 tablespoons powdered sugar
3 slices papaya

Preheat the oven to 450 degrees. Lightly beat the egg white and egg in a medium-size bowl. Gradually beat the flour into the eggs; do not overbeat. Stir in the milk, baking powder, ginger, and melted margarine. Spray a 9-inch ovenproof skillet or round cake pan with nonstick cooking spray. Pour the batter into the pan and bake for 20 minutes. The pancake will puff up on the sides. Spoon the fruit into the center of the pancake, and sprinkle with powdered sugar. Loosen the pancake from the pan with a wide spatula, and cut it into wedges with a sharp knife. Serve immediately; garnish with papaya.

Exchanges per serving: ½ meat, 1 bread, 1 fruit, 1 fat, ½ milk

Calories per serving: 323
Fat per serving (gm): 7.9
Cholesterol per serving (mg): 93

MULTI-GRAIN BREAD

The goodness of oats, whole wheat, and corn in one loaf.

Yield: 8 servings

⅓ cup cornmeal
⅓ cup whole-wheat flour
½ cup rolled oats
1 tablespoon baking powder
½ teaspoon salt
4 egg whites
2 tablespoons light olive oil
⅓ cup honey
1 cup buttermilk

Blend cornmeal, flour, oats, baking powder, and salt in a large bowl. In a separate bowl, mix egg whites, olive oil, honey, and buttermilk. Add the liquid ingredients to the dry ones, stirring only until dry ingredients are moistened; do not overmix. Pour the batter into a greased 9-inch cake pan and bake at 350 degrees until a toothpick inserted in the center comes out clean, about 35 minutes. Serve warm.

Exchanges per serving: 1 bread, 1 fat

Calories per serving: 148
Fat per serving (gm): 4.3
Cholesterol per serving (mg): 1.1

CHI CHI BANANA MUFFINS

Like other trendy jumbo muffins, these are not lacking in calories, even though they are quite low in fat. Savor one with a friend or save half for an evening snack, if weight control is your goal.

Yield: 8 muffins (1 muffin/serving)

2 cups all-purpose flour
1 cup quick-cooking oats
1 tablespoon plus 1 teaspoon baking powder
¾ teaspoon salt
1¼ cups mashed bananas (3 to 4 small ripe bananas)
⅓ cup honey
2 tablespoons vegetable oil
2 egg whites
⅓ cup nonfat milk
½ teaspoon vanilla extract
½ cup dried fruit (raisins, finely chopped apricots, etc.)

Preheat oven to 400 degrees. Grease eight 3-by-1½-inch muffin cups. Combine the flour, oats, baking powder, and salt in a large mixing bowl. In a separate bowl combine the mashed bananas, honey, oil, egg whites, milk, and vanilla, and blend. Add the banana mixture to dry ingredients all at once and stir just until dry ingredients are moistened. Batter will be lumpy. Scrape the bowl and spoon. Fold in the dried fruit. Fill muffin cups with batter. Bake until a toothpick inserted in the center comes out clean, 25 to 30 minutes. Immediately remove the muffins from the pan.

Exchanges per serving: 2 bread, 2 fruit, 1 fat

Calories per serving: 291
Fat per serving (gm): 4.6
Cholesterol per serving (mg): .2

HOLIDAY GINGERBREAD

*Remembered particularly at holiday time, this healthful, low-fat ginger-
bread can readily be enjoyed throughout the year.*

Yield: 12 servings

1 cup sifted whole-wheat flour
1 cup sifted all-purpose flour
½ teaspoon salt
1 teaspoon baking soda
1 teaspoon baking powder
1 tablespoon grated fresh ginger, or 1 teaspoon ground ginger
1 teaspoon ground cinnamon
1 egg, beaten
3 tablespoons light olive oil
¾ cup molasses
¼ cup honey
1 cup buttermilk

Preheat the oven to 325 degrees. In a large mixing bowl, stir the
wheat flour, all-purpose flour, salt, baking soda, baking powder, ginger, and cinnamon together. In a separate bowl, combine the egg, oil,
molasses, honey, and buttermilk. Stir the liquid ingredients into the dry
ones, just until blended. Pour the batter into a lightly greased
8-inch square baking pan. Bake until a toothpick inserted near the
center comes out clean, about 50 minutes. Serve with Orange Sauce
(p. 310), if desired.

Exchanges per serving: 1 bread, 1 fruit, 1 fat
Exchanges per serving (with sauce): 1 bread, 1½ fruit, 1 fat

Calories per serving: 185; with sauce, 225
Fat per serving (gm): 4.0; with sauce, 4.1
Cholesterol per serving (mg): 23.0; with sauce, 23.0

GARLIC BREAD

Yield: 4 servings

4 1-ounce slices Italian bread
4 teaspoons margarine
½ teaspoon garlic salt

Spread each slice of bread with margarine; sprinkle it with garlic salt. Wrap the slices in foil and bake them at 350 degrees until warm (about 15 minutes).

Exchanges per serving: 1 bread, 1 fat

Calories per serving: 118
Fat per serving (gm): 4.1
Cholesterol per serving (mg): .3

Desserts

COUNTRY CLASSIC COOKIES

Everyone loves chocolate, but for those trying to limit their fat intake, it is usually taboo. These cookies can be enjoyed without worry, however; they're low in fat, high in fiber, and cholesterol-free!

Yield: 4 dozen (¾–1 ounce each)

1 cup packed light brown sugar
½ cup light corn syrup
¼ cup light olive oil
¾ cup plain nonfat yogurt
1 teaspoon vanilla
4 cups quick-cooking oats
⅔ cup oat bran
1¾ cups sifted whole-wheat flour
½ teaspoon baking soda
¾ teaspoon salt
2½ teaspoons baking powder
3 ounces (½ cup) chocolate chips, chopped
Nonstick cooking spray

Preheat the oven to 350 degrees.

Combine the brown sugar, corn syrup, olive oil, yogurt, and vanilla in a large mixing bowl. Stir in the oats and oat bran. In a separate bowl, mix the flour, baking soda, salt, and baking powder. Add the dry ingredients to the liquid mixture, and stir until the dry ingredients are dissolved. (The dough will be stiff.) Stir in the chocolate-chip pieces. Drop the dough by spoonfuls onto baking sheets sprayed with nonstick cooking spray; flatten the cookies with the bottom of a glass dipped in water. Bake until the cookies are lightly browned on the bottom (9 to 11 minutes).

Exchanges per serving (1 cookie): 1 bread, ½ fat

Calories per serving: 94
Fat per serving (gm): 2.4
Cholesterol per serving (mg): .1

POACHED PEARS

This dessert is sure to impress—and it's low in calories, too!

Yield: 6 servings

6 small pears
Juice of 1 lemon
¼ cup water
2 cups dry red wine
1 cup granulated sugar
1 2-inch stick cinnamon
2 cloves
Mint leaves for garnish

Peel the pears without removing their stems. Combine the lemon juice and water. Dip the pears into the lemon-water to prevent browning; discard the lemon-water. Heat the wine, sugar, cinnamon, and cloves in a small saucepan, stirring constantly, until the sugar is dissolved and the mixture boils. Reduce the heat and add the pears. Simmer, uncovered, until the pears are soft but not mushy when pierced with a sharp knife. Cool the pears in the syrup until they are lukewarm; discard the cinnamon and cloves.

Spoon a little syrup onto six dessert plates. Remove the pears from the saucepan; set them in the center of the plates. Spoon more syrup onto the pears. Garnish them with mint leaves. Serve warm or chilled. (Extra syrup can be refrigerated in a covered container for later use as a topping for ice milk, frozen yogurt, or fruit salad.)

Exchanges per serving: 2 fruit

Calories per serving: 142
Fat per serving (gm): .6
Cholesterol per serving (mg): 0

ORANGE SORBET

This is a light, refreshing dessert.

Yield: eight ½-cup servings

Grated zest of 1 orange
1½ cups water
1 cup granulated sugar
2 cups fresh orange juice
1 cup orange-flavored mineral water
3 large oranges
Mint leaves for garnish

In a medium-size saucepan, simmer the orange zest with the water and sugar for 20 minutes; cool. Pour the sugar water through a strainer into a medium-size bowl, reserving the zest for later. To the sugar water, add the orange juice and mineral water. Pour the mixture into the canister of an ice cream maker; freeze according to the manufacturer's instructions for sorbet. Fold in the zest just before the sorbet firmly freezes. (If an ice cream maker is unavailable, the sorbet may be successfully made by freezing over night in a metal bowl.)

Cut the oranges in half between the blossom and stem ends; peel or cut out the fruit, leaving the skins intact. Slash off the end of each half so that it will stand upright, being careful not to cut through the skin. Just before serving, fill the "cups" with sorbet; garnish with mint leaves.

Exchanges per serving: 3 fruit

Calories per serving: 174
Fat per serving (gm): .2
Cholesterol per serving (mg): 0

EASY PLUM-AND-HONEY BAKE

Satisfy your brunch guest's sweet tooth with this dessert and forego the fat and calories of the traditional coffee cake.

Yield: 6 servings

1 16-ounce can whole plums, packed in water or in their own juice
1 cup Bisquick
⅓ cup nonfat evaporated milk
2 egg whites
¼ cup honey
1 tablespoon margarine, softened
½ teaspoon vanilla extract
¼ cup Grapenuts cereal

Preheat the oven to 350 degrees. Drain the plums well; pat them dry with paper towels. Slice the plums, remove the pits, and chop them; set them aside.

   In a mixing bowl, combine the Bisquick, milk, egg whites, honey, margarine, and vanilla. With the mixer at low speed, beat the ingredients just until blended, constantly scraping the bowl with a rubber spatula. Beat 2 minutes at medium speed, occasionally scraping the bowl. Fold the plums and cereal into the batter. Spread the batter into a greased 9-inch pie pan. Bake for 25 to 30 minutes, until a toothpick inserted in the center comes out clean.

Exchanges per serving: 1 fruit, 1½ bread, 1 fat

Calories per serving: 218
Fat per serving (gm): 4.7
Cholesterol per serving (mg): 5.0

OLD-FASHIONED APPLE CRISP

This long-forgotten treat from days gone by can be returned to your active recipe file. Its homey taste and aroma will bring back fond memories, and its low-fat, high-fiber content is great for you, too!

Yield: 9 servings

4 cups sliced tart apples (about 3 medium apples)
½ cup packed light brown sugar
⅓ cup all-purpose flour
⅔ cup quick-cooking oats
1 tablespoon honey
2 teaspoons nonfat milk
2 tablespoons margarine, softened
1 teaspoon ground cinnamon
¾ teaspoon ground nutmeg

Preheat the oven to 375 degrees. Arrange the apple slices in a greased 8-inch square pan. Mix the remaining ingredients thoroughly; sprinkle the mixture over the apples. Bake until the topping is golden brown and the apples are tender (about 30 minutes).

Exchanges per serving: 1½ fruit, ½ bread, ½ fat

Calories per serving: 144
Fat per serving (gm): 3.2
Cholesterol per serving (mg): 0

KIWI CUPS

These are refreshingly delicious!

Yield: 4 servings

4 Almond Cookie Cups (p. 327)
2 kiwis, peeled and cut into ¼-inch slices
½ cup Ginger Sauce (p. 307)

Prepare the Almond Cookie Cups as directed. Arrange the kiwi slices in the cookie cups. Prepare the Ginger Sauce as directed. Pour the sauce over the slices.

Exchanges per serving: 2½ fruit

Calories per serving: 151
Fat per serving (gm): 1.1
Cholesterol per serving (mg): 0

ALMOND COOKIE CUPS

Use these for Kiwi Cups (p. 326), or fill them with frozen yogurt.

Yield: about 16 cups (1 cup/serving)

¾ cup granulated sugar
¾ cup all-purpose flour
1 teaspoon vanilla extract
⅓ cup egg white (about 3 large egg whites)
¼ cup finely ground almonds

Preheat the oven to 400 degrees. In a medium-size bowl, mix all of the ingredients thoroughly. Drop the cookies evenly by spoonfuls onto three or four well-greased cookie sheets. Using a knife dipped in cold water, spread the batter for each cookie into a thin 4-inch-diameter circle, leaving 2-inch spaces between the cookies. Bake, one tray at a time, until the cookies are golden at the edges (5 to 6 minutes). Remove them quickly with a spatula, and, holding the cookies with your fingers, gently turn up the edges and place each cookie in a muffin tin or similar-size cup. Let the cookies sit to cool; then remove them from the tin(s) or cups.

Exchanges per serving: 1 fruit

Calories per serving: 72
Fat per serving (gm): .9
Cholesterol per serving (mg): 0

BLUEBERRY SWIRL

This dessert is simple and light!

Yield: 8 servings

2 cups frozen or canned blueberries, thawed and drained (reserve juice)
2 tablespoons reserved juice and/or water
2 tablespoons cornstarch
½ cup granulated sugar
2 cups plain nonfat yogurt
Mint leaves (optional)

Put 1 cup of the blueberries in a blender or food processor with the reserved juice and/or water, cornstarch, and sugar, and blend until smooth. Cook the mixture in a saucepan over low heat until it is thickened, stirring constantly. Stir in the remaining blueberries; cool. Whip the yogurt until it is smooth and light. Swirl the yogurt and blueberry mixture in a parfait glass or dessert dish. Garnish with mint leaves.

Exchanges per serving: 1 fruit, ½ milk

Calories per serving: 108
Fat per serving (gm): .7
Cholesterol per serving (mg): 1.0

BANANA CUSTARD WITH CHOCOLATE LEAVES

Yield: 6 servings

½ cup nonfat dry milk
1 12-ounce can nonfat evaporated milk
1 egg
3 egg whites
½ cup granulated sugar
2 cups pureed banana (about 4½ bananas)
1 teaspoon vanilla extract
½ teaspoon banana extract
2 tablespoons semisweet chocolate chips
6–12 rose, gardenia, or ivy leaves, washed

Preheat the oven to 350 degrees.

Blend the dry milk into the evaporated milk. Beat the egg and egg whites together slightly. Combine them with the sugar, banana, and vanilla and banana extracts. Stir in the milk gradually. Pour the mixture into six 6-ounce custard cups. Place the cups in a 9 × 13-inch pan on a rack in the oven. Pour very hot water into the pan to within ½ inch of the tops of the cups. Bake until a knife inserted halfway between the center and the edge comes out clean (about 45 minutes). Remove the cups from the water.

To make chocolate leaves, melt the chocolate chips in a small pan over hot water. Trail the leaves, one at a time, over the top of the melted chocolate, covering only one side. Cool, chocolate-side up. When the chocolate has hardened, carefully peel off the leaf. Garnish each custard cup with one or two chocolate leaves.

Exchanges per serving: 3 fruit, 1 milk

Calories per serving: 256
Fat per serving (gm): 2.8
Cholesterol per serving (mg): 49

OATMEAL-RAISIN BARS

These slightly sweet bars make a great midday snack and are a good source of cholesterol-lowering fiber.

Yield: thirty-two 2-by-1-inch bars

¾ cup all-purpose flour, sifted
2 teaspoons baking powder
1 teaspoon ground cinnamon
2 cups quick-cooking oats
2 egg whites, slightly beaten
⅔ cup brown sugar
¼ cup light olive oil
½ cup skim milk
1 teaspoon vanilla extract
⅔ cup seedless raisins

Preheat the oven to 350 degrees.

Blend the flour, baking powder, and cinnamon together well. Stir in the oats. In a larger bowl, mix the egg whites, brown sugar, oil, skim milk, and vanilla extract. Add the flour-oat mixture a little at a time, blending after each addition. Stir in the raisins. Spread onto a greased 8-inch square pan. Bake until golden brown (about 20 minutes). Cool before cutting.

Exchanges per serving: 1 bread

Calories per serving: 74
Fat per serving (gm): 2.0
Cholesterol per serving (mg): 7.0

MOM'S APPLESAUCE CAKE

A family favorite.

Yield: 16 pieces

⅓ cup oil
1½ cups granulated sugar
2 eggs
2 cups all-purpose flour
2 tablespoons cocoa
¾ teaspoon salt
1½ teaspoons ground cinnamon
¼ teaspoon ground cloves
½ teaspoon baking soda
1½ teaspoons baking powder
1⅔ cups applesauce
1½ cups raisins

Combine the oil, sugar, and eggs and beat for 4 minutes. Blend the flour, cocoa, salt, cinnamon, cloves, baking soda, and baking powder thoroughly. Mix the dry ingredients into the liquid, a little at a time, alternating with the applesauce. Stir in the raisins. Pour into a greased and floured 9-by-13-inch pan; bake in a preheated 350-degree oven for 50 to 55 minutes (until a toothpick inserted in the center comes out clean).

Exchanges per serving: 1 bread, 2 fruit, 1 fat

Calories per serving: 232
Fat per serving (gm): 5.7
Cholesterol per serving (mg): 34.1

KIWI CHEESECAKE

A light, elegant dessert.

Yield: 12 slices

2 tablespoons margarine
1¼ cups vanilla wafer cookie crumbs (about 30 wafers)
⅓ cup granulated sugar
1 tablespoon cornstarch
1 tablespoon lemon juice
⅓ cup fruity white wine
1 cup Yogurt Cheese (p. 313)
7 tablespoons powdered sugar
1 teaspoon vanilla
7 medium-size, firm-ripe kiwi fruit

In a food processor or with a fork, cut the margarine into the cookie crumbs until it disappears. Press the crumbs into the bottom and sides of a 9-inch pie pan. Bake at 375 degrees for 8 minutes. Set aside to cool. Meanwhile, in a small saucepan, stir together the granulated sugar and cornstarch. Add the lemon juice and wine, and bring to a boil over medium heat, stirring constantly. Set aside to cool. Beat the Yogurt Cheese, powdered sugar, and vanilla until very smooth. Spread the mixture over the bottom of the cooled pie crust. Remove skin from the kiwi fruit and cut the fruit crosswise into ¼-inch slices. Arrange the slices in a pie pan so that they overlap slightly and cover the Yogurt Cheese completely. Spoon or pour the wine mixture evenly over the fruit.

Cover the pie without touching the glaze, and refrigerate for at least 1 hour before serving.

Exchanges per serving: 2 milk, 1 fruit, ½ fat

Calories per serving: 148
Fat per serving (gm): 3.4
Cholesterol per serving (mg): 6.0

FAT-FREE WHIPPED TOPPING

This low-calorie, low-cholesterol topping can be used instead of whipped cream on pie, cake, or in dessert recipes. For best results, use very cold milk, bowl, and beaters.

Yield: about 6½ cups (twenty-six ¼-cup servings)

1 cup nonfat evaporated milk, chilled
1½ tablespoons lemon juice
¼ cup granulated sugar
1 teaspoon vanilla

Pour the milk into a chilled bowl and beat with chilled beaters until foamy. Add the lemon juice and beat until firm. Add the sugar and vanilla and beat until stiff. Whipped milk will hold its shape for up to 1 hour, if refrigerated.

Exchanges per serving: free exchange

Calories per serving: 16
Fat per serving (gm): trace
Cholesterol per serving (mg): .4

Beverages

FORTIFIED HOT CHOCOLATE

Yield: 1 serving

1 packet sugar-free hot-chocolate mix
2½ tablespoons nonfat dry milk
6 to 8 ounces hot water

Mix together the hot-chocolate mix and the nonfat dry milk in a coffee cup. Add the hot water and stir until blended.

Exchanges per serving: 1 milk

Calories per serving: 89
Fat per serving (gm): .4
Cholesterol per serving (mg): 4.0

TOFU BREAKFAST SHAKE

Yield: 6 servings

3 cups orange juice
1 14-ounce package soft tofu
1 cup frozen strawberries, unsweetened
2 ripe bananas
1 tablespoon honey

Blend the orange juice and the tofu in a blender. Add the strawberries and blend. Slice in the bananas and add the honey; blend until smooth.

Exchanges per serving: 2 fruit, ½ meat

Calories per serving: 160
Fat per serving (gm): 3.7
Cholesterol per serving (mg): 0

SPARKLING FRUIT JUICE

Yield: 1 serving

⅓ cup orange juice
⅔ cup sparkling water or Diet 7-Up

Pour both ingredients into a tall glass with ice cubes.

Exchanges per serving: ½ fruit

Calories per serving: 39
Fat per serving (gm): .2
Cholesterol per serving (mg): 0

APPENDIX A:
RESEARCH DESIGN OF THE
ROCKPORT WALKING
PROGRAM STUDY

A six-month scientific study of the effects of walking combined with a low-fat diet on cholesterol levels, weight control, and aerobic capacity.

Subjects

Both men and women who met the following criteria were included:

1. A sedentary life-style
2. Not on any diet for the last six months
3. Between 30 and 60 years of age
4. Not taking beta blockers, blood-pressure, cholesterol, or thyroid medications
5. At least 20 percent overweight according to the Metropolitan Life Insurance tables
6. Not planning to go out of town more than two weeks during the first four months of the study (Phase one)

Division of Subjects

Eighty men and women were divided randomly into four groups:

1. A control group
2. A diet-only group
3. A walking-only group
4. A combination diet-and-walking group

Each group had 8 men and 12 women.

Design of Study

Phase one consisted of 16 weeks of supervised intervention, divided as follows:

1. The diet-only group met about every two weeks with a dietitian to discuss changes in eating habits.
2. The walking-only group met three times a week for supervised walking, 60 to 75 minutes per day, and walked on their own four times a week, 60 to 75 minutes per day.
3. The diet-and-walking group met about every two weeks with a dietitian to discuss changes in eating habits, three times a week for supervised walking, 60 to 75 minutes per day, and walked on their own four times a week, 60 to 75 minutes per day.
4. The control group had no intervention. All subjects were weighed weekly (including the controls).

Phase two consisted of eight weeks of unsupervised intervention. The four groups followed the same programs on their own (without supervision).

Testing

VISIT ONE

1. The study was explained and informed consent signed.
2. Subjects met with dietitian to fill out food diary records.
3. Second appointments were scheduled.

4. Instructions for testing were given to subjects, including:
   a. All tests to be done in early morning after a 12-hour fast
   b. No exercise allowed 24 hours before a test
   c. No cigarettes or caffeine allowed before a test
   d. All tests to be given at approximately the same time of day

VISIT TWO

1. Blood samples drawn
2. Resting heart rate and resting blood pressure taken
3. Resting Metabolic Rate (RMR)
4. Subjects given a VO2MAX treadmill test (a Balke test that consists of raised elevations every two minutes as ECG—electrocardiograms—and blood-pressure measurements, etc., are monitored)

VISIT THREE

1. Underwater weighing
2. Anthropometric measurements taken (numerous skin folds and girths)

VISIT FOUR

1. One-mile walk test performed at outdoor track.

Study Timetable

From February 16 through March 18, subjects were recruited, interviewed extensively, and gathered together for a general orientation meeting.

From March 21 through April 30, the subjects were all tested.

On April 18, the first 40 subjects started intervention and phase one. On May 2, the other 40 subjects started intervention and phase one. The walking-only and the combination diet-and-walking groups met for supervised exercise three times a week. All four groups filled out four-day food diaries periodically.

On August 8, testing began on the completion of phase one for all subjects.

On October 16, testing began on the completion of phase two for all subjects.

On November 30, all testing was completed, and data analysis began.

Specific Characteristics of Study

The diet portion of the study followed the American Heart Association guidelines for low-fat and low-cholesterol diets. It was designed for a one- to two-pounds-a-week weight loss in both the diet-only and the combination diet-and-walking groups. The diet used an exchange plan based on the American Diabetes Association/The American Dietetic Association.

Supervised walks were conducted at the Lake Quinsigamond tracks in Worcester, Massachusetts.

Walks were designed to expend about 3,000 kilocalories per week.

One blood sample per subject was drawn before the study began, after phase one, and again after phase two. Blood sample parameters were:

1. Total cholesterol
2. HDL-cholesterol
3. LDL-cholesterol
4. Triglycerides

The control group received a fee of $100 for their participation. They also received the Diet and Walking Program at the end of the six-month study.

APPENDIX B:
COOKBOOK
RECOMMENDATIONS

Heart-Healthy Cookbooks

The American Heart Association Cookbook. New York: David McKay Co., 1984.

Becker, Gail, R.D. *Heart-Smart: A Plan for Low-Cholesterol Living.* New York: Merrell Dow Publications, 1984.

Brody, Jane. *Jane Brody's Good Food Book: Living the High-Carbohydrate Way.* New York: W. W. Norton, 1985.

Connor, Sonja, R.D., and William Connor, M.D. *The Best from the Family Hearts Kitchen.* Portland, OR: Oregon Health Sciences University, 1984.

———. *The New American Diet.* New York: Simon & Schuster, 1986.

Goor, Ron and Nancy. *Eater's Choice: A Food Lover's Guide to Lower Cholesterol.* Boston: Houghton Mifflin Co., 1987.

Lowry, Eve, R.D., and Carla Mulligan Ennis. *Living Lean and Loving It.* "Classic Flavors Without the Fat." C. V. Mosby Company, 1988.

Piscatella, Joseph and Bernie. *Don't Eat Your Heart Out Cookbook.* New York: Workman Publishing Co., 1982.

Polak, Jeanne. *Fat and Calorie Controlled Meals.* Philadelphia: F. Stickley Co., 1982.

Recipes for Your Heart's Delight: The Stanford Guide to Healthy Cooking. Stanford, CA: Health Policy and Research Building, Room 8, 1983.

APPENDIX C:
EXERCISE LOG

The exercise logs on the following pages should be used to record the mileage and duration of your walks for each day of the 20-Week Walking Program. Use the sample on page 343 as a guide for filling out your personal log. The exercise log is an important tool in making your 20-Week Walking Program work for you. See pages 220–25 for more detailed instructions.

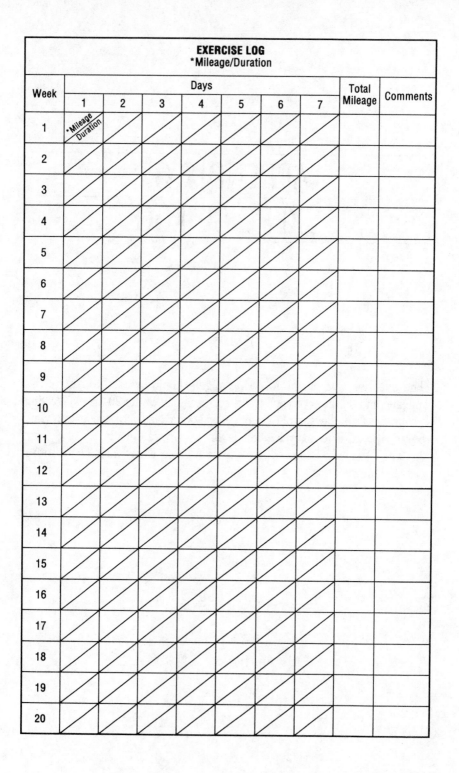

Week	Days							Total Mileage	Comments
	1	2	3	4	5	6	7		
1	*Mileage Duration								
2									
3									
4									
5									
6									
7									
8									
9									
10									
11									
12									
13									
14									
15									
16									
17									
18									
19									
20									

EXERCISE LOG
*Mileage/Duration

EXERCISE LOG
*Mileage/Duration

Week	Days							Total Mileage	Comments
	1	2	3	4	5	6	7		
1	2.0 / 40	2.0 / 39	2.0 / 38	2.0 / 40				8	
2	2.0 / 41	2.0 / 40	2.0 / 38	2.0 / 40	2.0 / 38	2.0 / 39		12	
3	2.5 / 49	2.5 / 52	2.5 / 50	2.5 / 48	2.5 / 48			12.5	
4									
5									
6									
7									
8									
9									
10									
11									
12									
13									
14									
15									
16									
17									
18									
19									
20									

APPENDIX D:
FOOD DIARY

The food diaries on the following pages should be used to determine your knowledge of the fat content in various foods. Use the blank food diary to record everything you eat and drink on the day you have chosen to do this exercise. Follow the instructions on pages 26–7 and the examples on pages 345–48 to complete the exercise and learn to identify "hidden" fat.

FOOD DIARY

H = Home
R = Restaurant (please specify)
C = Cafeteria
O = Other (please specify)

Name: _____
Date Food Consumed: _____

Time	Place	Food Item: Description	Quantity

PRE
DIET

Obvious Fats

■ butter(2tsp.)=2pats

■ mayonnaise(2tsp.)=2pats

Total = 4 pats

FOOD DIARY

H = Home
R = Restaurant (please specify)
C = Cafeteria
O = Other (please specify)

Name: John Diary
Date Food Consumed: Mon. January 1, 1991

Time	Place	Food Item: Description	Quantity
8:00	H	wheat toast with (butter)	2 slices/2tsp. butter
		cheerios with milk (whole)	2 cups/1 cup milk
		orange juice	6 oz.
		coffee with cream	8oz. coffee/1 tbsp. cream
10:00	O	bran muffin with butter	1 large/2 tsp. butter
	office	decaf coffee with cream (half + half)	8oz. coffee/1 tbsp. cream
	desk		
1:00	C	ham + cheese sandwich on bulky roll	2oz. ham/1oz. Am. cheese
		(mayonnaise)	(2 tsp.)
		potato chips	25 chips
		tossed salad (iceberg lettuce, onions, carrots, cukes)	2 cups
		italian dressing	2 tbsp.
		cherry pie	1/8 of pie
		milk (whole)	12 oz.
3:00	O	delicious apple	1 large
	break	can of coke	12 oz.
	room		
7:00	R	extra crispy thigh + breast	1 of each
	Kentucky	cole slaw	1 serving
	Fried	mashed potato with gravy	1 serving/1 tbsp
	Chicken	biscuit with butter	1 pat butter/1 medium
		Sprite	medium-15 oz.
9:00	H	mint chocolate chip ice cream (Hood)	2 scoops/1 1/2 cups

Fats incognito

- whole milk (20oz.)=5pats
- cream, regular(1tbsp.)=½pat
  half+half (1tbsp.)=½pat
- Cheese (1oz.) = 2pats
- salad dressing(2tbsp.)= 3pats
- ice cream(1½cups)= 4½pats

Total= 15½pats

PRE / DIET

FOOD DIARY

H = Home
R = Restaurant (please specify)
C = Cafeteria
O = Other (please specify)

Name: John Diary
Date Food Consumed: Mon. January 9, 199?

Time	Place	Food Item: Description	Quantity
8:00	H	wheat toast with butter	2 slices/2tsp. butter
		cheerios with milk (whole)	2cups/1 cup milk
		orange juice	6oz.
		coffee with (cream)	8oz. coffee (1tbsp. cream)
10:00	O office desk	bran muffin with butter	1 large/2tsp. butter
		decaf coffee with cream (half+half)	8oz. coffee/1 tbsp. cream
1:00	C	ham + (cheese) sandwich on bulky roll	2oz ham (1oz Am cheese)
		mayonnaise	2tsp.
		potato chips	25 chips
		tossed salad (iceberg lettuce, onions, carrots, cukes)	2 cups
		(Italian dressing)	(2 tbsp)
		cherry pie	1/8 of pie
		MILK (whole)	12 oz
3:00	O break room	delicious apple	1 large
		can of coke	12 oz.
7:00	R Kentucky Fried Chicken	extra crispy thigh + breast	1 of each
		cole slaw	1 serving
		mashed potato with gravy	1 serving/1 tbsp
		biscuit with butter	1 pat butter/1 medium
		Sprite	medium - 15 oz.
9:00	H	mint chocolate chip (ice cream) (Hood)	3 scoops (1½ cups)

347

H = Home
R = Restaurant (please specify)
C = Cafeteria
O = Other (please specify)

FOOD DIARY

Name: _John Diary_
Date Food Consumed: _Mon. January 1, 1981_

Time	Place	Food Item: Description	Quantity
8:00	H	wheat toast with butter	2 slices/2 tsp butter
		cheerios with milk (whole)	2 cups/1 cup milk
		orange juice	6 oz.
		coffee with cream	8 oz. coffee/1 tbsp. cream
10:00	O office desk	bran muffin with butter	1 large/2 tsp. butter
		decaf coffee with cream (half + half)	8 oz. coffee/1 tbsp. cream
1:00	C	ham + cheese sandwich on bulky roll	2 oz ham/1 oz Am cheese
		mayonnaise	2 tsp.
		potato chips	25 chips
		tossed salad (iceberg lettuce, onions, carrots, cukes)	2 cups
		italian dressing	2 tbsp.
		cherry pie	1/8 of pie
		milk (whole)	12 oz.
3:00	O break room	delicious apple	1 large
		can of coke	12 oz.
7:00	R Kentucky Fried Chicken	extra crispy thigh + breast	1 of each
		cole slaw	1 serving
		mashed potato with gravy	1 serving/1 tbsp
		biscuit with butter	1 pat butter/1 medium
		Sprite	medium-15 oz.
9:00	H	mint chocolate chip ice cream (hood)	3 scoops/1½ cups

Fats undercover

- muffin (1 large)= 2 pats
- potato chips (25)= 3½ pats
- fried chicken (1 thigh, 1 breast) = 6 pats
- cole slaw (1 serving)=1 pat
- gravy (1 tbsp.)=1 pat
- biscuit (1) = 1 pat

Total = 14½ pats
Grand Total = 34 pats

APPENDIX E:
FAT AND CHOLESTEROL
COMPARISON CHARTS

MEATS

PRODUCT (3½ ounces, cooked)*	SATURATED FATTY ACIDS (Grams)	CHOLESTEROL (Milligrams)	TOTAL FAT[1] (Grams)	CALORIES FROM FAT[2](%)	TOTAL CALORIES
Beef					
Kidneys, simmered[3]	1.1	387	3.4	21	144
Liver, braised[3]	1.9	389	4.9	27	161
Round, top round, lean only, broiled	2.2	84	6.2	29	191
Round, eye of round, lean only, roasted	2.5	69	6.5	32	183
Round, tip round, lean only, roasted	2.8	81	7.5	36	190
Round, full cut, lean only, choice, broiled	2.9	82	8.0	37	194
Round, bottom round, lean only, braised	3.4	96	9.7	39	222
Short loin, top loin, lean only, broiled	3.6	76	8.9	40	203
Wedge-bone sirloin, lean only, broiled	3.6	89	8.7	38	208
Short loin, tender-loin, lean only, broiled	3.6	84	9.3	41	204

PRODUCT (3½ ounces, cooked)*	SATURATED FATTY ACIDS (Grams)	CHOLESTEROL (Milligrams)	TOTAL FAT[1] (Grams)	CALORIES FROM FAT[2](%)	TOTAL CALORIES
Chuck, arm pot roast, lean only, braised	3.8	101	10.0	39	231
Short loin, T-bone steak, lean only, choice, broiled	4.2	80	10.4	44	214
Short loin, porter-house steak, lean only, choice, broiled	4.3	80	10.8	45	218
Brisket, whole, lean only, braised	4.6	93	12.8	48	241
Rib eye, small end (ribs 10–12), lean only, choice broiled	4.9	80	11.6	47	225
Rib, whole (ribs 6–12), lean only, roasted	5.8	81	13.8	52	240
Flank, lean only, choice, braised	5.9	71	13.8	51	244
Rib, large end (ribs 6–9), lean only, broiled	6.1	82	14.2	55	233
Chuck, blade roast, lean only, braised	6.2	106	15.3	51	270
Corned beef, cured, brisket, cooked	6.3	98	19.0	68	251
Flank, lean and fat, choice, braised	6.6	72	15.5	54	257
Ground, lean, broiled medium	7.2	87	18.5	61	272
Round, full cut, lean and fat, choice, braised	7.3	84	18.2	60	274
Rib, short ribs, lean only, choice, braised	7.7	93	18.1	55	295
Salami, cured, cooked, smoked, 3–4 slices	9.0	65	20.7	71	262
Short loin, T-bone steak, lean and fat, choice, broiled	10.2	84	24.6	68	324
Chuck, arm pot roast, lean and fat, braised	10.7	99	26.0	67	350
Sausage, cured, cooked, smoked, about 2	11.4	67	26.9	78	312
Bologna, cured, 3–4 slices	12.1	58	28.5	82	312
Frankfurter, cured, about 2	12.0	61	28.5	82	315

PRODUCT (3½ ounces, cooked)*	SATURATED FATTY ACIDS (Grams)	CHOLESTEROL (Milligrams)	TOTAL FAT[1] (Grams)	CALORIES FROM FAT[2](%)	TOTAL CALORIES
Lamb					
Leg, lean only, roasted	3.0	89	8.2	39	191
Loin chop, lean only, broiled	4.1	94	9.4	39	215
Rib, lean only, roasted	5.7	88	12.3	48	232
Arm chop, lean only, braised	6.0	122	14.6	47	279
Rib, lean and fat, roasted	14.2	90	30.6	75	368
Pork					
Cured, ham steak, boneless, extra lean, unheated	1.4	45	4.2	31	122
Liver, braised[3]	1.4	355	4.4	24	165
Kidneys, braised[3]	1.5	480	4.7	28	151
Fresh, loin, tenderloin, lean only, roasted	1.7	93	4.8	26	166
Cured, shoulder, arm picnic, lean only, roasted	2.4	48	7.0	37	170
Cured, ham, boneless, regular, roasted	3.1	59	9.0	46	178
Fresh, leg (ham), shank half, lean only, roasted	3.6	92	10.5	44	215
Fresh, leg (ham), rump half, lean only, roasted	3.7	96	10.7	43	221
Fresh, loin, center loin, sirloin, lean only, roasted	4.5	91	13.1	49	240
Fresh, loin, sirloin, lean only, roasted	4.5	90	13.2	50	236
Fresh, loin, center rib, lean only, roasted	4.8	79	13.8	51	245
Fresh, loin, top loin, lean only, roasted	4.8	79	13.8	51	245
Fresh, shoulder, blade, Boston, lean only, roasted	5.8	98	16.8	59	256
Fresh, loin, blade, lean only, roasted	6.6	89	19.3	62	279
Fresh, loin, sirloin, lean and fat, roasted	7.4	91	20.4	63	291
Cured, shoulder, arm picnic, lean and fat, roasted	7.7	58	21.4	69	280

PRODUCT (3½ ounces, cooked)*	SATURATED FATTY ACIDS (Grams)	CHOLESTEROL (Milligrams)	TOTAL FAT[1] (Grams)	CALORIES FROM FAT[2](%)	TOTAL CALORIES
Fresh, loin, center loin, lean and fat, roasted	7.9	91	21.8	64	305
Cured, shoulder, blade roll, lean and fat, roasted	8.4	67	23.5	74	287
Fresh, Italian sausage, cooked	9.0	78	25.7	72	323
Fresh, bratwurst, cooked	9.3	60	25.9	77	301
Fresh, chitterlings, cooked	10.1	143	28.8	86	303
Cured, liver sausage, liverwurst	10.6	158	28.5	79	326
Cured, smoked link sausage, grilled	11.3	68	31.8	74	389
Fresh, spareribs, lean and fat, braised	11.8	121	30.3	69	397
Cured, salami, dry or hard	11.9	—	33.7	75	407
Bacon, fried	17.4	85	49.2	78	576
Veal					
Rump, lean only, roasted	—	128	2.2	13	156
Sirloin, lean only, roasted	—	128	3.2	19	153
Arm steak, lean only, cooked	—	90	5.3	24	200
Loin chop, lean only, cooked	—	90	6.7	29	207
Blade, lean only, cooked	—	90	7.8	33	211
Cutlet, medium fat, braised or broiled	4.8	128	11.0	37	271
Foreshank, medium fat, stewed	—	90	10.4	43	216
Plate, medium fat, stewed	—	90	21.2	63	303
Rib, medium fat, roasted	7.1	128	16.9	70	218
Flank, medium fat, stewed	—	90	32.3	75	390

Source: *Eating to Lower Your Blood Cholesterol.* Developed by the National Heart, Lung, and Blood Institute.

Composition of Foods: Beef Products—Raw • Processed • Prepared, Agriculture Handbook 8–13. United States Department of Agriculture, Human Nutrition Information Service (August 1986).

Composition of Foods: Pork Products—Raw • Processed • Prepared, Agriculture Handbook 8–10. United States Department of Agriculture, Human Nutrition Information Service (August 1983).

Home and Garden Bulletin. Nutritive Value of Foods. No. 72. United States Department of Agriculture. Human Nutrition Information Service (1986).

*3½ oz = 100 grams (approximately)

[1]Total fat = saturated fatty acids plus monounsaturated fatty acids plus polyunsaturated fatty acids.

[2]Percent calories from fat = (total fat calories divided by total calories) multiplied by 100; total fat calories = total fat (grams) multiplied by 9.

[3]Liver and most organ meats are low in fat, but high in cholesterol. If you are eating to lower your blood cholesterol, you should consider your total cholesterol intake before selecting an organ meat.

— = Information not available in the sources used.

POULTRY

PRODUCT (3½ ounces, cooked)*	SATURATED FATTY ACIDS (Grams)	CHOLESTEROL (Milligrams)	TOTAL FAT[1] (Grams)	CALORIES FROM FAT[2](%)	TOTAL CALORIES
Turkey, fryer-roasters, light meat without skin, roasted	0.4	86	1.9	8	140
Chicken, roasters, light meat without skin, roasted	1.1	75	4.1	24	153
Turkey, fryer-roasters, light meat with skin, roasted	1.3	95	4.6	25	164
Chicken, broilers or fryers, light meat without skin, roasted	1.3	85	4.5	24	173
Turkey, fryer-roasters, dark meat without skin, roasted	1.4	112	4.3	24	162
Chicken, stewing, light meat without skin, stewed	2.0	70	8.0	34	213
Turkey roll, light and dark	2.0	55	7.0	42	149
Turkey, fryer-roasters, dark meat with skin, roasted	2.1	117	7.1	35	182
Chicken, roasters, dark meat without skin, roasted	2.4	75	8.8	44	178
Chicken, broilers or fryers, dark meat without skin, roasted	2.7	93	9.7	43	205
Chicken, broilers or fryers, light meat with skin, roasted	3.0	85	10.9	44	222
Chicken, stewing, dark meat without skin, stewed	4.1	95	15.3	53	258
Duck, domesticated, flesh only, roasted	4.2	89	11.2	50	201

PRODUCT (3½ ounces, cooked)*	SATURATED FATTY ACIDS (Grams)	CHOLESTEROL (Milligrams)	TOTAL FAT[1] (Grams)	CALORIES FROM FAT[2](%)	TOTAL CALORIES
Chicken, broilers or fryers, dark meat with skin, roasted	4.4	91	15.8	56	253
Goose, domesticated, flesh only, roasted	4.6	96	12.7	48	238
Turkey bologna, about 3½ slices	5.1	99	15.2	69	199
Chicken frankfurter, about 2	5.5	101	19.5	68	257
Turkey frankfurter, about 2	5.9	107	17.7	70	226

Source: *Eating to Lower Your Blood Cholesterol.* Developed by the National Heart, Lung, and Blood Institute.

Composition of Foods: Poultry Products—Raw • Processed • Prepared, Agriculture Handbook 8–5. United States Department of Agriculture, Science and Education Administration (August 1979).
*3½ oz = 100 grams (approximately)
[1]Total fat = saturated fatty acids plus monounsaturated fatty acids plus polyunsaturated fatty acids.
[2]Percent calories from fat = (total fat calories divided by total calories) multiplied by 100; total fat calories = total fat (grams) multiplied by 9.

FISH AND SHELLFISH

PRODUCT (3½ ounces, cooked)*	SATURATED FATTY ACIDS (Grams)	CHOLESTEROL (Milli-grams)	OMEGA-3 FATTY ACIDS (Grams)	TOTAL FAT[1] (Grams)	CALORIES FROM FAT[2](%)	TOTAL CALORIES
Finfish						
Haddock, dry heat	0.2	74	0.2	0.9	7	112
Cod, Atlantic, dry heat	0.2	55	0.2	0.9	7	105
Pollock, walleye, dry heat	0.2	96	1.5	1.1	9	113
Perch, mixed species, dry heat	0.2	42	0.3	1.2	9	117
Grouper, mixed species, dry heat	0.3	47	—	1.3	10	118
Whiting, mixed species, dry heat	0.3	84	0.9	1.7	13	115
Snapper, mixed species, dry heat	0.4	47	—	1.7	12	128
Halibut, Atlantic and Pacific, dry heat	0.4	41	0.6	2.9	19	140
Rockfish, Pacific, dry heat	0.5	44	0.5	2.0	15	121
Sea bass, mixed species, dry heat	0.7	53	—	2.5	19	124
Trout, rainbow, dry heat	0.8	73	0.9	4.3	26	151
Swordfish, dry heat	1.4	50	1.1	5.1	30	155
Tuna, bluefin, dry heat	1.6	49	—	6.3	31	184

PRODUCT (3½ ounces, cooked)*	SATURATED FATTY ACIDS (Grams)	CHOLESTEROL (Milli- grams)	OMEGA-3 FATTY ACIDS (Grams)	TOTAL FAT[1] (Grams)	CALORIES FROM FAT[2](%)	TOTAL CALORIES
Salmon, sockeye, dry heat	1.9	87	1.3	11.0	46	216
Anchovy, European, canned	2.2	—	2.1	9.7	42	210
Herring, Atlantic, dry heat	2.6	77	2.1	11.5	51	203
Eel, dry heat	3.0	161	0.7	15.0	57	236
Mackerel, Atlantic, dry heat	4.2	75	1.3	17.8	61	262
Pompano, Florida, dry heat	4.5	64	—	12.1	52	211
Crustaceans						
Lobster, northern	0.1	72	0.1	0.6	6	98
Crab, blue, moist heat	0.2	100	0.5	1.8	16	102
Shrimp, mixed species, moist heat	0.3	195	0.3	1.1	10	99
Mollusks						
Whelk, moist heat	0.1	130	—	0.8	3	275
Clam, mixed species, moist heat	0.2	67	0.3	2.0	12	148
Mussel, blue, moist heat	0.9	56	0.8	4.5	23	172
Oyster, Eastern, moist heat	1.3	109	1.0	5.0	33	137

Source: *Eating to Lower Your Blood Cholesterol.* Developed by the National Heart, Lung, and Blood Institute.

Composition of Foods: Finfish and Shellfish Products—Raw • Processed • Prepared, Agriculture Handbook 8–15. United States Department of Agriculture (in press).

*3½ oz = 100 grams (approximately)

[1]Total fat = saturated fatty acids plus monounsaturated fatty acids plus polyunsaturated fatty acids.

[2]Percent calories from fat = (total fat calories divided by total calories) multiplied by 100; total fat calories = total fat (grams) multiplied by 9.

— = Information not available in sources used.

DAIRY AND EGG PRODUCTS

PRODUCT	SATURATED FAT (Grams)	CHOLESTEROL (Milligrams)	TOTAL FAT[1] (Grams)	CALORIES FROM FAT[2](%)	TOTAL CALORIES
Milk (8 ounces)					
Skim milk	0.3	4	0.4	5	86
Buttermilk	1.3	9	2.2	20	99
Low-fat milk, 1% fat	1.6	10	2.6	23	102
Low-fat milk, 2% fat	2.9	18	4.7	35	121
Whole milk, 3.3% fat	5.1	33	8.2	49	150
Yogurt (4 ounces)					
Plain yogurt, low fat	0.1	2	0.2	3	63
Plain yogurt	2.4	14	3.7	47	70
Cheese					
Cottage cheese, low-fat, 1% fat, 4 oz.	0.7	5	1.2	13	82
Mozzarella, part- skim, 1 oz.	2.9	16	4.5	56	72

PRODUCT	SATURATED FAT (Grams)	CHOLESTEROL (Milligrams)	TOTAL FAT[1] (Grams)	CALORIES FROM FAT[2](%)	TOTAL CALORIES
Cottage cheese, creamed, 4 oz.	3.2	17	5.1	39	117
Mozzarella, 1 oz.	3.7	22	6.1	69	80
Sour cream, 1 oz.	3.7	12	5.9	87	61
American processed cheese spread, pasteurized, 1 oz.	3.8	16	6.0	66	82
Feta, 1 oz.	4.2	25	6.0	72	75
Neufchâtel, 1 oz.	4.2	22	6.6	81	74
Camembert, 1 oz.	4.3	20	6.9	73	85
American processed cheese food, pasteurized, 1 oz.	4.4	18	7.0	68	93
Provolone, 1 oz.	4.8	20	7.6	68	100
Limburger, 1 oz.	4.8	26	7.7	75	93
Brie, 1 oz.	4.9	28	7.9	74	95
Romano, 1 oz.	4.9	29	7.6	63	110
Gouda, 1 oz.	5.0	32	7.8	69	101
Swiss, 1 oz.	5.0	26	7.8	65	107
Edam, 1 oz.	5.0	25	7.9	70	101
Brick, 1 oz.	5.3	27	8.4	72	105
Blue, 1 oz.	5.3	21	8.2	73	100
Gruyère, 1 oz.	5.4	31	9.2	71	117
Muenster, 1 oz.	5.4	27	8.5	74	104
Parmesan, 1 oz.	5.4	22	8.5	59	129
Monterey Jack, 1 oz.	5.5	25	8.6	73	106
Roquefort, 1 oz.	5.5	26	8.7	75	105
Ricotta, part-skim, 4 oz.	5.6	25	9.0	52	156
American processed cheese, pasteurized, 1 oz.	5.6	27	8.9	75	106
Colby, 1 oz.	5.7	27	9.1	73	112
Cheddar, 1 oz.	6.0	30	9.4	74	114
Cream cheese, 1 oz.	6.2	31	9.9	90	99
Ricotta, whole milk, 4 oz.	9.4	58	14.7	67	197
Eggs					
Egg, chicken, white	0	0	tr.	0	16
Egg, chicken, whole	1.7	274	5.6	64	79
Egg, chicken, yolk	1.7	272	5.6	80	63

Source: *Eating to Lower Your Blood Cholesterol.* Developed by the National Heart, Lung, and Blood Institute.

Composition of Foods: Dairy and Egg Products—Raw • Processed • Prepared, Agriculture Handbook 8–1, United States Department of Agriculture, Agricultural Research Service (November 1976).

[1]Total fat = saturated fatty acids plus monounsaturated fatty acids plus polyunsaturated fatty acids.

[2]Percent calories from fat = (total fat calories divided by total calories) multiplied by 100; total fat calories = total fat (grams) multiplied by 9.

oz. = ounce

tr. = trace

FROZEN DESERTS

PRODUCT (1 cup)	SATURATED FATTY ACIDS (Grams)	CHOLESTEROL (Milligrams)	TOTAL FAT[1] (Grams)	CALORIES FROM FAT[2](%)	TOTAL CALORIES
Fruit popsicle, 1 bar	—	—	0.0	0	65
Fruit ice	—	—	tr.	0	247
Fudgsicle	—	—	0.2	2	91
Frozen yogurt, fruit flavored	—	—	2.0	8	216
Sherbet, orange	2.4	14	3.8	13	270
Pudding pops, 1 pop	2.5	1	2.6	25	94
Ice milk, vanilla, soft serve	2.9	13	4.6	19	223
Ice milk, vanilla, hard	3.5	18	5.6	28	184
Ice cream, vanilla, regular	8.9	59	14.3	48	269
Ice cream, French vanilla, soft serve	13.5	153	22.5	54	377
Ice cream, vanilla, rich, 16% fat	14.7	88	23.7	61	349

Source: *Eating to Lower Your Blood Cholesterol.* Developed by the National Heart, Lung, and Blood Institute.

Composition of Foods: Dairy and Egg Products—Raw • Processed • Prepared, Agriculture Handbook 8–1. United States Department of Agriculture, Agricultural Research Service (November 1976).

Pennington, J., and Church, H. *Bowes and Church's Food Values of Portions Commonly Used.* 14th ed. Philadelphia: J.B. Lippincott Company (1985).
[1]Total fat = saturated fatty acids plus monounsaturated fatty acids plus polyunsaturated fatty acids.
[2]Percent calories from fat = (total fat calories divided by total calories) multiplied by 100; total fat calories = total fat (grams) multiplied by 9.
— = Information not available in sources used.
tr. = trace

FATS AND OILS

PRODUCT (1 Tablespoon)	SATURATED FATTY ACIDS (Grams)	CHOLESTEROL (Milligrams)	POLYUNSATURATED FATTY ACIDS (Grams)	MONOUNSATURATED FATTY ACIDS (Grams)
Rapeseed oil (canola oil)	0.9	0	4.5	7.6
Safflower oil	1.2	0	10.1	1.6
Sunflower oil	1.4	0	5.5	6.2
Peanut butter, smooth	1.5	0	2.3	3.7
Corn oil	1.7	0	8.0	3.3
Olive oil	1.8	0	1.1	9.9
Hydrogenated sunflower oil	1.8	0	4.9	6.3
Margarine, liquid, bottled	1.8	0	5.1	3.9

PRODUCT (1 Tablespoon)	SATURATED FATTY ACIDS (Grams)	CHOLESTEROL (Milligrams)	POLYUNSATURATED FATTY ACIDS (Grams)	MONOUNSATURATED FATTY ACIDS (Grams)
Margarine, soft, tub	1.8	0	3.9	4.8
Sesame oil	1.9	0	5.7	5.4
Soybean oil	2.0	0	7.9	3.2
Margarine, stick	2.1	0	3.6	5.1
Peanut oil	2.3	0	4.3	6.2
Cottonseed oil	3.5	0	7.1	2.4
Lard	5.0	12	1.4	5.8
Beef tallow	6.4	14	0.5	5.3
Palm oil	6.7	0	1.3	5.0
Butter	7.1	31	0.4	3.3
Cocoa butter	8.1	0	0.4	4.5
Palm kernel oil	11.1	0	0.2	1.5
Coconut oil	11.8	0	0.2	0.8

Sources: *Eating to Lower Your Blood Cholesterol*. Developed by the National Heart, Lung, and Blood Institute.

Composition of Foods: Fats and Oils—Raw • Processed • Prepared, Agriculture Handbook 8–4. United States Department of Agriculture, Science and Education Administration (June 1979).

Composition of Foods: Legumes and Legume Products—Raw • Processed • Prepared, Agriculture Handbook 8–16. United States Department of Agriculture, Human Nutrition Information Service (December 1986).

NUTS AND SEEDS

PRODUCT (1 ounce)	SATURATED FATTY ACIDS (Grams)	CHOLESTEROL (Milligrams)	TOTAL FAT[1] (Grams)	CALORIES FROM FAT[2](%)	TOTAL CALORIES
European chestnuts	0.2	0	1.1	9	105
Filberts or hazelnuts	1.3	0	17.8	89	179
Almonds	1.4	0	15.0	80	167
Pecans	1.5	0	18.4	89	187
Sunflower seed kernels, roasted	1.5	0	1.4	77	165
English walnuts	1.6	0	17.6	87	182
Pistachio nuts	1.7	0	13.7	75	164
Peanuts	1.9	0	14.0	76	164
Hickory nuts	2.0	0	18.3	88	187
Pine nuts, pignolia	2.2	0	14.4	89	146
Pumpkin and squash seed kernels	2.3	0	12.0	73	148
Cashew nuts	2.6	0	13.2	73	163
Macadamia nuts	3.1	0	20.9	95	199
Brazil nuts	4.6	0	18.8	91	186
Coconut meat, unsweetened	16.3	0	18.3	88	187

Sources: *Eating to Lower Your Blood Cholesterol*. Developed by the National Heart, Lung; and Blood Institute.

Composition of Foods: Legumes and Legume Products—Raw • Processed • Prepared, Agriculture Handbook 8–16. United States Department of Agriculture, Human Nutrition Information Service (December 1986).

Composition of Foods: Nut and Seed Products—Raw • Processed • Prepared, Agriculture Handbook 8–12. United States Department of Agriculture, Human Nutrition Information Service (September 1984).

[1]Total fat = saturated fatty acids plus monounsaturated fatty acids plus polyunsaturated fatty acids.

[2]Percent calories from fat = (total fat calories divided by total calories) multiplied by 100; total fat calories = total fat (grams) multiplied by 9.

BREADS, CEREALS, PASTA, RICE, AND DRIED PEAS AND BEANS

PRODUCT	SATURATED FATTY ACIDS (Grams)	CHOLESTEROL (Milligrams)	TOTAL FAT[1] (Grams)	CALORIES FROM FAT[2](%)	TOTAL CALORIES
Breads					
Melba toast, 1 plain	0.1	0	tr.	0	20
Pita, ½ large shell	0.1	0	1.0	5	165
Corn tortilla	0.1	0	1.0	14	65
Rye bread, 1 slice	0.2	0	1.0	14	65
English muffin	0.3	0	1.0	6	140
Bagel, 1, 3½" diameter	0.3	0	2.0	9	200
White bread, 1 slice	0.3	0	1.0	14	65
Rye krisp, 2 triple crackers	0.3	0	1.0	16	56
Whole-wheat bread, 1 slice	0.4	0	1.0	13	70
Saltines, 4	0.5	4	1.0	18	50
Hamburger bun	0.5	tr.	2.0	16	115
Hot dog bun	0.5	tr.	2.0	16	115
Pancake, 1, 4" diameter	0.5	16	2.0	30	60
Bran muffin, 1, 2½" diameter	1.4	24	6.0	43	125
Corn muffin, 1, 2½" diameter	1.5	23	5.0	31	145
Plain doughnut, 1, 3¼" diameter	2.8	20	12.0	51	210
Croissant, 1, 4½" by 4"	3.5	13	12.0	46	235
Waffle, 1, 7" diameter	4.0	102	13.0	48	245
Cereals (1 cup)					
Corn flakes	tr.	—	0.1	0	98
Cream of wheat, cooked	tr.	—	0.5	3	134
Corn grits, cooked	tr.	—	0.5	3	146
Oatmeal, cooked	0.4	—	2.4	15	145
Granola	5.8	—	33.1	50	595
100% Natural Cereal with raisins and dates	13.7	—	20.3	37	496
Pasta (1 cup)					
Spaghetti, cooked	0.1	0	1.0	6	155
Elbow macaroni, cooked	0.1	0	1.0	6	155
Egg noodles, cooked	0.5	50	2.0	11	160
Chow mein noodles, canned	2.1	5	11.0	45	220
Rice (1 cup cooked)					
Rice, white	0.1	0	0.5	2	225
Rice, brown	0.3	0	1.0	4	230

PRODUCT	SATURATED FATTY ACIDS (Grams)	CHOLESTEROL (Milligrams)	TOTAL FAT[1] (Grams)	CALORIES FROM FAT[2](%)	TOTAL CALORIES
Dried Peas and Beans (1 cup cooked)					
Split peas	0.1	0	0.8	3	231
Kidney beans	0.1	0	1.0	4	225
Lima beans	0.2	0	0.7	3	217
Black-eyed peas	0.3	0	1.2	5	200
Garbanzo beans	0.4	0	4.3	14	269

Source: *Eating to Lower Your Blood Cholesterol.* Developed by the National Heart, Lung, and Blood Institute.

Composition of Foods: Breakfast Cereals—Raw • Processed • Prepared, Agriculture Handbook 8–8. United States Department of Agriculture, Human Nutrition Information Service (July 1982).

Composition of Foods: Legume and Legume Products, Agriculture Handbook 8–16. United States Department of Agriculture, Nutrition Monitoring Division (December 1986).

Home and Garden Bulletin. Nutritive Value of Foods. No. 72. United States Department of Agriculture. Human Nutrition Information Service (1986).

[1]Total fat = saturated fatty acids plus monounsaturated fatty acids plus polyunsaturated fatty acids.
[2]Percent calories from fat = (total fat calories divided by total calories) multiplied by 100; total fat calories = total fat (grams) multiplied by 9.
— = Information not available in sources used.
oz. = ounce
tr. = trace

SWEETS AND SNACKS

PRODUCT	SATURATED FATTY ACIDS (Grams)	CHOLESTEROL (Milligrams)	TOTAL FAT[1] (Grams)	CALORIES FROM FAT[2](%)	TOTAL CALORIES
Beverages					
Ginger ale, 12 oz.	0.0	0	0.0	0	125
Cola, regular, 12 oz.	0.0	0	0.0	0	160
Chocolate shake, 10 oz.	6.5	37	10.5	26	360
Candy (1 ounce)					
Hard candy	0.0	0	0.0	0	110
Gum drops	tr.	0	tr.	tr.	100
Fudge	2.1	1	3.0	24	115
Milk chocolate, plain	5.4	6	9.0	56	145
Cookies					
Vanilla wafers, 5 cookies, 1¾" diameter	0.9	12	3.3	32	94
Fig bars, 4 cookies 1⅝" × 1⅝" × ⅜"	1.0	27	4.0	17	210
Chocolate brownie with icing, 1½" by 1¾" by ⅞"	1.6	14	4.0	36	100
Oatmeal cookies, 4 cookies, 2⅝" diameter	2.5	2	10.0	37	245
Chocolate-chip cookies, 4 cookies, 2¼" diameter	3.9	18	11.0	54	185

PRODUCT	SATURATED FATTY ACIDS (Grams)	CHOLESTEROL (Milligrams)	TOTAL FAT[1] (Grams)	CALORIES FROM FAT[2](%)	TOTAL CALORIES
Cakes and Pies					
Angel food cake, 1/12 of 10″ cake	tr.	0	tr.	tr.	125
Gingerbread, 1/9 of 8″ cake	1.1	1	4.0	21	175
White layer cake with white icing, 1/16 of 9″ cake	2.1	3	9.0	32	260
Yellow layer cake with chocolate icing, 1/16 of 9″ cake	3.0	36	8.0	31	235
Pound cake, 1/17 of loaf	3.0	64	5.0	41	110
Devils food cake with chocolate icing, 1/16 of 9″ cake	3.5	37	8.0	31	235
Lemon meringue pie, 1/6 of 9″ pie	4.3	143	14.0	36	355
Apple pie, 1/6 of 9″ pie	4.6	0	18.0	40	405
Cream pie, 1/6 of 9″ pie	15.0	8	23.0	46	455
Snacks					
Popcorn, air-popped, 1 cup	tr.	0	tr.	tr.	30
Pretzels, stick, 2¼″, 10 pretzels	tr.	0	tr.	tr.	10
Popcorn with oil and salted, 1 cup	0.5	0	3.0	49	55
Corn chips, 1 oz.	1.4	25	9.0	52	155
Potato chips, 1 oz.	2.6	0	10.1	62	147
Pudding					
Gelatin	0.0	0	0.0	0	70
Tapioca, ½ cup	2.3	15	4.0	25	145
Chocolate pudding, ½ cup	2.4	15	4.0	24	150

Source: *Eating to Lower Your Blood Cholesterol.* Developed by the National Heart, Lung, and Blood Institute.

Home and Garden Bulletin, Nutritive Value of Foods. No. 72. United States Department of Agriculture. Human Nutrition Information Service (1986).

[1]Total fat = saturated fatty acids plus monounsaturated fatty acids plus polyunsaturated fatty acids.

[2]Percent calories from fat = (total fat calories divided by total calories) multiplied by 100; total fat calories = total fat (grams) multiplied by 9.

oz. = ounce

tr. = trace

MISCELLANEOUS

PRODUCT	SATURATED FATTY ACIDS (Grams)	CHOLESTEROL (Milligrams)	TOTAL FAT[1] (Grams)	CALORIES FROM FAT[2](%)	TOTAL CALORIES
Gravies (½ cup)					
Au jus, canned	0.1	1	0.3	3	80
Turkey, canned	0.7	3	2.5	37	61
Beef, canned	1.4	4	2.8	41	62
Chicken, canned	1.7	3	6.8	65	95
Sauces (½ cup)					
Sweet and sour	tr.	0	0.1	<1	147
Barbecue	0.3	0	2.3	22	94
White	3.2	17	6.7	50	121
Cheese	4.7	26	8.6	50	154
Sour cream	8.5	45	15.1	53	255
Hollandaise	20.9	94	34.1	87	353
Bearnaise	20.9	99	34.1	88	351
Salad Dressings (1 Tablespoon)					
Russian, low-calorie	0.1	1	0.7	27	23
French, low-calorie	0.1	1	0.9	37	22
Italian, low-calorie	0.2	1	1.5	85	16
Thousand Island, low-calorie	0.2	2	1.6	59	24
Imitation mayonnaise	0.5	4	2.9	75	35
Thousand Island, regular	0.9	—	5.6	86	59
Italian, regular	1.0	—	7.1	93	69
Russian, regular	1.1	—	7.8	92	76
French, regular	1.5	—	6.4	86	67
Blue cheese	1.5	—	8.0	93	77
Mayonnaise	1.6	8	11.0	100	99
Other					
Olives, green, 4 medium	0.2	0	1.5	90	15
Nondairy creamer, powdered, 1 teaspoon	0.7	0	1.0	90	10
Avocado, Florida	5.3	0	27.0	72	340
Pizza, cheese, ⅛ of 15″ diameter	4.1	56	9.0	28	290
Quiche lorraine, ⅛ of 8″ diameter	23.2	285	48.0	72	600

Source: *Eating to Lower Your Blood Cholesterol.* Developed by the National Heart, Lung, and Blood Institute.

Composition of Foods: Fats and Oils—Raw • Processed • Prepared, Agriculture Handbook 8–4. United States Department of Agriculture, Science and Education Administration (June 1979).

Composition of Foods: Soups, Sauces, and Gravies—Raw • Processed • Prepared, Agriculture Handbook 8–6. United States Department of Agriculture, Science and Education Administration (February 1980).

Home and Garden Bulletin. Nutritive Value of Foods. No. 72. United States Department of Agriculture. Human Nutrition Information Service (1986).

[1]Total fat = saturated fatty acids plus monounsaturated fatty acids plus polyunsaturated fatty acids.

[2]Percent calories from fat = (total fat calories divided by total calories) multiplied by 100; total fat calories = fat (grams) multiplied by 9.

— = Information not available in the sources used.

SOURCES

Books

Alpert, Joseph S. *The Heart Attack Handbook: A Commonsense Guide to Prevention, Treatment, Recovery, and Staying Well*, 2d ed. Boston: Little, Brown and Company, 1978, 1985.

Getchell, Bud. *The Fitness Book*. Indianapolis: Benchmark Press, Inc., 1987.

Kashiwa, Anne, and James Rippe. *Fitness Walking for Women*. New York: Perigee Books, 1987.

Katch, Frank I., and William D. McArdle. *Nutrition, Weight Control, and Exercise*, 2d ed. Philadelphia: Lea & Febiger, 1983.

Rippe, James M. *Fit for Success*. New York: Prentice Hall Press, 1989.

———, and William Southmayd. *The Sports Performance Factors*. New York: Perigee Books, 1986.

Sharkey, Brian J. *Physiology of Fitness*, 2d ed. Champaign, Illinois: Human Kinetics Publishers, Inc., 1984.

Sweetgall, Robert, James Rippe, and Frank Katch. *Fitness Walking*. New York: Perigee Books, 1985.

Ulene, Art. *Count Out Cholesterol*. New York: Alfred Knopf, 1989.

Pamphlets

American Diabetes Association, Inc. and The American Dietetic Association. *Healthy Food Choices*. Alexandria, Virginia and Chicago: American Diabetes Association, Inc. and The American Dietetic Association, 1986.

———. *Exchange Lists for Meal Planning*. Alexandria, Virginia and Chicago: American Diabetes Association, Inc. and The American Dietetic Association, 1986.

American Heart Association. *Nutrition Labeling*. Dallas: American Heart Association, 1978.

———. *Dining Out*. Dallas: American Heart Association, 1984.

———, Minnesota Affiliate Nutrition Task Force. *Grocery Guide*. Dallas: American Heart Association, 1982.

Lean Life Food Series Sound/Slide Program
Eve Lowry, R.D.
NUTRIVISUALS
P.O. Box 1367, Shingle Springs, CA 95682

National Cholesterol Education Program. *High Blood Cholesterol in Adults*. Washington, D.C.: NIH Publication, 1988.

The Rockport Company. *Walking*. Marlboro, Massachusetts: The Rockport Company, 1987.

The Rockport Walking Institute. *Rockport Fitness Walking Test*. Marlboro, Massachusetts: The Rockport Company, 1987.

U.S. Department of Health and Human Services, Public Health Service, National Institutes of Health. *Eating to Lower Your High Blood Cholesterol*. Washington, D.C.: NIH Publication, 1987.

———. *So You Have High Blood Cholesterol . . .* Washington, D.C.: NIH Publication, 1987.

Ward, Ann, and James Rippe. *Starting Your Personal Fitness Walking Program*. Philadelphia: J. B. Lippincott, 1987.

———. *Walking for Health and Fitness*. Philadelphia: J. B. Lippincott, 1988.

Articles

Allen, W. D., and B. M. Quigley. "The Role of Physical Activity in the Control of Obesity." *Medical Journal of Australia* 2:434–38, 1977.

Bennett, W., and J. Gurin. "Do Diets Really Work?" *Science*, March 1982.

Birk, T. J., and C. A. Birk. "Use of Ratings of Perceived Exertion for Exercise Prescription." *Sports Medicine* 4:1–8, 1987.

Burns, C. M., R. Richman, and I. D. Caterson. "Nutrition Knowledge in the Obese and Overweight." *International Journal of Obesity* 11:485–92, 1987.

Charney, E., H. C. Goodman, M. McBride, B. Lyon, and R. Pratt. "Childhood Antecedents of Adult Obesity: Do Chubby Infants Become Obese Adults?" *New England Journal of Medicine* 295:1, 1976.

Chirico, A., and A. J. Stunkard. "Physical Activity and Human Obesity." *New England Journal of Medicine* 263:19, 1960.

Dahlkoetter, J., E. J. Callahan, and J. Linton. "Obesity and the Unbalanced Energy Equation: Exercise Versus Eating Habit Change." *Journal of Consulting and Clinical Psychology* 47:5, 1979.

Danforth, E., Jr. "Diet and Obesity." *American Journal of Clinical Nutrition* 41:1132–45, 1985.

Epstein, L. H., and R. R. Wing. "Aerobic Exercise and Weight." *Addictive Behaviors* 5:371–88, 1980.

Findlay, S., with T. Shryer and Bureau Reports. "Smart Ways to Shape Up." *U.S. News & World Report*, July 18, 1988.

Flynn, M. A., G. B. Nolph, Y. Osio, G. Y. Sun, B. Lanning, G. Krause, and J. C. Dally. "Serum Lipids and Eggs." *Journal of The American Dietetic Association* 86:11, 1986.

Hagan, D. R. "Benefits of Aerobic Conditioning and Diet for Overweight Adults." *Sports Medicine* 5:144–45, 1988.

————, S. J. Upton, L. Wong, and J. Whittam. "The Effects of Aerobic Conditioning and/or Caloric Restriction in Overweight Men and Women." *Medicine and Science in Sports and Exercise* 16:1, 1986.

James, P. T., M. E. J. Lean, and G. McNeill. "Dietary Recommendations After Weight Loss: How to Avoid Relapse of Obesity." *American Journal of Clinical Nutrition* 45:1135–41, 1987.

Kline, G. M., J. P. Porcari, R. Hintermeister, P. S. Freedson, A. Ward, R. F. McCarron, J. Ross, and J. M. Rippe. "Prediction of VO_2max from a One-Mile Track Walk." *Medicine and Science in Sports and Exercise* 19:3, 1987.

Pavlou, K. N., W. P. Steffee, R. H. Lerman, and B. A. Burrows. "Effects of Dieting and Exercise on Lean Body Mass, Oxygen Uptake, and Strength." *Medicine and Science in Sports and Exercise* 17:466, 1985.

Porcari, J. P., G. M. Kline, P. S. Freedson, A. Ward, J. Ross, and J. M. Rippe. "Is Fast Walking an Adequate Aerobic Training Stimulus in 30- to 69-Year-Old Adults?" *The Physician and SportsMedicine* 15:119, 1987.

————, A. Ward, W. Morgan, M. Mance, C. Ebbeling, A. Kline, S. O'Hanley, and J. M. Rippe. "Effect of Walking on State Anxiety and Blood Pressure." *Medicine and Science in Sports and Exercise* 20:585, 1988.

Rikli, R., and S. Busch. "Motor Performance of Women as a Function of Age in Physical Activity Level." *Journal of Gerontology* 41:645, 1986.

Rippe, J. M., moderator. "Roundtable Discussion: Walking for Fitness." *The Physician and SportsMedicine* 14:10, October 1986.

————, moderator. "Roundtable Discussion: The Health Benefits of Exercise (part 1 of 2)." *The Physician and SportsMedicine* 15:10, October 1987.

————, moderator. "Roundtable Discussion: The Health Benefits of Exercise (part 2 of 2)." *The Physician and SportsMedicine* 15:11, November 1987.

———. "29 Tips for Staying With It." *American Health*, June 1988.

———, A. Ward, and P. S. Freedson. "Exercise: Staying With It." *Encyclopaedia Britannica Medical and Health Annual*, 1988.

———. "Walking: Nothing Pedestrian About It." *Encyclopaedia Britannica Medical and Health Annual*, 1988.

———, A. Ward, J. P. Porcari, and P. S. Freedson. "Walking for Health and Fitness." *Journal of the American Medical Association* 259:18, 1988.

Segal, K. R., and F. X. Pi-Sunyer. "Exercise, Resting Metabolic Rate, and Thermogenesis." *Diabetes/Metabolism Reviews* 2:1–2, 1986.

Stunkard, A. J. "Your Genes Could Be Making You Fat." *Shape*, March 1987.

———, T. I. A. Sorensen, C. Hanis, T. W. Teasdale, R. Chakraborty, W. J. Schull, and F. Schulsinger. "An Adoption Study of Human Obesity." *New England Journal of Medicine* 314:4, 1986.

Thompson, J. K., G. J. Jarvie, and B. B. Lahey. "Exercise and Obesity: Etiology, Physiology, and Intervention." *Psychological Bulletin* 91:1, 1982.

Van Itallie, T. B. "Bad News and Good News About Obesity." *New England Journal of Medicine* 314:4, 1986.

———, and M. Yang. "Current Concepts in Nutrition: Diet and Weight Loss." *New England Journal of Medicine* 297:21, 1977.

Wadden, T., and A. J. Stunkard. "Why Crash Diets Crash: The Best Methods for Weight Loss." *Shape*, March 1987.

Wilmore, J. H., moderator. "Roundtable Discussion: Body Composition." *The Physician and SportsMedicine* 14:3, 1986.

INDEX

We'll Pay You $5 to Improve Your Health

Begin The Rockport Walking Program today! Start it in a pair of comfortable Rockport® ProWalker™ walking shoes.

We'll help you with a $5.00 rebate from The Rockport Company.

After you buy your shoes, just send the dated register receipt and style number cut from the side of the Rockport shoe box, as proof of purchase, to the address below and we will send you $5.00.

The Rockport Company
Dept: ROCKPORT WALKING PROGRAM^SM REBATE
72 Howe Street
Marlboro, MA 01752

Walk your way to better health in a pair of Rockport walking shoes made by the leaders of the fitness walking movement.

- -

Please send me a rebate check for $5.00. I have enclosed the required proof of purchase from a pair of Rockport® ProWalker™ walking shoes.

Name_____

Address_____

City_____

State_____ Zip_____

Void where prohibited.